WASATCH TOURS

Volume 1

An Introduction to Ski Touring in the Wasatch Mountains

Alexis Kelner and David Hanscom

WASATCH TOURS PUBLISHING
Salt Lake City, Utah

Dedicated to Brett and Eric and Greg.

Published by:
WASATCH TOURS PUBLISHING
Salt Lake City, Utah

ISBN 1-884744-02-8

©Copyright 1993 by Alexis Kelner and David Hanscom.

Printed in the United States of America. All rights reserved. No part of this book may be used or reproduced in any manner whatsoever without written permission except in the case of brief quotations embodied in critical articles and reviews. For information contact Alexis Kelner, 1201 First Avenue, Salt Lake City, UT 84103, or David Hanscom, 1451 Moray Court, Park City, UT 84060.

PREFACE

When *Wasatch Tours* was first published in 1976, it was intended for a rather limited population of skiers who practiced their sport mostly in the proximity of the Central Wasatch. The most optimistic expectation was that a couple thousand tourers might find the volume useful to their touring activities. By 1993, we estimate, some 40,000-50,000 backcountry visitors had utilized the first edition of *Tours* to plan and to execute their winter–and frequently summer–outings.

To meet the demands of this "new generation" of winter recreationists, a major revision was undertaken in 1989. Several criteria guided the revision process: to provide better and more detailed information for beginning tourers, to enlarge the geographical coverage to encompass the entire Wasatch, to increase the quality of maps and aerial photographs, to help winter recreationists become better informed about mountain hazards, and to update the avalanche safety chapter with the latest survival and rescue procedures.

Another important revision was the inclusion of a chapter discussing the history of canyon preservation. Since mountain recreation is generally conducted on public lands, we felt that a comprehensive account of Wasatch Front conservation efforts would help induce the growing ranks of backcountry users to become more active in the management processes of *their* public lands. We encourage other guidebook writers and publishers to include similar discussions.

The extensive revision process necessitated publication of the guide in three volumes. Volume 1 is an introduction to backcountry touring in and near the Wasatch. The volume commences with an overview of Wasatch ski touring and follows with comprehensive chapters on equipment, mountain hazards, and avalanches. The next two chapters describe numerous tours especially suited to beginners. The volume concludes with a discussion of canyon preservation issues and suggestions for community activism.

Having mastered the rudiments of mountain survival, the beginner can then progress into the realms of intermediate and advanced touring as described in subsequent volumes. Volume 2 details many touring routes in the regions of the Wasatch Mountains located north of the Salt Lake County/Utah County divide; touring areas east of Salt Lake Valley, Bountiful, Farmington, Ogden, and Willard are included. Volume

3 describes skiing options in the Wasatch located south of Salt Lake County. Touring areas east of Alpine, American Fork, Pleasant Grove, Provo, Springville, Payson, and Nephi are included.

We would like to acknowledge and thank a number of individuals who assisted in the preparation of both editions of *Wasatch Tours*. First and foremost is Larry Swanson, without whose time and flying skills the aerial photographs would not have been possible. Larry's expertise with an airplane made the use of telephoto lenses unnecessary.

Several experts provided valuable suggestions for the avalanche chapter: Ron Perla, recently retired Research Scientist for the Canadian Department of the Environment; Gerry Horton, Cliff Blake, and Jim Head of the Wasatch National Forest; Knox Williams and Pete Martinelli of the U.S. Forest Service's Snow and Avalanche Research Project in Fort Collins, Colorado; Brad Meiklejohn and Bruce Tremper of the Utah Avalanche Forecast Center.

The preservation chapter was reviewed by long-time environmental activists Gale Dick, Tom Berggren, Karin Caldwell, and Ann Wechsler. Numerous Forest Service officials provided helpful suggestions on this and other parts of the book.

Helicopter skiing regulation advocates Steve Lewis, Milt Hollander, and Bob Athay never turned down an opportunity to provide valuable information or to help with photography. Karin and Dennis Caldwell and Bob Woody endured, without complaints, numerous outings planned specifically for photographic purposes. Roly Pearson and Bill Stenquist suffered through many exploratory hikes and ski tours.

Charlie Butler and Riley Cutler of Wasatch Touring, Jerry Richardson of Kirkham's, and Charlie Sturgis of White Pine reviewed the equipment chapter. Their understanding of current technology and trends in the ski and clothing industries helped bring order to a very confusing subject. Howie Garber's detailed markup of the physiological hazards section was invaluable.

Special thanks go to Weber State University's Gary Willden and students in his beginner touring class for field testing the manuscript. Assistance provided by Bob Kessler and Joe Zachary with the LaTeX document preparation system was also greatly appreciated. Ruta Ehlers deserves a special accolade for design of the simple, yet striking covers.

These volumes would not have been possible without the patience and understanding of Karla and Mary. We thank them very much.

Alexis Kelner and *Dave Hanscom*
November 1993

TABLE OF CONTENTS

1. Introduction 7
2. Equipment 33
3. Mountain Hazards 69
4. Avalanche Safety 121
5. Wasatch Beginner Tours 167
6. Beginner Tours in Outlying Areas 215
7. Preserving the Wasatch 245

"We slept overnight at the Comstock Mine." The Arbor Day, 1923, ski trip from Park City to Brighton by the Wasatch Mountain Club. Long skis were common during the 1920's; turns were relatively rare. Photo by W. H. Hopkins, courtesy of the Wasatch Mountain Club.

Chapter 1

INTRODUCTION

The Wasatch Mountains east of Salt Lake City have long been a haunt of skiers from throughout the world. An abundance of powder snow, good terrain for any skiing ability, and clear sunny days have made the range a popular winter recreation mecca. Seven commercial ski areas are located within a 45-minute drive of downtown Salt Lake City. Two large resorts are located within a similar distance of Ogden and one ski area is equally close to Provo. The "white gold" that covers the Wasatch has enabled the development of a modest winter tourist industry.

While ski resorts—and associated real estate developments—have been multiplying, a *real* boom has been taking place in the Wasatch: ski touring has matured from the sport enjoyed by a few hardy mountaineers and racers to a pastime for almost anyone who has the desire and ambition to take a walk on a winter day. With increasing numbers of individuals looking for types of recreation that provide fresh air and exercise, ski touring is a natural during the season when outdoor tennis, golf, bicycling, and hiking aren't practical.

There are as many reasons for ski touring as there are participants in the sport. To some, touring is an extension of hiking. Some skiers want to take advantage of the seemingly unlimited trackless powder of the backcountry with no lift lines to wait in, no crowds to hassle. Others feel the need to ascend the highest peaks, regardless of adversities to be overcome. To many who've watched ski lift prices soar to unaffordable levels, ski touring offers the opportunity to practice the most fundamental of traditional family values: *thrift*!

Whatever the motivations for getting out, Wasatch tourers will find useful information in the pages and volumes that follow. The goal of *Wasatch Tours* is to help individuals enjoy pleasant and safe winter outings in the backcountry along the Wasatch Front.

This chapter introduces the novitiate to the history of ski touring in the Wasatch and provides an overview of different types of backcountry touring. The chapter lists sources of information available to the tourer and brings to notice the topic of touring etiquette. It concludes with a discussion of the ski tour classification system used in this and subsequent volumes.

EARLY HISTORY

The Mormon Pioneers had barely entered the Valley of the Great Salt Lake and already the lure of mountaineering on the nearby Wasatch Mountains began to attract its first disciples. On Friday, August 20, 1847, Albert Carrington, William Rust, John Brown, and two others departed the City of the Great Salt Lake to attempt an ascent of Twin Peaks, the prominent alpine summit at the south-eastern edge of Salt Lake Valley.

A full day was required to approach the foot of the mountain; three of the explorers reached the summit the following day. During their descent the trio achieved another first in Utah mountaineering: a bivouac necessitated by having become separated and lost. In his *Journal* Brown expressed satisfaction with the adventure, despite having spent the night "without bedding or coats" and "without either supper, dinner, or breakfast."

But it was not the pioneers who introduced skis and skiing to the Wasatch. It was the miners.

In her 1893 book, *My Summer in a Mormon Village*, F. A. Merriam depicts an Alta miner's use of "skees" fourteen feet long and six inches wide. In his manuscript, *An Account of Alta*, R. F. Marvin describes the Alta of 1916 as having "exactly two pairs of skis in the camp." Marvin recounts having to send "all the way to St. Paul" for his skis. "When the skis came," he writes, "they were hickory, thick and heavy, and exactly eleven feet long." Using a single long pole cut from a river birch, the miner "rowed" himself up and down the nearby mountains "to all the places your lifts and tows take you now, and beyond, to the top of Baldy on occasion."

By 1917, members of the rapidly-organizing Wasatch Mountain Club discovered skiing. Ski outings were scheduled to foothill areas above Salt Lake City. One of the first "community ski slopes" was located northeast of the University of Utah, near the present location of the Fort Douglas

EARLY HISTORY

Figure 1.1 *"Over the first mountain range, marching onward . . . no turning back."* Park City to Brighton, 1923. The single ski pole was used to maintain balance and to pivot about during turns. Photograph by W. H. Hopkins, courtesy of the Wasatch Mountain Club.

Country Club. The site was popular for ski jumping competitions, but before and after each meet much recreational skiing took place there. A *Salt Lake Tribune* reporter described the act of skiing as consisting of two parts: "a rapid descent, sometimes only part of the distance down the hill, and then a sudden tumble into the snow, which covered the ground to a depth of two feet."

The popularity of cross country skiing increased during the 1920's and 1930's. With unreliable snow conditions at the foothill sites, members of the Wasatch Mountain Club commenced organizing outings to such diverse locations as Parley's Summit, Park City, Brighton, Alta, Bountiful's Mueller Park, and Payson Canyon.

Anticipating continued growth of skiing and the eventual popularity of Brighton as a ski site, members of the outing club began construction of a lodge at the barely accessible mountain village. Completed in 1935, the Wasatch Mountain Club's lodge quickly became the "ski center of Utah." Rasmussen's Ranch, near Parley's Summit, also became a popular gathering place for local skiers. Snow Basin was a popular area near Ogden.

On January 2, 1937, the Community Camp Winter Sports Center

Figure 1.2 *"Enjoying the brisk breezes of winter."* February, 1935. Left to right: Edith Cook, Mary Spencer, Ethel Lenzi, Dorothy Green, Marie Bringhurst, Irintha Simmons, Helen Blaker, Nola Graham, and Florence Reich. Photo by S. Dean Green, courtesy of the *Salt Lake Tribune*.

(later renamed Spruces), in Big Cottonwood Canyon, was inaugurated by Wasatch National Forest officials as "Utah's newest and finest winter sports center." Constructed as part of a Great Depression employment program, the center was the first developed winter recreation site in the alpine regions east of Salt Lake City. At the time of its dedication, Community Camp boasted of 2.5 miles of ski trails, a toboggan slide, several small skiing hills, a large skating rink, and a ski jumping ramp that accommodated jumps of up to 150 feet.

Early during the 1940's, Alta's James Laughlin urged construction of alpine ski huts in the western forests, especially in proximity of skiing areas. "Until we have them," he wrote in 1941, "the run of American skiers will never know what it means to tour, and, as anyone knows who has toured abroad, touring is the real cream of skiing."

Officials of the Wasatch National Forest, Salt Lake County government, and members of the Wasatch Mountain Club endorsed Laughlin's concept. Some fourteen backcountry shelters were planned that would have connected Park City, Brighton, Alta, and American Fork Canyon into a "ski tourer's paradise." Three of the fourteen huts were completed by 1948, mostly through the efforts and craftsmanship of the mountain club.[1]

Popularity of Wasatch ski touring declined after World War II. Commercial lift skiing, commenced at Alta in 1937-38, had increased dramatically during the war years and continued growing until it leveled off

---

[1] Only the Point Supreme hut remains intact. The Germania Hut, once located along the south edge of Albion Basin, was sold at auction, dismantled, and reassembled at a residence in Bountiful. The hut located on Snake Creek Pass burned to the ground during a scouting campout.

TYPES OF TOURING

Figure 1.3 Tom and Mimi Stevenson, left, and Bill Conrod pause near the Germania ski hut. The hut contained double-decked bunks with mattresses, a cooking stove, and a small unisex toilet.

in the 1980's. Rediscovered during the mid-sixties, ski touring continues to grow at an unprecedented rate.[2]

TYPES OF TOURING

In the mid-1960's *ski touring* was defined as "going from hither to yon on skis" and "merely walking up and down on skis, moving easily, efficiently, rapidly if desired." Nearly thirty years later, the simple definitions still apply, although the term ski touring has become encompassed within the broader category of "non-motorized winter recreation." *Cross country skiing* is a generic term that best fits the definition of going from hither to yon on skis. *Backcountry touring* refers to ski touring in undeveloped areas such as wilderness areas or other locations not serviced by ski lifts or groomed by machines.

---

[2] For a comprehensive history of Utah skiing see: *SKIING IN UTAH—A History* by A. Kelner. The 256-page book details many fascinating aspects of skiing in Utah. The volume can be mail ordered from the author.

Figure 1.4 Marsha Rasmussen utilizes the "kick-and-glide" technique popular among nordic tourers for rapid travel on flat, or nearly-flat, terrain. Photo courtesy of Craig Hansell, the *Salt Lake Tribune*.

This section contains an overview of the various types of ski touring practiced in the Wasatch. Equipment associated with the different categories is discussed in Chapter 2.

Nordic Touring

The term *nordic* relates to the Northern European countries of Finland, Norway, and Sweden, where skiing is believed to have originated. Nordic ski equipment, traditionally made of lightweight woods, is designed for travel on gentle, rolling terrain. In the past, *nordic touring* generally referred to ski touring along such terrain on nordic-type equipment. Recent improvements in such equipment, however, have made its use on steep, mountainous terrain more practical for experienced skiers.

Alpine Touring

The term *alpine* originated with the mountainous countries of central Europe. "Alpine tours typically involve skiing a variety of snow conditions and types of terrain," write George Westbrook and Dave Smith in the Wasatch Mountain Club's *Rambler*. "Indeed, the challenge of skiing the entire mountain and all the snow conditions that it may throw at

TYPES OF TOURING 13

Figure 1.5 Dennis Caldwell descends a snowfield in the Lone Peak Wilderness. Many Wasatch Front ski tourers utilize downhill skis for outings into such rugged areas.

you is one of the chief joys of this type of touring." Figure 1.5 illustrates the type of terrain frequently encountered on alpine ski tours. Equipment used for this type of touring is generally heavier and more rugged than that used for nordic touring.

Ski Mountaineering

Ski mountaineering generally refers to the ascent of mountain peaks with the aid of skis. The Wasatch Mountains are an ideal range for ski mountaineering. The 150-mile length of the range includes 23 peaks over 11,000 feet in elevation. The proximity of the summits to population centers makes single-day ascents practical. As illustrated in Figure 1.6, ski mountaineering outings may involve steeper and more challenging terrain than that encountered on alpine tours.

Urban Touring

Urban touring is defined as cross country skiing in or near densely populated areas. The best opportunities for this activity are found in municipal parks and golf courses, where underlying terrain is smooth and free of rocks and other obstacles.

Nearby foothill areas are laced with old jeep roads and trails that can often be used without endangering one's limbs or equipment. Such

Figure 1.6 The final slope beneath the summit of Lone Peak is more challenging than most backcountry skiers would want to attempt. Ascent of such pitches may require use of climbing rope and ice axe.

areas, located to the east of the Great Salt Lake and Utah Lake, are frequently subjected to "lake effect" storms that may drop several inches—or even feet—of snow along the foothills. The best urban touring is usually found immediately after such storms; touring conditions deteriorate rather quickly when the snow is softened by mid-day heating and is refrozen during the night.

Related Activities

A number of winter recreation activities closely related to ski touring are gaining popularity.

Track Skiing. Track skiing may appear to the uninitiated as "mindlessly running about in circles," but it is an ideal method for tourers to practice their nordic skills. A number of commercial establishments maintain snowmobile-groomed "tracks" and reasonably-priced lessons for those wishing to improve their skiing techniques. Equipment and locales for track skiing will be described in later chapters.

TYPES OF TOURING 15

Figure 1.7 Under exceptional snow conditions it is possible to find ski trails immediately adjacent to the urban areas along the Wasatch Front.

Winter Camping. Availability of clothing and bedding made of modern waterproof textiles and lightweight insulating materials has contributed to the rising popularity of winter camping. Winter camping can take place in mountain tents, snow caves or igloos, or, as illustrated in Figure 1.8, within a semi-portable shelter known as a "yurt."

Cross Country Ski Racing. For a person who enjoys running and bicycling in the summer, "citizens races" provide opportunities to maintain fitness during the snowy months without risking life and limb on slippery city streets. Studies have shown that this form of exercise provides a better aerobic workout than almost any other sport. There is also much less risk of injury than would result from a high impact activity, such as running, or one that requires highly repetitive motions, such as bicycling. Cross country ski racing enables an athlete to maintain good physical condition while allowing injuries caused by summer activities to heal.

Skiers of all fitness and ability levels may participate in events scheduled throughout December, January, and February. Contact one of the local ski touring centers for more information.

Snowboarding. Snowboarding is an unusual, hybrid sport combining some aspects of skiing, skateboarding, and surfing. This challenging new wintersport is practiced by a uniquely talented group of

Figure 1.8 After a ski tour, Bob Woody (left), Russel and Lynne Taylor socialize in a *yurt,* a style of movable shelter popular among natives of northern Asia and Siberia. Thanks to The Utah Nordic Alliance, area tourers needn't enplane for Asia. A small fee, to offset maintenance, is charged for overnight use of the shelter.

young eccentrics who like to call themselves "shredders." Despite rapid growth of the sport around the country, some Utah ski resorts still decline to permit snowboarding on their high-priced terrain. As a result,

TYPES OF TOURING 17

Figure 1.9 Cross country ski races in Utah are social activities as much as they are competitive events. Proudly displaying their awards from the final race of the 1990 season are (l. to r.) Nan Chalat, Herb and Sam Lepley, and Cindy Cromer.

snowboarders are forced to use the backcountry, where they must walk straight up hillsides in waist-deep snow in order to enjoy carving turns on descent or jumping from high prominences.

Snowboarding will not be discussed further in this book, but participants would be wise to learn about physiological and natural hazards. Several boarders have been injured or killed in avalanches and other backcountry accidents in recent years.

Snowshoeing. An important mode of over-snow transportation for some 6,000 years, snowshoeing is rapidly gaining popularity as a winter recreation. Snowshoes are ideal for hikers who wish to continue their sport throughout the year, but who do not enjoy skiing. Snowshoes outperform skis on narrow trails with little room for turns and are ideal for terrain that is not too steep. Snowshoeing demands less skill than alpine or nordic touring and is generally less dangerous for winter travel. This method of travel is an excellent complement to winter camping.

Many of the ski touring routes, especially those described as beginner and intermediate, are well-suited for recreational snowshoeing. As snowshoers gain proficiency in safe winter travel, many of the more advanced routes become practical for them. New technologies and materials utilized in snowshoe construction are partially responsible for the rapid rise in popularity. Equipment will be discussed in Chapter 2.

Nordic Sledding. Commencing in the early 1980's, various winter recreation opportunities have become available for the mobility-impaired or the differently-abled individual. The non-profit organiza-

Figure 1.10 Salt Lake snowboarder Dan Gorder illustrates a popular maneuver as he gets "big air" in the foothills above Salt Lake City.

tion known as *S'PLORE* (Special Populations Learning Outdoor Recreation and Education) conducts numerous backcountry winter outings for individuals with physical or intellectual impairments. Operating with funds provided by corporate and individual donors, user fees, and special fund-raising activities, the organization helps over 300 individuals enjoy winter recreation each year. Staffed by several full-time professionals, *S'PLORE* relies on numerous community volunteers to help implement its programs.

S'PLORE maintains sleds specially designed to meet the needs of persons experiencing mobility impairments. Novices can learn about nordic sledding on groomed trails at specified centers, then progress into the realms of backcountry touring.

Gourmet Touring. For many participants, ski touring is as much a social event as it is a physical activity. Early in the 1960's, Gale Dick added yet another level of enjoyment to backcountry touring: *eating*. Members of Salt Lake's Wasatch Mountain Club found the first test of his new tri-athletic (skiing, eating, and socializing) event to their liking and immediately incorporated it into their winter outings program.

According to Prof. Dick, the theory of the club's annual Gourmet Ski Tour is quite simple: "to go no farther than you can carry what

Figure 1.11 Snowshoeing has increased in popularity among runners as lightweight equipment has become available. Arnold Ziffel and Rufous Firefly are shown here participating in the Wasatch Overland race from Brighton to Park City.

you intend to consume." It is not unusual for an unaffiliated backcountry tourer to arrive at his destination to discover some dozen or more club members already there—attired in tuxedo and formal—fussing over fondue pots, cranking an ice cream freezer, or whipping cream to top strawberry shortcakes. Prof. Dick has led this gastronomic delight continuously for over 25 years; only rarely has it been cancelled due to inclement weather.

INFORMATION/INSTRUCTION

During the past two decades, *Wasatch Tours* was the only comprehensive guide to touring in the Wasatch Mountains. As the Information Age moves into the mid-1990's, numerous publications exist—and several others are planned—to help make the would-be tourer's outings more enjoyable. The materials can be described as official agency materials, books and articles, and maps. Just as the quantity of published matter has increased, so has the availability of ski touring instruction.

During the 1960's and early 1970's, the only known copy of the Wasatch National Forest's "Ski Touring Routes" map was a rapidly-

Figure 1.12 Nordic sleds, specially-designed to meet the needs of individuals experiencing mobility impairments, have skis mounted on the bottom. Ski poles are used to gain and to maintain momentum.

oxidizing copy tacked inside the privy of the Wasatch Mountain Club Lodge at Brighton. Today, in response to the sky-rocketing popularity of winter backcountry recreation, nearly all Forest Service headquarters or district ranger offices carry brochures, pamphlets, and maps that describe—in a rudimentary manner—winter recreation opportunities within their jurisdictions.

The U.S. Department of Agriculture *Winter Recreation Safety Guide* is must reading for anyone venturing into the backcountry during winter. The small booklet covers—quite briefly—everything from altitude sickness to sanitation and contains an extensive bibliography of winter recreation books. Best of all, it's free! Agency-produced "Recreational Opportunities" maps are especially useful since they indicate areas of potential conflicts with snowmobiles. A visit to the local District Ranger's office is wise before commencing a season of touring. (This is also an excellent place to deposit your letter commending—or condemning—recent agency actions that affect backcountry recreation.)

Some Forest Headquarters and District Ranger Offices have been staffed with volunteers from an "interpretive association" who can sell you, or direct you to, materials not of the agency's making.

Figure 1.13 Organized by Gale Dick (arrow), the Wasatch Mountain Club's annual Gourmet Ski Tour is a popular end-of-the-season activity.

A number of guidebooks to the Wasatch have been published recently. The best deal with summer recreation. Since tourers ought to be familiar with possible touring areas during the snowless seasons, the hiking guides will serve them well. John Veranth's *Hiking the Wasatch*

Figure 1.14 Many publications, produced privately and by governmental agencies, are available for the backcountry winter recreationist.

(published by the Wasatch Mountain Club) is an excellent publication that describes hikes in the mountains east of Salt Lake City.[3] Another excellent summer guide book (geared for those interested in short, basically beginner hikes) is Tom Berggren's forthcoming *Family Hikes and Walks in Northern Utah*. John Veranth's *Wasatch Winter Trails* briefly describes a few of the tours covered in this book, but is less comprehensive than his *Wasatch Trails*.

Some of the best "guides" to winter recreation are a series of ski touring columns in the *Salt Lake Tribune* authored by long-time backcountry skier/hiker/writer/photographer Craig Hansell. Under the heading "The Touring Column," the articles appear periodically in the paper's sports pages. Tom Wharton, the newspaper's Outdoors Editor, also contributes frequent articles describing various aspects of touring.

Due to the basic simplicity of canyons and ridges in the Wasatch Mountains, the authors have rarely—if ever—relied on topographical maps to aid them on their outings. A series of oblique, closeup photographs, however, can be quite useful for studying traditional touring routes and in planning variations.

Those who find maps and photographs—and routes superimposed on maps and photographs—useful will enjoy purchasing Alpentech's Wasatch and Uinta touring and hiking maps. Engineer Beat vonAllmen has done an admirable job of placing everything one ever wanted

---

[3] A trail map of the Tri-Canyon Area (Millcreek, Big Cottonwood, and Little Cottonwood canyons), intended as a supplement to *Hiking the Wasatch*, will soon be published by long-time Wasatch Mountain Club volunteer Dale Green.

to know about touring on a series of area maps. Each one is a high altitude, vertical aerial photograph that has been overprinted with contours and touring routes. Also superimposed are many avalanche paths with little symbols showing where fatalities have occurred. The maps make an excellent decoration for an office wall and are easily carried in a pack.

Ski Touring Instruction

Instruction in the art and mysteries of ski touring is a buyers' market. Nearly every Wasatch Front university has a class—or an entire program of classes—that deals with winter backcountry recreation. Touring instruction is also available from commercial recreational entities, some area churches, scouting organizations, and several non-profit outing clubs.

The Universities. University instructional programs are exceptionally sensitive to budgetary considerations as well as to availability of qualified—and enthusiastic—instructors. If a physical education department has an active ski tourer on its faculty, it's likely that excellent courses will be offered. Registering for such courses may require admission to the university. Some Wasatch Front universities offer *for their students, staff, and faculty* opportunities to participate in "cooperative adventure" programs.

The brief descriptions that follow are meant to illustrate the types of instruction or programs that may be available. It is best to contact each campus to learn what courses are available at the time of need.

University of Utah. Initially organized by Utah mountaineering leader—now living legend—Harold Goodro, the University of Utah's Department of Recreation and Leisure offers many courses dealing with mountain recreation. During winter, enrollees can take courses in cross country skiing, alpine or telemark skiing, wilderness snow-camping, ski mountaineering and even ice climbing and snowshoeing. Though designed primarily for skill development, all courses have academic components that may require submission of term papers and participation in written examinations. The classes are taught either by Harold Goodro or by one of many departmental instructors. During the winter of 1991-92 some 200 novice tourers participated in the classes.

Most of the classes described are also offered to the community-at-large through the Division of Continuing Education. The cost depends upon the total number of credit hours a student is taking.

The University of Utah also offers a "cooperative adventure trips"

Figure 1.15 Still teaching classes at the age of 77, University of Utah's Harold Goodro organized Utah's first college instructional programs emphasizing backcountry recreation.

program for its students, faculty, staff, and alumni. The Outdoor Recreation Program is based on shared responsibility for trip planning and participation. It is free for students, but a modest membership fee ($25/year in 1993) is required for others. In the past, trips have varied from full-moon Bryce Canyon National Park ski tours, to introduction to winter camping, to advanced 5-day backpacks in the High Uintas Wilderness.

Weber State University. Department of Physical Education Professor Gary Willden teaches what are among the state's finest classes in backcountry winter recreation. His "Beginning Cross Country Skiing" class has a heavy emphasis on activity and deals with equipment, clothing, and techniques suited for beginners. The "Intermediate Cross Country Skiing" class emphasizes cross country downhill techniques and involves more challenging terrain. Dr. Willden's "Winter Camping" class deals with equipment, trip planning and shelter construction. Students are given two overnight field trips to test their skills in snow-cave and igloo construction; one trip is made on snowshoes, the other is completed on cross country skis.

Brigham Young University. B.Y.U. does not have any curricular programs in cross country skiing or touring at this time. An "Introduc-

Figure 1.16 Weber State University's Dr. Gary Willden relaxes with his students beside an igloo constructed during his popular winter camping class. Note the innovative use of a plastic "thermopane" window to add light to the interior.

tion to Outdoor Recreation" class includes one session in cross country skiing among many recreational sports overviewed.

Outdoors Unlimited, a not-for-profit enterprise at Brigham Young University, provides recreational opportunities in a number of fields, including cross country and backcountry touring. The largely "user fee" funded program is directed by David Webb. Outdoors Unlimited is truly unlimited. Anyone with cash, check, or Visa card can participate in the program. To those interested in touring, the organization offers equipment rental and ski repair service as well as numerous opportunities for winter adventure. A Learn to Ski Day—held annually along the Wasatch Plateau above Fairview Canyon—introduces novices to cross country touring. Other outings are convened throughout winter. Past outings have included moonlight ski trips, overnight excursions to develop winter camping skills, and every few years, winter outings to Yellowstone National Park.

Commercial Instruction. Most Wasatch Front nordic skiing centers, or touring centers, offer some degree of instruction to their clientele. These will be discussed in Chapter 5. Touring equipment stores may

Figure 1.17 No snow is necessary during the first instructional session of the Deseret News Ski School. With cooperation of Alta's Alf Engen, the newspaper's ski school has been teaching area residents ski techniques since the late 1940's. Photo courtesy of the *Deseret News*.

also offer backcountry skiing instruction. It is best to check early during the season for particulars.

Eleemosynary Touring Instruction Programs. A number of Wasatch Front organizations provide free (or nearly-free) instruction in the basics of cross country touring.

Deseret News Ski School. Held annually since 1947, the Deseret News Ski School is one of the nation's oldest instructional programs for beginning skiers. Originally established to teach downhill ski techniques, the school has recently branched out to offer instruction in the rudiments of cross country skiing. The school is usually convened early in November, and consists of four two-hour instructional sessions on consecutive Saturdays through November and early December. The first session, illustrated in Figure 1.17, is a "dry-land clinic" generally held at one of the local parks. Subsequent sessions are convened at area resorts, whose managers have in the past contributed lift rides as part of the basic fee. The cost for the four two-hour sessions has been held for many years at $10.

A number of local stores usually offer students specially-priced equipment rental packages; other sponsors provide participants with a "goodie bag" filled with gifts. During the 1992/93 season, over 1,000 downhill, and nearly 200 cross country, students participated in the program. Advance registration for this fine ski school is required; watch for announcements in the *Deseret News* during the last weeks of October or call them at their listed number.

The Wasatch Mountain Club. Since the early 1920's—well before construction of the area's first ski lifts—Utah's Wasatch Mountain Club has been a leader in backcountry touring. Though the club has no formal program of touring instruction, it organizes, for its members and guests, small seminars and clinics that deal with various aspects of touring.

To the beginner, the club's most valuable touring resource is its comprehensive schedule of backcountry outings. The outings are organized and led by experienced tourers familiar with every nook and nuance of the Wasatch Mountains. Tourers can proceed from beginner tours to outings requiring progressively advanced skills. The club's annual dues are currently only $25.

The Church of Jesus Christ of Latter-day Saints. The Utah Central Area Single Adults organization sponsors a cross country skiing interest group. Backcountry touring outings are organized twice monthly; one is for beginning tourers, the other for those with intermediate capabilities. Near the beginning of the winter season, instructional clinics are convened to provide participants with basic cross country training. In the past, topics of discussion included avalanche safety, touring equipment, waxing techniques, and overviews of Wasatch Front ski touring areas.

Individuals interested in participating should contact their ecclesiastical leaders for details.

Scouting Programs. Since the Boy Scouts of America are generally associated with local churches, they depend on volunteer leaders for organization of instructional programs and outings. Troops fortunate enough to recruit an active tourer to a leadership position will generally have an active touring program. Those who aren't so fortunate, won't.

Utah Sierra Club. Utah's chapter of the Sierra Club conducts winter outings, though their schedule in not nearly as comprehensive as that of the Wasatch Mountain Club.

The Utah Nordic Alliance. Abbreviated to *TUNA*, The Utah Nordic Alliance emerged from a union of the Park City Nordic Club and the Utah Nordic Ski Association. *TUNA* is a non-profit organization whose main purpose is to promote all forms of nordic skiing. Its activities include organization of races, social events, clinics, and a few ski tours, sponsorship of a junior cross country ski team, and operation of the previously mentioned yurt. *TUNA News*, their monthly newsletter, keeps cross country skiers informed on issues of importance. Copies may be obtained at most Utah outdoors shops and ski touring centers.

SKI TOURING ETIQUETTE

The recent explosion in backcountry winter recreation has renewed interest in discussions of touring etiquette. A few suggestions from Utah's most experienced ski tourers are provided here.

"As a rule, skiers who travel the backcountry have deliberately selected to stay away from the bustling resorts for the purpose of enjoying some solitude in a pristine setting," Karin Caldwell writes. "Given that there is only a limited amount of backcountry terrain available, ... it is unavoidable that two or more parties might find themselves competing for their solitude on a particular ski tour. It is certainly unpleasant, as happens from time to time, to find yourself and your party breaking trail in deep powder, and to be suddenly joined by a totally unknown group, moving much faster thanks to the broken path, and breathing down your neck while listening to your conversations."

In order to optimize the pleasure for everyone, Caldwell suggests that parties try to stay away from one another as best they can. "Touring is often a form of socializing between good friends, and just as one would not march into one's neighbor's house every time they have a private gathering, one should avoid intruding on other ski touring parties out in the backcountry."

Brad Meiklejohn, former hazard forecaster for the Utah Avalanche Forecast Center, writes that "people need to be encouraged to keep their tracks close together in crowded areas, to respect the rights of those who broke the trail, to avoid skiing near other groups, and to break trails that will be useful to everyone who follows." He advises tourers to pay special attention to inter-party safety considerations, such as not skiing above other groups, and sharing observations about potentially dangerous snow and avalanche conditions.

Tourers Bob Athay and Steve Lewis suggest that descent of slopes should be in the order of ascent. The first touring party to arrive at the top of a slope should be extended the courtesy of skiing it first. Descent tracks should be "spooned" (i.e., made close together, as in Figure 1.18) so as to leave untracked snow for others to ski on.

While the foregoing discussion has dealt with interparty etiquette, a number of intraparty "rules of conduct" have been suggested.

"Equipment chatter," discourses on one's touring equipment, and

Figure 1.18 "Spooning" of ski tracks (placing them close together) assures uncut snow for other tourers to enjoy.

"shop talk," discourses relating to work, should be strictly limited to five minutes per person per ski tour. "Whimpering" about a route or quality of the snow or any other element of a tour is similarly limited to five minutes. A variation on this rule allows the privilege to be transferable from individual to individual. If one tourer's whimpering is exceptionally melodramatic or entertaining, others in the party may wish to transfer their five-minute limits to that person.

CLASSIFICATION OF TOURS

We have chosen to categorize tours principally by their level of difficulty.

- *Beginner tours* range from outings suitable for anyone, to those requiring a reasonable amount of stamina. Most beginner tours are on relatively gentle terrain, so the only required skiing skill is the ability to slow down and/or to stop when necessary.
- *Intermediate tours* have downhill sections that are steep enough to make it unwise for a novice skier to attempt them. They typically involve much more climbing, so a higher level of physical conditioning is often required.
- *Advanced tours* require both endurance and expert skiing skills. All but the most competent and knowledgeable should use mountaineering or downhill equipment.
- *Super tours* speak for themselves. Anyone who undertakes one of these marathons needs an intimate knowledge of the mountains and weather, the ability to ski any slope under any snow condition, the strength to keep going for a full day or longer, and the willingness to spend a night on the mountain if circumstances dictate.

This volume is devoted exclusively to beginner tours. The second and third volumes of *Wasatch Tours* will contain descriptions of intermediate, advanced, and super tours.

In addition to classifying ski tours by their level of difficulty, we have labeled many of them according to existing and potential threats to their continuing availability and enjoyment for human-powered backcountry users.

When ski touring became a recreational diversion during the early 1920's, tourers could trek unimpeded anywhere in the Wasatch. Commercial ski lift recreation began in Utah during the late 1930's to serve the needs of *local* skiers. It expanded somewhat during the war, then continued growing slowly through the mid-60's. During the 1970's, when commercial skiing made the transition to become a "destination industry," Salt Lake Valley residents and local backcountry recreation advocates voiced concerns that if left unchecked, continued exploitation of the Wasatch could well lead to the *de facto* expulsion of local canyon users from their back yard canyons.[4]

Two labels are found in *Wasatch Tours* that relate to this problem:

- *Rest In Peace*, abbreviated to *R.I.P.*, is a notation used by the authors to describe backcountry touring terrain that has been converted to commercial skiing since the initial publication of *Wasatch Tours* in 1976.
- *Endangered*, abbreviated to *End.*, is a notation used to warn tourers that an area has high potential for being absorbed into a commercial ski area operation.

Some "endangered" areas are so classified due to *Interconnect,* a marketing gimmick initiated early in the 1980's by the Utah Ski Association. At present, *Interconnect* is a commercial guided "ski tour" between Park City and Alta or Snowbird that is intended to provide well-heeled tourists with a "backcountry experience." Long-term plans envision a more sinister incarnation of the interconnect concept; several chair lifts—with associated packed trails—would be constructed in areas that are currently popular for cross country skiing.

Helicopter skiing is another major deterrent to enjoyable ski touring in the Wasatch. Contracted to "heli-skiing," this form of commercial skiing substitutes helicopters for ski lifts. Most ski tourers, as well as some canyon business and property owners, consider heli-skiing to be a noisy, disruptive, and dangerous form of mountain exploitation. This very controversial form of commercial recreation made its Wasatch Front debut in 1973.

Hazards and annoyances associated with heli-skiing have become so commonplace that officials of the Wasatch-Cache National Forest—who have the responsibility of regulating the heli-ski concession—have published a map showing terrain and landing sites approved for helicopter skiing. Copies are available free of charge at all Forest Service offices.

- *Helicopter Permit Area*, abbreviated as *H.P.A.*, is the notation used by the authors to warn tourers that a particular outing may be affected—or disrupted and endangered—by the presence of the recreational 'copter.

---

[4] Even lift skiers frequently expressed concerns over the "destination market" philosophy of exploitation. Ski lift ticket prices, many felt, would be increased to reflect the high incomes of out-of-state visitors and would tend to outprice the locals, who became known among industry officials as "brown baggers."

As *Wasatch Tours* goes to press, the worst fears of local skiers have become reality. Some daily lift fees now exceed $40 and 60% of Wasatch Front resort usage is by destination visitors whose annual family incomes often exceed $100,000.

Proper dress is vital for the comfort and safety of cross country skiers. It is important not to dress too warmly for climbing. Clothing should not be so confining as to restrict the movements of the tourer. Photograph of Dorde Wright Woodruff by Jack White, courtesy of O'Dell Peterson.

Chapter 2

EQUIPMENT

The recent revolution in materials and equipment manufacturing techniques has spurred the continuing rapid growth of ski touring. Since the initial publication of *Wasatch Tours* in 1976, the advance of equipment technology has accelerated. Space-age materials are being used in skis, boots, poles, clothing, avalanche beacons, and other accessories. Wooden skis and poles, used by past generations of tourers, have been exiled to museums or to serve as decorations above fireplaces. Leather boots and wool clothing are still common, though similar attire made of synthetics is gaining popularity. Today, cross country skiers face even more alternatives in selecting equipment than they did fifteen years ago, and the debate over what is "best" is increasingly confusing.

This chapter does not attempt to answer all of the questions that relate to equipment; technology changes too rapidly. We attempt only to help the tourer ask the right questions and to provide a few examples of the possibilities that exist today. We recommend a visit to one of several specialty shops in the Wasatch Front to obtain details on current products before making any major equipment purchases.

The most important consideration in selecting equipment is the type of touring to be done and the terrain to be visited. Will you expect to restrict yourself to commercial cross country ski centers and other groomed trails, or will you venture into the backcountry? Will you stay on relatively flat terrain, or will the lure of steep powder slopes tempt you? Will you be satisfied with ski tours in protected areas at low elevations, or will ascent of a mountain be your winter goal? Will you be taking a ski lift wherever possible and choosing trips with a minimum amount of climbing? Will your outings span only a few hours, or might your excursions last many hours or even days? Will you limit your

Figure 2.1 The use of natural materials in skiing related equipment, such as wool, wood, and leather, has given way to space-age synthetics, like lycra, fiberglass, and plastics. Photos courtesy of the Wasatch Mountain Club.

touring activities only to periods of good weather?

Most individuals find that answers to these questions lead to compromises as they contemplate equipment needs. It is not uncommon for active tourers to own two or more outfits, each suitable for a different variety of touring.

A second consideration is the tourer's skiing proficiency. A rank beginner's equipment needs are quite different from those of a person with intermediate or advanced skiing skills. The desire to continue improving one's technique may also dictate the types of equipment to examine.

Safety is an extremely important consideration. Do you feel the need for release bindings for your skis, or are you willing to incur some risk to legs, knees, and ankles in order to minimize equipment weight? Are snowshoes, perhaps, the best alternative for your winter recreation?

Cost need not be the determining factor in equipment acquisition; the most expensive gear may not necessarily be the best for a particular individual. Renting or borrowing equipment before purchase will help to predetermine its usability and may prevent a costly mistake.

The remainder of this chapter discusses equipment requirements for

CLOTHING

Figure 2.2 Effective headgear for winter weather must protect the ears and neck. Christine Young (left) shows one of her neck gaiters, a product manufactured by her local company, Christine's. The powder hood in the center photo, usually worn under a warm hat, is an effective option for severe weather conditions. The locally-made Roly Cap (modeled at right by Roly Pearson, a long-time area ski tourer) has a retractable ear flap for cold days.

safe and enjoyable backcountry winter excursions. Clothing needs will be considered first. Analysis of ski equipment and packs will follow. General principles are introduced at the beginning of each section; descriptions of specific equipment follow, along with analysis of strengths, weaknesses, and hints for the buyer.

CLOTHING

Clothing is the most important element of safe and comfortable touring. What one wears on a ski tour will be determined by the type and length of tour to be attempted. A run around Sugarhouse Park, obviously, will not require as much clothing as would a tour in one of the high canyons. A general requirement for *all* tours is to *always carry extra clothing*.

Headgear

Due to the immense blood flow volume in and around the brain, the head has the potential for greatest heat loss. A wool or synthetic-fiber head-band provides the lightest degree of protection, primarily serving to keep the ears warm and to soak up perspiration. For colder weather, a wool, wool/cotton blend, or synthetic fiber stocking cap large enough to be pulled over the ears, forehead, and upper neck is more suitable. The

Figure 2.3 Greg Hanscom shows the versatility of the balaclava as a headgear option for winter outings. In the folded position shown at left, it can cover the ears or just the top of the head. For colder conditions, it is pulled down around the neck. More intense weather may require that it be used to protect the mouth and nose as shown at right.

locally produced wool "Roly Cap," shown in the right part of Figure 2.2, is an excellent alternative to the stocking cap; one of its particularly useful features is the small visor that protects the eyes from wind, sun glare, and deep powder.

In particularly cold and windy conditions, it is necessary to cover the neck and chin. Several products are available for this purpose, but a simple "neck gaiter"(shown at left) works very well. Another alternative (middle) is a thin nylon "powder hood."

Still more protection is afforded by a wool "ski mask" hat that can be pulled over the head and neck. Such caps are popular among alpine skiers who finance purchase of exorbitantly-priced lift passes by robbing banks. A wool balaclava provides the most protection and is especially useful for extended or weather-exposed outings. As shown in Figure 2.3, this type of headgear provides graduated protection that's determined by how the hat is unfolded.

Headgear needs are somewhat different during springtime; ventilation and protection from sun glare become the dominant objectives. The smartly stylish and politically correct "Heli-Free Wasatch" ski cap achieves both objectives admirably.

Sunglasses. Sunglasses are an extremely important item of headgear that should be carried on a ski tour. Direct and reflected ultraviolet (UV) rays can cause *permanent* damage to the lining of the eye. The glare of sun on snow can also be harmful. Since not all commercial sunglasses block UV rays, the buyer should be especially careful to select only those that assure protection against such rays.

Sidepieces that block side glare are highly recommended, particularly for late winter and spring tours when the sun is higher in the sky. Some sunglass lenses are coated with a polarizing film that reduces reflected light; mirrored lenses may provide still more protection against glare. A cord, or commercially-available eye-glass keeper, can be used to secure eye glasses or sun glasses snugly to the head; unsecured glasses are easily lost during a tumble in deep powder snow. Some tourers prefer to use glacier goggles, which provide maximum protection against glare and UV rays and have the added advantage of providing protection from wind and driven snow.

Upper Body Garments

The principle of "layering" is the basic rule to be followed in protecting the torso and its appendages from cold.

The first layer of clothing next to the skin should pull moisture away from the skin so that it can evaporate. A light turtleneck made of a dual-component synthetic material[1] makes an excellent first layer.

A second layer should provide insulation by trapping air that can be kept warm by body heat. A wool shirt, or loose-fitting sweater are appropriate for this purpose. Clothing items made of synthetic materials such as polyester fleece or closer fitting stretch polyesters are popular alternatives.[2]

An outer layer should be waterproof and windproof to keep out rain, snow, and wind, while allowing perspiration to transpire away from the body. The ability of a fabric to keep atmospheric moisture from entering, while allowing body moisture to leave, is known as breathability. A number of waterproof, breathable alternatives such as Gore-Tex (a laminate) and nylon with a microporous coating are used in the manufacture of shell parkas, wind breakers, and other outer layer garments.

Many western skiers prefer to use hooded down or synthetically-insulated parkas for use as the outer shell. If kept dry, insulated parkas are exceptionally warm for their weight. The outer shells of such parkas are often made of breathable, yet waterproof materials.

---

[1] Dual-component materials consist of an inner layer that wicks perspiration away from the skin; the outer layer absorbs the liquid and allows it to evaporate. This process eliminates the coldness that comes from a wet layer next to the skin. The two layers are typically made from different polyesters.

[2] Many materials lose a large percentage of their insulating qualities when they get wet, particularly cotton. Wool has good properties when damp because its fibers are hollow, and some of the new synthetic fabrics are even better. A great deal of research is being conducted to develop fabrics that maintain insulation when wet.

Figure 2.4 Sharyl Smith models a *cagoule*, a long wind-proof garment that is particularly effective during tours in stormy weather. In an emergency, it can completely protect the wearer from the elements.

Some Wasatch Front tourers carry with them a cagoule, a calf or ankle-length waterproof parka illustrated in Figure 2.4. Unlike ordinary parkas, which are hip or waist-length, this extra-long garment provides excellent wind protection to the lower body and helps to contain more body heat within the shell. The cagoule becomes especially useful if a tourer is forced to spend the night in the woods. A candle, kept lighted under the cagoule, can help keep an individual from freezing on a cold winter night.

Other Clothing

The principle of layering is similarly applicable to hands, feet, and legs.

Special attention must be paid to hands and feet. Fingers and toes have large surface areas that contribute to rapid cooling. At cold temperatures finger and toe blood vessels start to constrict, reducing circulation of warm blood from the torso.

Hands can be protected from cold by the use of light gloves, wool mittens that fit easily over the gloves, and wind and water-resistant overmittens. When equipment needs to be adjusted the light gloves allow finger movement while protecting them from cold. Tourers who have particular difficulty keeping their hands warm will find that mittens are preferable to gloves, since they have less surface area where heat can escape. When temperatures aren't too cold, gloves (with or without liners) may suffice. Many quality products are made of modern synthetics such as Thinsulate and Thermolite. Some gloves contain a pocket that accommodates a small, chemically activated heating packet.

The battle to keep one's feet warm commences with liner socks manufactured of light wool or an appropriate synthetic fiber. Warm, knee-length wool socks follow. Leather or plastic boots serve as the outer wind, snow, and water barrier. Gaiters, either ankle or knee-high, keep loose snow from working its way into the boot where it can melt to destroy insulation. The higher gaiters also retard heat loss from the lower leg. Insulated gaiters are available for those needing additional lower leg and foot protection.

Individuals who are plagued with cold feet no matter what they wear may want to consider purchasing electrically-heated insoles for their ski boots. Such insoles position a small, electrical heating element directly under the toes. A rechargeable battery pack, attached to the boot or strapped to the lower leg, provides power. Advertising literature claims that the battery pack will provide "up to 8 hours of heat." The batteries can be recharged, the ad claims, "in excess of 1,000 times."

Light-weight synthetic longjohns are worn over the legs. A pant made of wool or some equivalent synthetic material is worn over the long johns. Wind pants, a lightweight garment made of a thin windproof material such as nylon, can be worn over the wool ski pants. "Warm-up pants", made of heavier, insulated garment, can be used in place of the wind pants, but are generally too hot during the ascent phase of a ski tour. They are ideal during a long descent, however, especially through deep and cold powder snow.

Practical Layering. Layering of clothing works best when all garments are absolutely dry. It is therefore best to remove layers *before* commencing the heavy exercise of a tour. Damp clothing caused by perspiration early in the tour can make the tourer feel cold all day. At the beginning of a tour, the parka, mittens, and wind pants should be stuffed into one's pack along with the hat, sweater, and overmitts. The dry garments should be saved for lunch stops, changes in the weather, and for the trip back to the car. Most knowledgeable tourers carry an extra pair of gloves and socks, as well as a spare turtle-neck shirt or insulated vest, to change into when their principal clothing becomes dampened.

Figure 2.5 Skiers have been around for a long time! The tracing of a Stone Age pictograph discovered in Russia (left) depicts what may well be "male bonding" associated with skiing. A section of an eleventh century rune stone discovered in Sweden (right) links use of skis with hunting.

SKI EQUIPMENT

In its most elemental form a ski is an extension of the foot that enhances its user's ability to travel over snow. A boot and a binding attaches the ski to the foot. Spread along the ski's bottom, substances such as wax reduce friction between ski and snow and enable the ski to slide forward; other materials or substances (including some forms of wax) increase friction to restrain the ski from sliding backward when climbing. A pole of some sort helps the skier to maintain balance and to control momentum. These basic principles were as applicable to ski gear of ancient Laplanders as they are to the equipment used today by recreational skiers.

Resembling a modern-day snowboard, the pine wood "Hoting" ski is the oldest ski known to man. The 4,500 year old artifact was discovered by Swedish archeologists in a peat bog in 1921. A sufficient number of prehistoric skis have been found in Scandinavia, Russia, and Siberia to allow categorizations with ethnic distinctions. Skis within the "Central Nordic" category are the most unusual of prehistoric skis. Each pair consisted of one long, grooved ski and one short, fur-covered ski. The long ski was used for sliding; the short one was for pushing against the snow to maintain forward momentum. Some prehistoric and historic rock carvings of skiers are depicted in Figure 2.5.

SKI EQUIPMENT

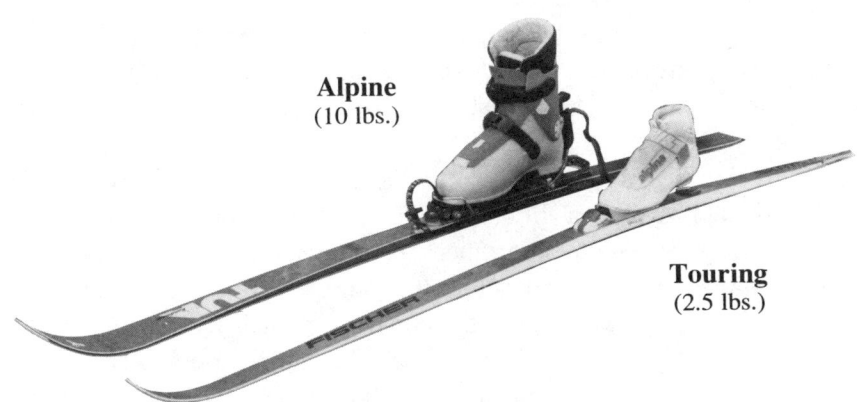

Figure 2.6 Alpine skiing equipment provides greater stability and turning power in the descent than equipment used for touring. Alpine equipment, however, is less desirable for climbing since it weighs approximately four times as much. Equipment courtesy of Wasatch Touring Company.

The major technological advances in ski design and construction have occurred in the twentieth century. Steel edges were added to wooden skis in the 1930's. Metal skis were developed after World War II and became popular during the 1950's. Skis made of composite polymeric materials are common today.

This section contains descriptions of modern cross country skis, boots, poles, and bindings, as well as discussions of waxing and climbing skins. The final part details equipment combinations suited for different types of touring.

Skis

Today, skis are manufactured to serve many diverse needs. Equipment used for jumping, for cross country, and for downhill (lift-serviced) skiing are all distinctively different. The family of skis used for cross country travel are generally referred to as "touring skis" or "cross country skis." Skis used for recreational downhill skiing are commonly called "alpine skis."[3] A representative of each type is illustrated in Figure 2.6.

---

[3] Technological advances in equipment design have made cross-use common. It is not unusual to see competent skiers descending groomed slopes of ski areas on cross country equipment, and it's not unusual to see alpine skis being used on ski tours. Mongrel crossbreed skis, which have evolved with the emergence of new and exotic manufacturing materials, are also beginning to blur the traditionally sharp demarcation between alpine and touring equipment.

Unlike alpine skis, which are designed specifically to slide at high speeds down a snowslope, touring skis must be designed for a duality of purposes—they must stick to the snow sufficiently to permit a skier to ascend a mountain *and* they must slide freely along flatlands and down the gentlest of slopes.

Three technologies have evolved to resolve this seeming contradiction of functions. (1) Waxes of different softness—and thus different ability to stick to the snow—can be applied to the smooth running surface of skis. Such waxes, often called "climbing waxes," are designed to retard backward slippage. Skis especially constructed to utilize such waxes are commonly called "waxable skis." (2) The ski is manufactured with a specially-textured sliding surface that permits easy forward sliding, but restricts the ability to slide backward. Skis with such a modified running surface are called "waxless skis." (3) A rough material such as rope, ribbed wood or plastic, or a strip of finely-textured material known as a "climbing skin" or "climber" can be attached temporarily to the sliding surface of the ski to prevent, or to retard, its ability to slide.

Waxable Skis. Modern waxable skis have a smooth sliding surface and are arched (technically, "cambered") in a manner that will not allow the center portion of the ski to touch the snow when the weight of the skier is evenly distributed over both skis. When weight is concentrated over one ski, however, the central area of the ski presses into the snow. This principle is illustrated in Figure 2.7.

In use, the front and rear of the sliding surface are coated with a wax that enhances slidability; the center part of the surface is coated with a softer wax that adheres to the snow. The softer wax is called a "climbing" or a "kick" wax, or simply "kicker." A skier moves forward by pressing one ski at a time into the snow. The kick wax allows him to move along using a "scooting" or "kick and glide" motion. On downhill or flat slopes, the skier weights both skis evenly, so the kick wax does not drag on the snow to impede progress.

For waxable skis to function properly it is important that the stiffness of the ski matches the weight of the skier. The less experienced skier may want to consider acquiring softer skis that make it easier to push the center portion of the ski into the snow.

Advantages: Properly waxed skis generally perform better than any other alternative since they slide very well and hence are easier to turn.

Disadvantages: Choosing proper wax is not always a simple matter, particularly when the temperature is near or above freezing, or when the snow conditions vary greatly during a tour.

SKI EQUIPMENT

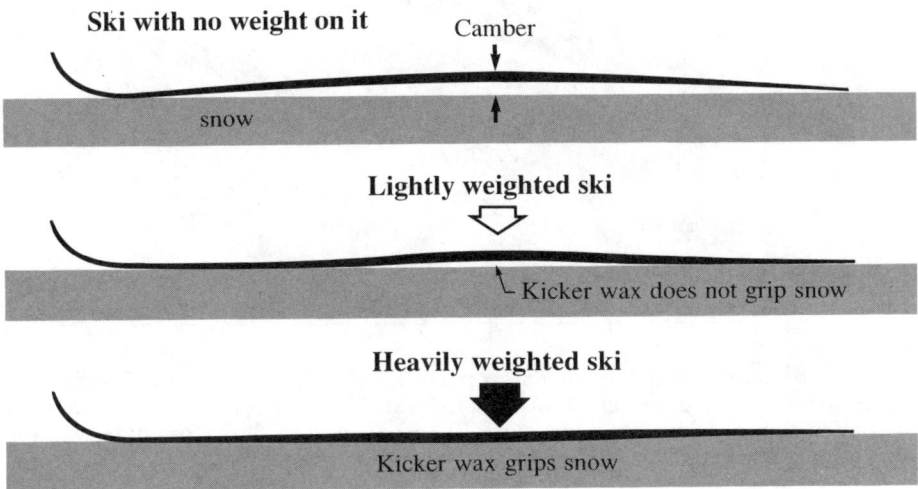

Figure 2.7 Waxable skis have a large amount of camber, which prevents the center section from touching the snow when weight is distributed evenly over both skis. In order for the kick wax to adhere to the snow, the skier pushes down very hard with one ski at a time.

Waxless Skis. The same principle is involved with this alternative as with the waxable ski, except no kicker wax is required. The key to success for waxless skis is the way the sliding surface is constructed. During manufacture, a step pattern is molded or machined into the center section of the ski's base (Figure 2.8). When the skier pushes the ski down on the snow with all of his or her weight, the step digs into the snow and prevents the ski from sliding backward. When the skier goes down the hill with skis evenly weighted, however, the steps don't drag on the snow, and the skis slide quite well. Waxless ski technology has evolved over the years to make this type of ski very effective in most snow conditions. They work particularly well when the snow is neither extremely hard nor very soft.

Advantages: The waxless ski is the simplest, most hassle-free alternative. The skis are always ready to go with no worry about selecting the proper wax; no time is required to put on wax or to attach climbing skins.

Disadvantages: Waxless skis don't work well on icy or very loose snow surfaces. Also, they don't slide as well as a properly waxed ski, so they are much slower and more difficult to turn.

Climbing Skins. Another alternative to the use of sticky wax for climbing is to attach climbers to the skis. A later section will describe

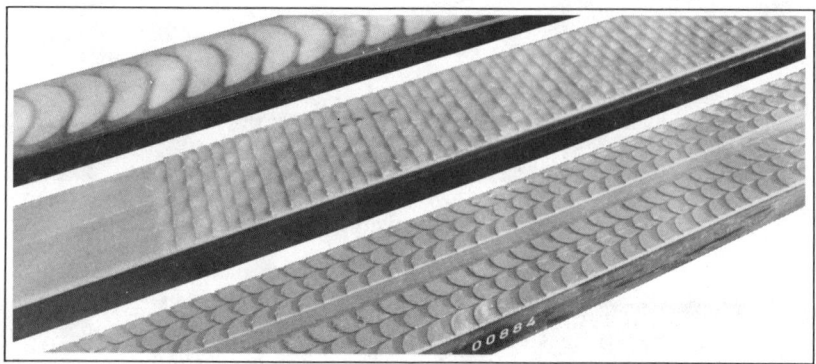

Figure 2.8 Waxless skis have a step pattern manufactured into the ski's running surface. When the skier pushes the ski down onto the snow surface, it will slide forward but not backward. The patterns of three popular waxless skis are shown here.

the selection and use of skins.

Advantages: Skins enable a skier to take a steeper route up a mountain than is practical with either waxed or waxless skis. They may also be used on any skis without regard to their camber or stiffness.

Disadvantages: Considerable time is required to attach and to remove skins. This can be particularly inconvenient if the tour involves several ascents and descents.

Hints For Selecting Skis. Touring skis should be a few centimeters longer than what one would use for downhill skiing. Short skis sink too far into deep snow and make climbing and turning difficult. For the same reason, skis are easier to handle in the powder if the tips are more flexible. This allows them to "float" to the surface between turns. Stiff tips tend to "dive" during a turn, which often leads to uncomfortable head plants.

Waxes

The basic theory behind climbing waxes is relatively simple: *one has to match the viscosity of the wax to the snow it is to be used on.* In practice, waxing is more complicated; the snow's temperature, density, humidity, granularity, and even its history, have to be considered. The complexities are even more pronounced in racing than in touring. Here, it is rumored that a very select group of monk-like vagabonds, resembling 13th century Goliards, travels the annual racing circuit, dispensing their earthy waxing wisdom to the racers. It is well-known that races are won as much by the "wax wonks" as they are by the racers.

SKI EQUIPMENT

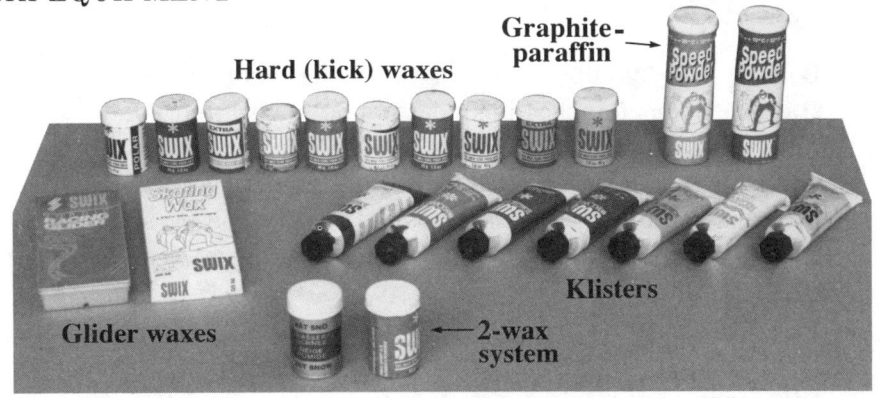

Figure 2.9 A small percentage of the waxes manufactured by one popular company is included in this photo. The two-wax system is adequate for most snow conditions encountered in the Wasatch.

Types of Waxes. It is not the authors' intention to detail the techniques of waxing; that would take more volumes than *Wasatch Tours*. A few suggestions, however, might be of value to the would-be tourer.

Modern cross country waxes are available in a variety of viscosities. The hardest (least viscous) waxes are slightly firmer than a household candle. Designated by the name "klister," the Swedish word for glue, the softest waxes have the consistency of cool honey. The harder waxes come in convenient, peel-away containers; klisters come in squeezable tubes.

Most touring waxes are color-coded and designated for a range of snow temperatures. The harder waxes are used on the coldest snow; the softer waxes are used on snow that is warmer. "Glider" waxes are especially formulated to enhance the ski's ability to slide; "kick" waxes allow the skier to ascend a slope. The top part of Figure 2.9 illustrates the wide range of waxes being manufactured by one company.

There are many brands of touring wax, all of which work well in the snow conditions for which they were designed. Beginning tourers are urged to select a single brand and to become familiar with the range of its waxes, rather than to try coping with waxes of several brands.

Some two-wax systems—one wax for cold snow, the other for wet snow—are available for tourers who do not wish to purchase the entire selection of waxes within a brand. Some companies manufacture spray-on waxes in environmentally safe pressurized or pump-operated containers.

Waxing Hints. During mid-winter Wasatch snow conditions are generally consistent, making waxing quite simple. Even at that, the neophyte tourer should consider the following suggestions:

- Begin a tour by applying kick wax on the center section of the ski, starting about 6 inches behind the boot's heel and going forward to a point about half way between the boot's toe and the ski tip. Glider wax can be applied to the tips and tails of the skis. By avoiding sticky wax on the rear of the ski, it is possible to glide on the downhills by leaning back and putting most of the weight on the tails of the skis.
- Wax lasts longer if it is rubbed into the ski with a cork or a foam block, or with a glove. Heat generated by rubbing enhances it's adherence to the skis and makes the surface smoother for better sliding.
- If the wax doesn't grip sufficiently well to climb, first add more of the same wax to the middle of the skis. If that still doesn't work, apply the same wax to a longer section of the ski base. If you still don't get enough grip, apply a softer wax on top of what was already there.[4]
- Use of klister is inevitable when the snow begins to melt in the spring. When snow texture varies between granular and powder during a tour, a layer of snow and ice may build up on the klister whenever the skis encounter dry snow. This problem can often be avoided by applying a layer of hard wax over the klister after it has cooled.
- Keep opened tubes of klister in separate plastic bags. Also, put klistered skis in a plastic ski bag (airlines have them) before putting them in your car. It's easier to prevent a mess than to clean it up.
- When removing wax from skis, excessive heat must be avoided, so it is best to use a solvent and/or a scraper. Particularly sticky waxes may require use of an abrasive, such as steel wool or a scouring pad, to assist the solvent.
- Early and late-season tourers often encounter an extremely wide range of snow temperatures during a tour, complicating the selection of the correct wax. Faced with the necessity of several wax changes during the course of a day, even the most devout waxer may resort to use of waxless skis.

Climbing Skins

Some ski historians believe that "very marked" tool scars along the prehistoric Hoting ski are "an indication of its having been skin-covered."

---

[4]Randy Gregg, ski technician at REI, describes this concept in a March 1993 Sports Guide article as the "thicker, longer, softer rule."

SKI EQUIPMENT   47

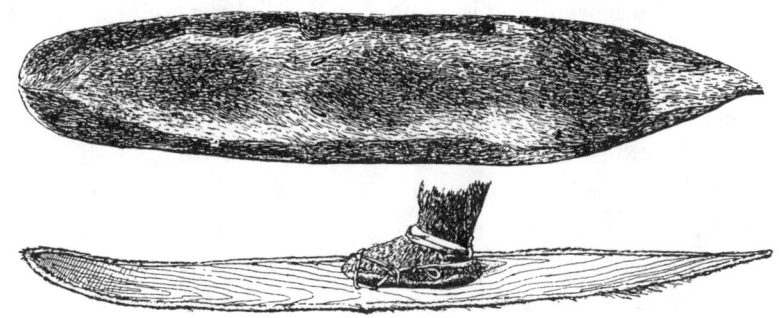

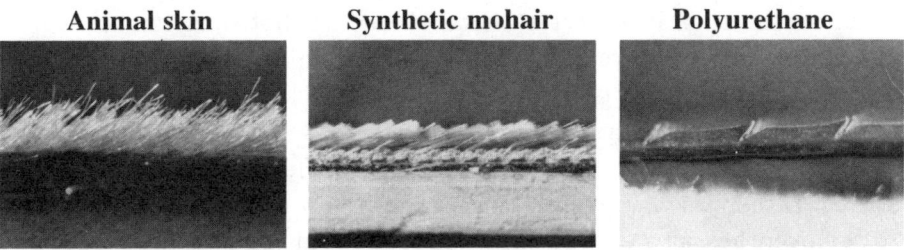

Figure 2.10   The bottom surface of some prehistoric skis, such as the Yukaghir ski pictured above, were entirely covered with animal skin, often taken from the legs of reindeer. The micrographs illustrate the surface texture of several varieties of modern climbing skins.

Some skis, described (or acquired) by various 18th and 19th Century expeditions into the extreme northern regions of Europe, were permanently covered with skins along their bottoms; reindeer skin, and skin taken from the legs of elk, were the commonly used. The top portion of Figure 2.10 illustrates the bottom and side views of the fur-covered, 149 cm. long Yukaghir ski. Several early historical versions of detachable skins (or "climbers," as they became known later) appear in various Norwegian and Swedish museums.

Modern (early 20th Century) detachable climbers were commonly made from the skin of seals. Today's improved—and environmentally conscientious—climbing skins are made from goat hair or synthetic materials such as mohair. "Snake Skins," climbers manufactured locally by Voilé, are constructed entirely of urethane plastic. The micrographs reproduced at the bottom of Figure 2.10 detail the surface characteristics of each variety of climber.

Traditionally, skins have been used only on heavy touring skis, particularly for steep climbs, but it is increasingly common to see them on narrower, medium-weight skis. The width of skins should closely match that of the skis. Wider skins have more surface area to adhere to the snow, but it is important that they not cover the ski's edges, especially if the tour traverses steep or icy slopes. One company manufactures a shorter model called "kicker skins" that are only about half the length of the ski; these are lighter, but not as effective for steep slopes.

Most modern climbers are attached to skis with glue that is applied to the cloth backing. The glue adheres best when it is warm and when the ski surface is clean and dry. Skins must be handled with care, and the glue-coated surface must remain clean when not in use. The base of the skis must be kept free of sticky climbing waxes. When putting skins on the skis, it is best to wipe off the ski bottoms as thoroughly as possible. If skins are repeatedly taken off and put back on during a tour, it is advisable to carry them inside the jacket. The glue must also be renewed periodically.

Some climbers are designed to attach to the skis with clamps and straps, rather than with glue. These are less convenient to attach and to remove; they also tend to slip from side to side on side hills, but they don't require a perfectly clean ski. (A little wax, in fact, may help to hold them in place.) One problem with straps is that they prevent the metal edges of the skis from biting into hard snow, which can make it difficult (and possibly dangerous) to traverse steep slopes. The bottom line is that adhesive skins, like waxable skis, are generally more effective, but require more care and maintenance.

When storing climbing skins, they should first be folded in half with the glued surface on the inside as shown in Figure 2.11. (It's best not to fold them in *exactly* the same place each time.) They may then be rolled or folded to fit into a plastic or cloth bag for storage in a pack or an inner coat pocket. It is important that climbers be dried between tours.

Boots

The two main purposes of touring boots are (1) to protect the feet from snow and cold, and (2) to efficiently transfer the wearer's commands to the skis during turning. The first requirement leads to boots that are well insulated (often with more than one layer), and the second leads to boots that are sufficiently stiff to allow leg movements to be easily transferred through the boots to the skis. A third consideration, which leads to compromises in boot selection, is comfort. Factors that influence structural and outward features of the boot are the type of

SKI EQUIPMENT

Figure 2.11 Karin Caldwell illustrates an advantage of climbers over wax; she easily walks straight up an approximately 30° slope. In the inset, Chris Erickson demonstrates a technique for quickly folding skins that works well even in windy weather. He first folds the skins together at the mid-point, then pulls the folded part down through a loop that he makes with his other hand, gently squeezing the two parts as they come together.

terrain, weather, and snow conditions to be encountered.

Close examination of historical Utah ski photographs suggests that common workboots (sometimes worn with rubbers) or hiking boots were used for skiing during the early 1920's. Boots crafted specifically for skiing appear in photos taken during the 1930's and 1940's. Leather boots manufactured for alpine (lift) skiing dominate touring photos taken in the 1950's and 1960's. Today, some local tourers scour second-hand stores and thrift shops in search of the beautifully hand-crafted leather boots popular in those decades.

Touring boots suitable for use in the Wasatch vary from moderately light, ankle-high models to heavier ones that extend well above the ankle and have fairly thick soles. The outer layer of the boots is made of leather or plastic. A soft lining, made of foam or fleece, adds comfort and insulation. An elastic or padded cuff bars loose snow from entering the boot. The front edge of the sole protrudes somewhat beyond the front of the boot to provide an interlock area for the ski's binding, and the heel is often grooved to accept a cable binding. *In selecting touring boots, it is necessary to consider boots and bindings in combination.* The

Figure 2.12 A wide variety of boots is available to tourers. The heavier models provide more control on the downhill, but the lighter ones are easier to carry to the top of the mountain. Equipment courtesy of White Pine Touring.

different types of binding will be discussed in a subsequent section.

Heavy touring boots provide considerably more lateral stability for turning and more warmth than lighter models. Some heavy touring boots are also built with thick lug soles desirable for outings that may involve hiking stretches of snow-free terrain, ascending or traversing hardpacked or icy snow, and scrambling on rocky ridges.

Hints for Choosing Touring Boots. The most important consideration when buying boots is the fit. There are many brands of good quality boots, and all have slightly different lasts. It is wise to try on several pair before making a purchase. Touring boots should be large enough to wear a light and a heavy pair of socks and still leave room for plenty of toe movement. The *toes* of the boots should be sufficiently loose to prevent pinched toes during telemark turns or whenever a ski slips back while climbing. It is equally important that the *heels* of the boots fit snugly, however, to prevent blisters. Tight boots can lead to cold feet, but loose boots make turning more difficult.

The sole of touring boots should have enough flexibility to permit full forward motion of the leg, but it should resist *twisting*. This tortional stiffness enables the skier's leg movements to be transmitted through the boot to the ski during turning.

Bindings

The primary function of a ski binding is to attach the boot to the ski. Automatic releasability during a bone-threatening fall is a relative

SKI EQUIPMENT

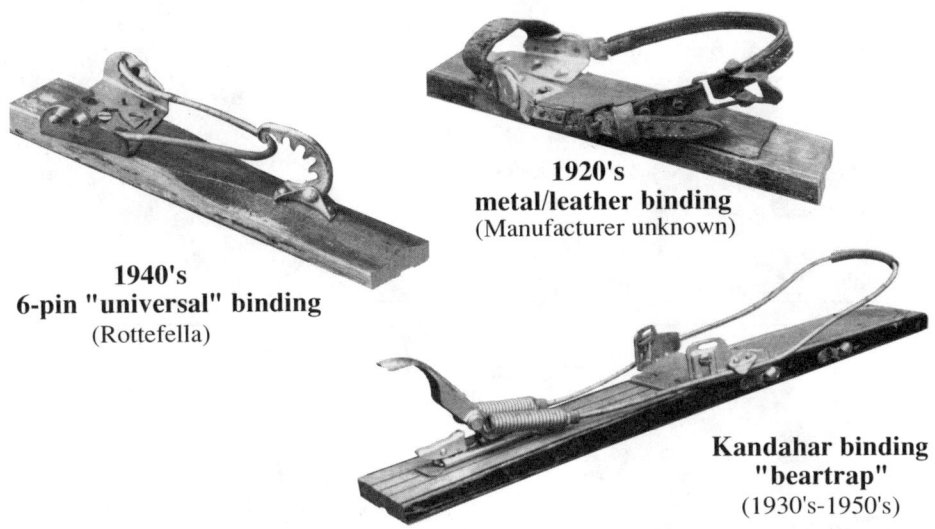

Figure 2.13 Note the similarity of the early and mid-20th century bindings shown here to the "modern" bindings used by tourers more than 50 years later.

newcomer to the functional requirements of bindings.

Sweden's 4,500 year old Hoting ski had no binding when it was discovered; a wide slot carved laterally through the ski suggests the possibility of a toe strap. Norway's 2,500 year old Overbö ski had a vertical hole bored through it, which indicates that thongs may have been used to attach the boots. Seventeenth century illustrations picture skis with toe loops and loop-and-strap combinations. Use of the loop/strap system of binding continued well into the twentieth century. In Utah, several early-1900's photographs clearly show thonged snowshoe harnesses mounted on skis as bindings.

As skiing (at that time exclusively cross country) began to gain popularity in the late 1800's, ski bindings began to receive technological attention. The first major advance occurred near the turn of the century when a U-shaped piece of metal with a strap across its top was developed to give greater lateral support for the front of the boot while still allowing the boot to pivot forward. This system, with a later provision of a heel clampdown, evolved into the universally popular Kandahar or "bear trap" binding of the thirties and forties. Modern variations of this system are still utilized today. A variety of historical bindings is illustrated in Figure 2.13.

In the post-war era, as skiing on packed slopes at lift-served ski areas gained popularity, safety release bindings were developed to meet

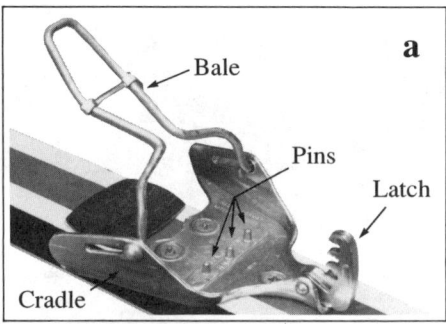 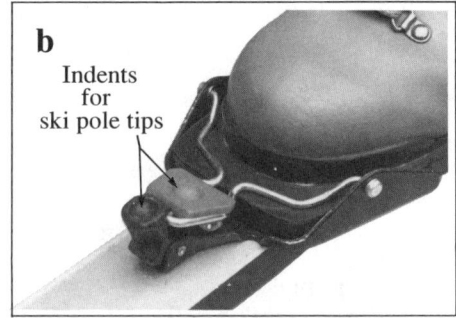
 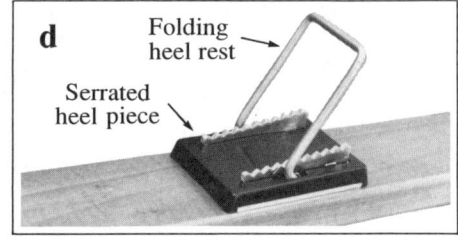

Figure 2.14 The most popular boot-binding combination is still the "3-pin." The metal plate built into the boot sole (c) prevents damage to the sole. A serrated metal heel plate (d) enhances the skiers' ability to turn the skis; the heel rest prevents the Achilles tendons from overstretching during steep ascents.

new demands of speed, control, and reliability. Advancement of release bindings continues today.

If ever the saying "whatever goes around comes around" applies to ski equipment, it is most true of ski bindings. With the advent of lift skiing, continued development of bindings for cross country skiing came nearly to a standstill. But not for long! With the resurgence of popularity of backcountry recreation in the 1970's and 1980's, new attention was focused on equipment for cross country use. Evolution of touring bindings parallels that of downhill bindings: first refinements for control of stability, then addition of releasability. Two Utah companies (Voilé and Black Diamond) are today involved in design and manufacture of some excellent cross country bindings.

Universal Bindings. While the present trend of cross country binding development is leading toward boot-and-binding combinations, three types of "universal" bindings are still available today. These are commonly known as "3-pin," "cable," and "plate." The chief advantages of such bindings is their compatibility with a variety of boots. Switching of equipment among friends is possible without worrying about incompatibility.

3-Pin Bindings. The 3-pin binding (illustrated in Figure 2.14 is one of the simplest and lightest of bindings used on skis.[5] It consists of a molded metal cradle that is mounted to the ski. Three metal pins protrude upward from the base of the cradle and engage into three matching holes in the sole of the boot. A latch clamps the boot firmly over the pins. These are often referred to as "75 mm. bindings," since that is the width of the toe of the boot that fits into them.

Pin bindings are available in traditional hand-latching models as well as spring-loaded, step-in types. In selecting a pin binding for backcountry use, tourers should choose a model that is quite sturdy and that will stand up to the amount of twisting required for turning (or falling) in deep snow. External latches (called "bales") made of thin wire should be avoided as they are more likely to pop out and to be lost in the powder. In purchasing boots for use with 3-pin bindings, it is important to make sure that the soles are internally reinforced *with metal plates* (as shown in Figure 2.14c) to prevent the pins from ripping out the holes.[6] Touring bindings are not complete without a heel piece that prevents the boot from sliding off the ski in a turn. Without this simple fixture, even a good powder skier would have difficulty in deep snow.

Many companies make 3-pin bindings, so it is possible to switch brands and to exchange skis with companions. Voilé has recently added a full safety release feature to one of their 3-pin binding designs.

Cable Bindings. The cable cross country binding consists of brackets that hold the toe of the boot and metal cables that cinch around the heels to hold them in. Such cable bindings were traditionally called "bear traps." Light-weight variants of the bear traps were quite popular during the 1960's and early 1970's, but they soon lost favor. Cable bindings resurfaced in the late 1980's in response to the need for heavy duty cross country ski bindings that would be less likely to damage the toes of the boots and hence be more reliable for ski mountaineering.

A major advantage of the cable binding is its usability with boots of different types. Many light touring boots, heavier ski boots, and even mountaineering boots will fit into a cable system. Another advantage is that cables give the skier more control during turning than 3-pin bindings, particularly if they allow the heel to be clamped to the ski during descent. Some also provide *limited* releasability during falls.

---

[5] Technically, this statement is incorrect. In the mid-1940's, Harold Goodro won a cross country ski race using no binding at all. He simply screwed the front of his racing boots permanently to his skis.

[6] To minimize this kind of damage to your boots, be sure to clean off all snow and ice, and to clamp the boots down firmly each time they are placed in the bindings.

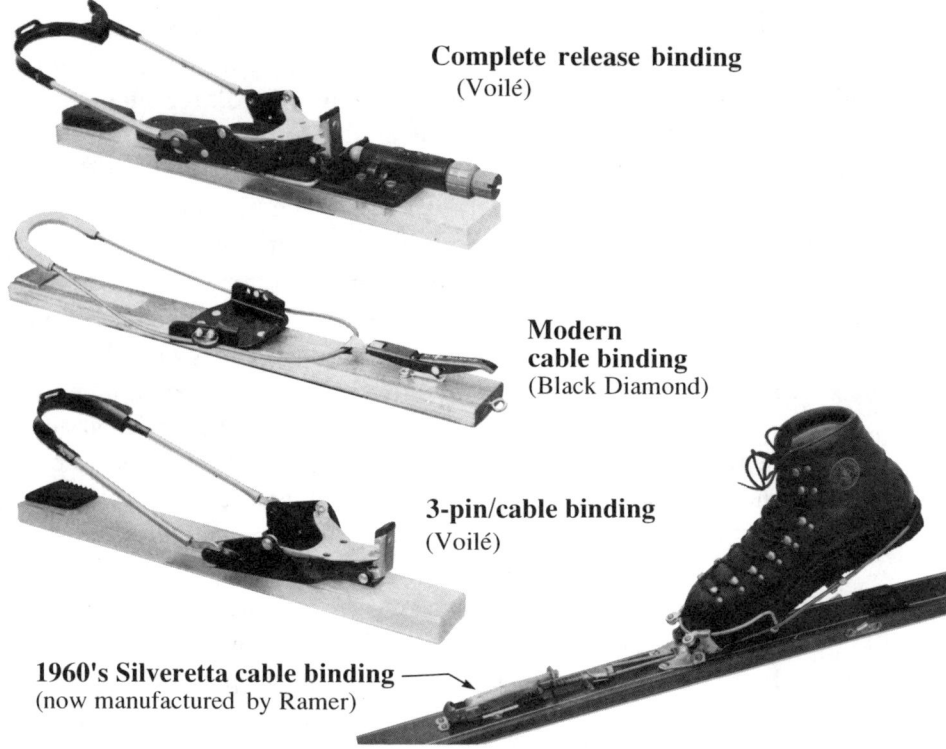

Figure 2.15 A number of cable binding models are available. The Voilé and Black Diamond products are manufactured in Salt Lake City.

Several types of cable bindings are illustrated in Figure 2.15.

Plate Bindings. In its elemental form the plate binding consists of a frontally-hinged platform that is attached to the ski, with the ski boot secured tightly to the plate. Illustrated in Figure 2.16, this type of binding was introduced in Europe early in the 1900's. The Austrian Bilgeri binding was adopted by the Austrian-Hungarian ski troops and was advertised as "best for Alpine skiing" in 1911.

A major modern-day improvement to the plate is a releasability feature. Some plates are attached to the ski with a mechanism that allows them to break free in a twisting fall. These are usually used with heavy-duty touring boots or with boots used for downhill skiing. The binding is quite heavy and has the added disadvantage of placing the skier higher above the top surface of the ski.

A very effective variation on the plate binding is produced by Voilé, a Salt Lake City company founded and run by ski tourers. This product consists of thin plastic strips that are permanently attached to the skis under 3-pin bindings and clamp to the back of the boots like cables.

SKI EQUIPMENT

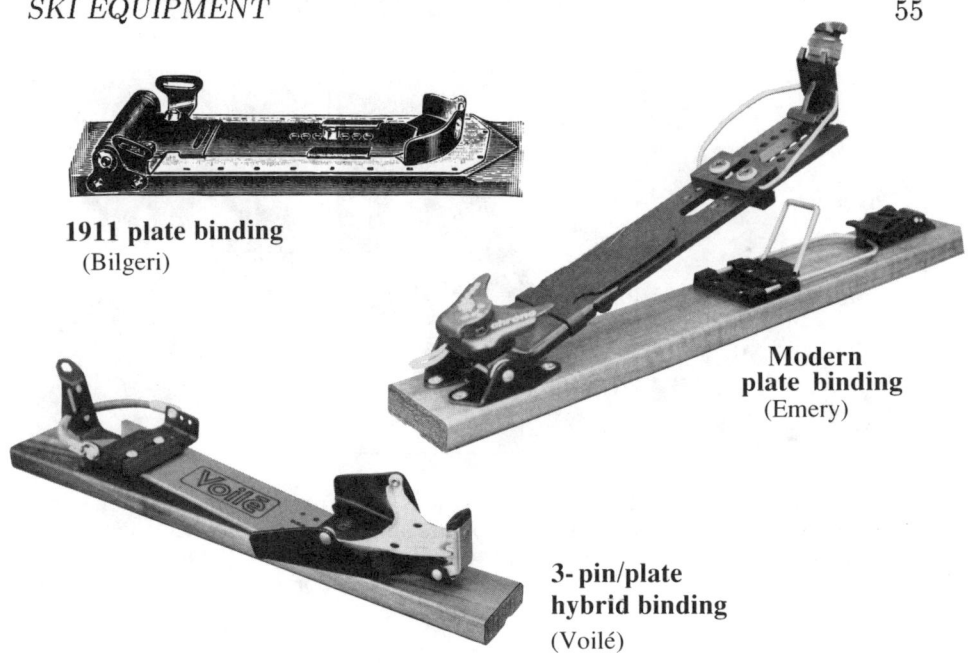

Figure 2.16 Plate bindings are designed to relieve the stress placed on boots by eliminating flexing of the soles. Many plate bindings allow the heels to be attached to the skis for easier turning, and some incorporate a release feature. Equipment courtesy of Recreational Equipment Inc. (REI).

They essentially act as an extra layer in the soles of the boots that improves their tortional rigidity without significantly increasing resistance to lifting the heels. Voilés also protect the holes in the toes of the boots and give the skier better control during turns. Their disadvantage is the increased potential for twisting injuries.

Other Boot/Binding Combinations. A good example of the application of modern technology to solve an existing problem is the *New Nordic Norm–Back Country* boot/binding system. Abbreviated to *NNN–BC*, this system is manufactured by several companies.

The *NNN–BC* boot has a horizontal bar built into the front of the sole that clamps into a slot in the binding. The bar acts as a hinge that allows the heel of the boot to lift freely. The bottom of the boot has a slot along its length that fits over a plastic piece attached to the ski to keep the boot from slipping off the ski in a turn. The *NNN–BC* is an excellent system for medium touring skis. Figure 2.17 illustrates the three components of the system.

The major advantage of the *NNN–BC* combination is the ease with which boots can be attached and detached. The binding also provides greater steering power and is less likely to damage the toe of the boot

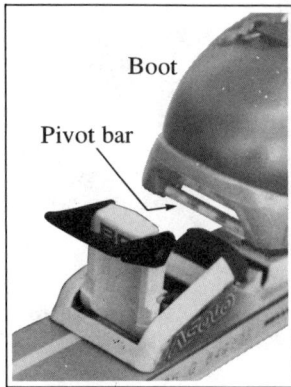 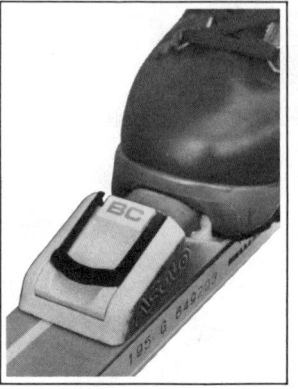 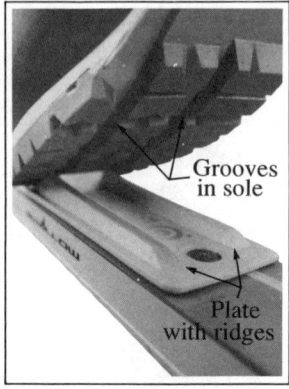

Figure 2.17 The NNN–BC binding includes a clamping mechanism that attaches to a pivot bar molded into the toe of the boot. A plate with ridges (that fit into grooves in the boot sole to prevent twisting during turns) is mounted on the ski. Equipment courtesy of Kirkham's Outdoor Products.

after repeated high-stress falls. A chief disadvantage is the binding's "unfriendliness" toward repairs in the field. If the boot's toe were to break during an outing, it would be quite difficult to perform a backcountry repair.

- Regardless of the boots and bindings that are selected, it is wise to use safety straps on touring skis. A runaway ski in deep snow is rarely found, and a lost ski in the backcountry can be a disaster. Most bindings have some point where straps can be attached, and two short pieces of nylon cord could save hours of misery.

Ski Poles

When archeologists extracted the 3,900 year old Kalutrask Ski from a Swedish marsh, it lay near a stick with a hollowed out blade at one end. It is tempting to conclude that the stick may be the world's oldest ski pole. Little is known of prehistoric ski poles. An early historical illustration shows a bearded, fur-clad skier/hunter carrying a pike-like pole. In 1673, a German writer published a text illustrating, among other things, Lapp skiers utilizing long disk-bearing poles to push themselves along the snow, to pivot about on a turn, and to maintain balance while descending. One historian suggests that the Lapps also utilized the single pole as a weapon of warfare.

In Utah, early skiers used a single, long pole. Some early to mid-1920's photographs picture use of two poles, one long and the other short. The single pole and the asymmetric dual poles disappear from

SKI EQUIPMENT

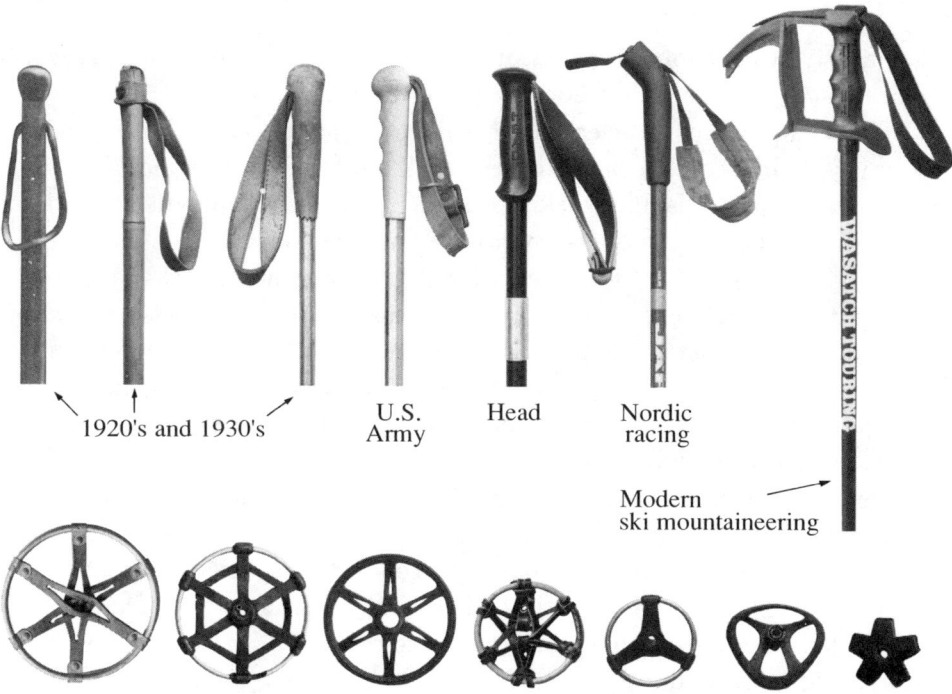

Figure 2.18 Ski pole handles and baskets, antique and contemporary. The larger baskets are more effective in deep powder; smooth handles are less likely to cause discomfort and wrist/hand fatigue on long tours.

photographs taken after that time.

Since the popularization of skiing sports, ski poles have undergone numerous changes—some functional, many cosmetic. Early poles were made of bamboo; aluminum, magnesium, and steel were used later. Some contemporary poles are constructed of composite materials containing glass or carbon fibers. Handles, wrist-loops, and baskets have also changed. Early bamboo poles rarely exhibit handles. Grips made of leather and cork were later added. Handles molded of plastics are common today. Basket design has followed the trends in skiing. Large baskets—to keep the pole from sinking in loose snow—were common among pre-ski lift tourers. As skiing on packed slopes became popular basket size was reduced. Today, a great variety of basket sizes and styles is available for the backcountry skier.

Hints for Selecting Ski Poles. Pole length should be greater for touring than for downhill skiing to allow for more pushing power. A good rule of thumb is to select poles that are armpit height. These longer poles may get in the way during the downhill part of the tour, but the extra length will pay dividends during the climb. An expensive alternative that eliminates this problem is adjustable poles that allow a skier to vary the length according to the terrain.

It is important to select poles that are durable enough to survive many falls in deep snow. Climbing with a broken pole is not an easy task. It is not advisable to skimp on this item of equipment. Bamboo and flimsy fiberglass models are not recommended for backcountry use.

Extra large baskets for poles are a good investment in the Wasatch, where the snow can be very soft and deep. Tourers may also want to consider buying ski poles with break-away handles for the time when a basket gets hung up on a tree branch. A dislocated shoulder is no fun at all, particularly in the backcountry. Alternatively, wrist straps should be removed when skiing down through heavily vegetated terrain.

Some poles are designed to be joined together to form an avalanche probe. Usually the handles must first be removed, and the two shafts are then screwed together to make a probe that is twice the length of one pole. This extremely useful feature will be discussed in Chapter 4.

Reconsider purchasing poles that are "trendy." Aerodynamically-shaped handles may appear inviting, but at certain angles their sharp edges may cause blisters and fatigue palm muscles after several hours of pushing oneself up a mountain. A smooth, round handle (as in Figure 2.18) works equally well at all angles.

EQUIPMENT COMBINATIONS

The primary consideration when deciding on cross country skiing equipment is the type of touring that will be done. The following sections describe the most common forms of ski touring, along with equipment combinations that are most appropriate for each.

Track Skiing

Track skiing is recommended for those who have no desire to leave the groomed trails at the cross country ski areas or the roads that have been packed by and for snow machines. Skis, boots, and poles for this type of skiing are extremely light and somewhat fragile. The skis are very narrow (about 45 mm) and quite stiff, so they are not suitable for deep snow or steep slopes. They also have very straight sides and do not turn easily. This kind of equipment is ideal for covering long distances in short periods of time, or for skiing any distance with a minimum of effort.

Track skiing is also a good choice for those interested in being stylish in their dress (and for those who enjoy observing others being so). Stretchy lycra clothing is available for bodies slim enough to do it justice. This material is extremely comfortable, but not particularly warm or wind-proof. Extra layers of warmer clothing and overboots are needed for cold days and long tours.

Most track skiers use "classical" technique, which is similar to walking. The skis are pushed along on the snow in a forward direction to take advantage of their slippery bottoms. Classical skiing may be done on waxable or waxless skis.

The other technique alternative is "skating", which is a method of propulsion that requires a very wide and well-packed trail. The skier uses a skating motion to push and glide along the track. The ski poles are also used for propulsion, usually in conjunction with skating motions to one side or to the other.

Skating is done on waxable skis, but the complexity of waxing is greatly reduced. Since forward momentum is gained by pushing off the edge of the ski, no kick wax is needed. More effort is involved in skating than in classical skiing, particularly for the beginner, but this technique is extremely efficient and very fast on gentle terrain. Anyone interested in learning to skate is advised to start with normal kicking and gliding on waxed skis, then mix in a bit of skating on gentle downhill sections. As the technique is mastered, the amount of kick wax can be gradually reduced. It is wise to carry kick wax for long tours so it can be added if the skating muscles get too tired to function.

Skis for packed trails should be longer than the skier is tall. Skating skis are stiffer and a bit shorter than classical skis, with more rounded tips. Poles should be shoulder height for classical skiing, longer for skating; the maximum length in any case is about nose level. Skating boots have extremely stiff soles, while classical boots must flex upward to allow the skier to kick and glide. Boots and bindings must be purchased together, since many different noncompatible combinations are available.

For both classical and skating techniques, there must be a good interlocking mechanism between the boot sole and the ski to allow the skis to be turned.[7]

---

[7]High performance track skis are relatively difficult to turn, regardless of the quality of the binding; they are not recommended for beginners, and they are not suitable for skiing in unpacked snow.

Figure 2.19 Leslie Thompson, one of the foremost American cross country ski racers, illustrates proper skating technique in a 1993 Wasatch Citizens Series event at the White Pine Touring Center in Park City. *Inset:* The high boots provide lateral support needed for long races and high-speed turns.

Light Touring

Many beginners spend most—or all—of their time at touring centers or on roadways. It is common for them to purchase sturdier equipment and warmer clothing than that described in the preceding section. Light touring equipment is suitable for skiers who wish to stay on packed trails and very moderate terrain, but it is not a wise choice for those who decide to venture into steeper terrain and deeper snow.

Light touring skis are wider than track skis (about 50 mm.), so they are more stable and a better choice for the novice. They have very little side camber,[8] so turning is difficult. They are designed for classical technique and are available with waxable or waxless bottoms.

Light touring boots are higher than those described previously, which means that they provide more warmth and more ankle support. Suitable boots can be found in either leather or plastic. Many boot/binding combinations exist that have good interlocking mechanisms to maximize

---

[8] "Side camber" is the term used to describe the difference between the width of the center of the ski and that of the tip and tail. Skis are usually designed to be wider at the front and back than in the middle to allow them to be turned more easily.

control. Boot soles should not be difficult to bend forward in a normal walking motion, but they should have good tortional stability; i.e., the soles should not *twist* easily.

General Touring

The lightest weight touring equipment suitable for general use in the Wasatch Mountains consists of 55 to 60 mm wide skis and ankle-high boots. The wider skis tend to sink less into the soft snow that prevails in Utah. This extra width, along with significant side camber, also makes them easier to turn. A major advantage of heavier skis is that they break less easily; saving a few ounces is not a good trade-off for mountain touring. The higher boots provide more warmth and support for long days in deep snow.

Waxable versus waxless is still an important issue. As discussed in an earlier section, a properly waxed ski is hard to beat, as long as its stiffness is appropriate for the skier. Many general touring skis are too stiff for soft snow.

There are numerous suitable alternatives for boots and bindings. Many tourers still utilize the traditional leather boots with 3-pin bindings. Other systems work fine, but low cut boots should be avoided. Many boots have very thin plastic soles, which provide neither warmth nor enough stiffness to allow one to turn the skis. The soles should have a smooth, long-radius flex with no sharp angles, and they should be difficult to twist. A soft lining and padded cuff improve warmth and comfort. Also, it is important to get heel pieces for the skis so the boots don't slide off the skis when they are pushed down and sideways during turns.

Light boots can be made warmer with a pair of insoles and with gaiters that come down over the toe. A large pair of wool socks over the boot also works, but be sure that the bindings function properly with them on.

One possibility that has not been mentioned in this section is to use climbing skins on general touring skis, rather than wax. Climbers defeat the advantage of light weight gear, since they weigh several ounces and do not slide very well, but they allow a skier to climb steep slopes more easily and safely.

General touring equipment is at its best on terrain that is not too steep and in moderately deep powder snow. It is delightful for climbing all but the steepest slopes, but most people have difficulty turning the skis in heavy or very deep snow. An expert skier can usually manage quite well as long as the snow is relatively consistent. The problem is not so much that the skis won't turn, but that the margin for error is very small. Mistakes often result in a cold landing.

Heavy Touring

The current trend for those who enjoy the "steep and deep," whether in the backcountry or at downhill skiing areas, is mountaineering or "telemark" skis with steel edges, heavy duty bindings (3-pin or cable), and stiff boots. Climbing skins are the best alternative for those who choose to propel themselves up the hills. The skis are essentially the same as alpine skis, but a little narrower (60 to 75 mm). Many skis provide the performance required for hard packed slopes and slalom racing, while others are softer and more appropriate for powder and backcountry skiing. This type of equipment is highly recommended for mountaineering outings where variable snow conditions are often encountered and steep slopes must be climbed. It is also the option of choice for winter camping, when heavy loads must be carried.

Heavy touring boots come well above the ankle and have fairly thick soles. Thus, they provide more lateral stability for turning and more warmth than the lighter boots discussed previously. They should be large enough for heavy and light socks with plenty of toe room; if extra warmth is desired, a pair of insoles and gaiters help considerably. Some of these boots have heavy lug soles suitable for mountaineering expeditions that involve hiking on rocky surfaces. Both leather and plastic models are available.

A skier using heavy equipment can exert considerable stress on boots and bindings, so it is wise to use Voilé plates as mentioned in a previous section. Remember, however, that the boot is no longer as free to twist or to pull out of the binding during a bad fall. Increasing numbers of knee injuries are occurring as boots and bindings become less forgiving. This problem can be eliminated by adding release plates underneath the bindings for safety.

It should be obvious that mountaineering ski equipment is much better for downhill, but less advantageous for climbing, than the lighter options. It provides more stability and allows more margin for error in deep or wind-packed snow. The boots are warmer and thus more suitable for extended tours in very cold weather. Heavy touring gear is good for the learning powder skier who can't resist the steep slopes, and for the person who does a variety of tours, but can't afford a second set of equipment.

Alpine Touring

Thirty years ago ski touring in the Wasatch was done almost exclusively on downhill skis with heavy boots and cable bindings, and with sealskins strapped to the bottom for climbing. This is still an option for tours that have very steep ascents and downhill runs that are of sufficient difficulty to require maximum control. The equipment is very heavy and makes climbing more tiring, but there are times when touring skis just won't suffice. This alternative is sometimes called alpine touring; in Europe it is known as "radonee skiing" and is extremely popular.

The bindings used for alpine touring allow heel lift for climbing and convert to normal release bindings for the downhill run. There are several brands available, most of which have some kind of plate mechanism that attaches the boot to the ski. The rear of the plate can be detached from the ski to allow heel lift.

The cost of skis, boots, bindings, and climbers is higher for this alternative than for regular touring equipment, although new telemark skis certainly cost more than a good pair of used downhills. If one does any lift skiing, however, the same set of gear could be used for both, so this could be the least expensive in the long run.

Snowshoeing

Last but not least are the snowshoes. They provide a good firm foundation both going up and coming down, with no slipping and sliding except on really steep terrain or on very hard snow surfaces. Snowshoes are suitable for most beginner and intermediate tours. Anyone who worries about going too fast and taking a dangerous spill on skis will be more comfortable on snowshoes. To a confirmed skier, snowshoeing appears dull, but the snowshoers get the last laugh on very narrow trails with insufficient room for turning or slowing down on skis. If hiking is enjoyable but skiing is not, snowshoes are a good way to get into the mountains in the winter.

Snowshoes are available in wood, metal, or plastic, with decking and laces made of rawhide or neoprene-coated nylon. Aluminum or magnesium framed snowshoes are more expensive than those framed with wood, but they are lighter and require less maintenance. Neoprene decking resists water absorption and is easier to take care of than rawhide. Most plastic snowshoes are not a good buy for someone seriously undertaking the sport.

The most important consideration when buying snowshoeing equip-

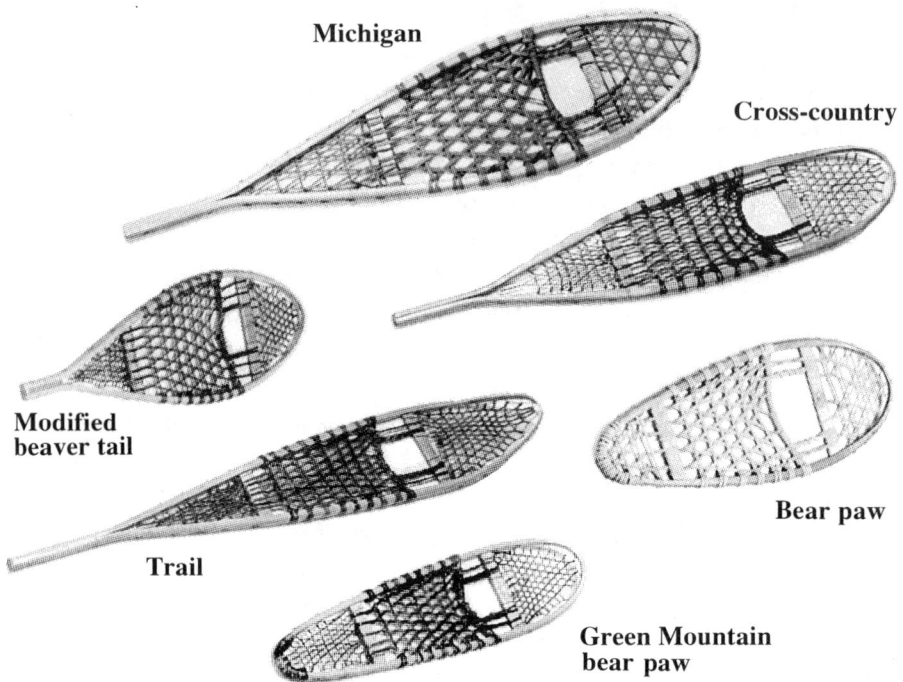

Figure 2.20 A large variety of snowshoe models is available for hikers who wish to expand their backcountry activities into winter. Larger shoes are more effective in deeper snow; smaller ones work better for those who enjoy running on packed snow surfaces. Photos courtesy of the Faber Safesport Snowshoe Company of LaCrosse, Wisconsin.

ment is the quality of the bindings. They must hold the boots firmly but allow enough freedom for comfortable walking. They must be strong enough to allow pulling and twisting without breaking. Poor quality bindings can cause endless problems.

One feature that can be very helpful on hard snow is the "snowshoe crampon." This device attaches to the bottom of the frame or binding to provide additional traction. It usually has several sharp teeth that bite into the snow surface and prevent the shoe from sliding. This would be a valuable item for tours that include steep slopes and/or windblown ridges.

Snowshoeing is probably the least expensive form of winter touring, especially for someone who already owns hiking boots. Other than the snowshoes, the only other equipment needed are gaiters, ski poles, and appropriate winter clothing.

EQUIPMENT

Figure 2.21 After years of coaching from his father, Eric Kelner has learned that the Deseret Industries ski bin is an excellent place to find bargains.

Budget Touring

As mentioned in the Preface, backcountry skiing permits one to practice the most fundamental of family values: *Thrift*. A prohibitively expensive lift pass is not the only cost the budget-conscious tourer is able to avoid. Careful bargain hunting can save bundles in touring equipment acquisition.

Where should the cost-conscious tourer look for bargains?

Autumn and spring are the best seasons for finding bargains. Thrift stores, such as the Mormon Church's Deseret Industries, is an excellent start. Look for the 1960's-vintage Head Model 240 skis, old ski poles with large baskets, and leather ski boots made by European companies such as Henke. Cross-country skis may sometimes be obtained from university-associated surplus outlets. Universities that sport ski teams will often sell their equipment at the end of the racing season; university "co-op adventure" and recreation programs also periodically dispose of their used equipment.

Equipment rental companies periodically renew their stocks and sell their used equipment at very reasonable prices. Military surplus stores sometimes carry large-basketed ski poles and mohair climbers. The Ski Truck, an enterprise operated out of the back of a large truck, can be a source of bargain equipment. Many clubs, civic organizations, and some communities annually organize "ski swaps;" one of the best sources for

Figure 2.22 Three types of pack are popular among ski tourers. The waist pack at left is manufactured by local entrepreneur Roly Pearson. The small day pack and the more substantial internal frame pack are made by Wave Products, also of Salt Lake City.

budget-priced new or used equipment is the Park City Ski Swap, held at the beginning of each ski season.

PACKS

Nearly every ski tourer carries some kind of a pack. Packs can be as small as a fanny pack, with room only for a few small items, or as large as necessary to carry loads as heavy as 100 pounds. Small fanny packs are most useful for track skiing or for short outings close to civilization. Small rucksacks or large fanny packs[9] are generally needed for longer tours when a skier must carry extra layers of clothing, plenty of food and water, and, of course, a camera.

Even larger packs are required for more advanced tours and ski mountaineering outings. Many large packs are available with internal frames to keep their contents away from the back. Some of the more specialized packs have side slots or straps for skis. This feature is valuable for tours that have steep pitches, ridges, or cornices that must be surmounted on foot. In such circumstances, the hands are often needed

---

[9] An important advantage of a fanny pack relates to the fact that the heaviest area of perspiration for most people is their back. Wearing a pack that covers the back tends to increase that perspiration, which can result in the skier being wetter and colder after a strenuous climb.

for climbing, and a dropped ski would be a disaster.

Two types of equipment are generally carried on tours: frequent use items and materials for emergencies. Frequent-use supplies include waxes, a scraper to remove waxes, glass fiber tape, and a pocket knife. All kinds of scrapers are commercially available. A 2-inch wide plastic paint scraper is an excellent low-cost alternative. A small roll of glass filament tape is handy for securing the heel of a climber, and a small pocket knife helps remove that tape. Frequent use articles , as well as food and drink, are best stored in easily-accessible utility pockets of the pack.

Materials for emergencies include repair kit, first aid kit, avalanche rescue equipment, and survival gear. These are described in the next two chapters.

The Wasatch mountains are especially beautiful in winter. The combination of steep terrain, snow, water, rock, and weather, however, can lead to tragedies for those unfamiliar with dangers posed by the alpine environment.

Chapter 3

MOUNTAIN HAZARDS

Winter arrived early in 1975. By Thanksgiving weekend the ski resorts near Salt Lake City could boast of a snowpack many feet deep. Down in the nearby valleys several Boy Scout troops planned to utilize the holiday to fulfill merit badge requirements in cross country skiing and winter camping. Small parties of unaffiliated tourers scheduled similar outings throughout the nearby Wasatch.

Two young ski tourers—one 15, the other 16 years of age—left Alta on Thanksgiving Day for a campout on Catherine Pass, along the ridge between Alta and Brighton. They set up camp on a barren spot high on the ridge and settled down for the night.

During the night the weather began to deteriorate, and by Friday morning a full-fledged blizzard had enveloped the Wasatch Mountains. On Friday afternoon one of the Catherine Pass campers staggered exhausted into a cabin in Alta's Albion Basin. He had become separated from his companion, he told members of the area's ski patrol, during that morning's descent from the pass. The Salt Lake County Sheriff's Department was notified and planning commenced for a search and possible rescue.

The first opportunity for an organized search by helicopter came the next morning. A pair of abandoned skis, positioned in an "X" (an international distress signal), were spotted in a meadow below the pass, but there was no sign of their owner. Examination of the skis revealed that repair of a binding or a boot had been attempted. The weather deteriorated again, prohibiting further flights. Some ground parties were dispatched to search the vicinity of the crossed skis, but they were forced to retreat as the storm intensified.

Saturday night's wind chill neared −40°F. By Sunday morning the

Figure 3.1 Mountain hazard-related newspaper clippings gathered during the 1992-93 snow season attest to a growing number and diversity of winter recreation accidents.

48-hour blizzard had deposited three feet of fresh snow in Albion Basin. Ten search teams began what by then many feared had become a recovery. Probing located the 16-year old's body some 400 yards downslope of the crossed skis. Both boys, it was later learned, had abandoned packs containing food and clothing somewhere along the route of their retreat.

The Albion Basin tragedy reinforces several basic winter backcountry commandments:

- *Always be aware—and wary—of mountain hazards, especially the possibility of avalanches.*
- *During an outing anticipate your body's physiological needs: food, water, and insulation.*

- *Always be prepared for the worst eventuality; carry repair, survival, and first aid equipment as well as extra food and clothing.*
- *Plan outings with enough companions to affect rescue and evacuation should a member of the party become ill or injured.*
- *Inform someone of the destination, route, planned time of return, and who to notify in the event of suspected trouble.*

This chapter expands on these commandments by surveying hazards associated with backcountry winter recreation and with specific dangers common to the Wasatch.[1] It concludes with discussions of survival equipment to be carried on ski tours.

NATURAL HAZARDS

While avalanches (to be discussed in the next chapter) pose the major winter hazard in the Wasatch, other "natural" hazards occasionally injure or kill the unwary backcountry recreationist. Some of these hazards are associated with weather, others with terrain. The presence of wildlife may also lead to a dangerous situation—either for the tourer or for the animal.

Hazards Associated with Weather

The area's relatively benign winters—with periods of fair weather between intense storms—makes the Wasatch one of the finest ski touring areas in the country. Yet under certain circumstances, such as occurred during the Catherine Pass incident described earlier, the weather can become a vicious killer.

Storms. According to Ronald I. Perla, recently retired co-author of the U.S. Forest Service's *Avalanche Handbook*, the primary moisture supply for the Wasatch is the Pacific Ocean. Wasatch Front storms generally arrive via a southeastwardly flow from the Pacific Northwest region. Storms in the Wasatch can start very suddenly and last several days, with snowfall intensities reaching 5-6 inches per hour. It is not unusual for a single storm to leave 3-4 feet of fresh powder on the mountains.

---

[1] Most of the information presented in this chapter is derived from the authors' personal observations and experience gained during an accumulated total of 60 years of Wasatch touring, hiking, and mountaineering. Additional insight was gained from consultations with several individuals possessing vast practical wisdom in winter travel, survival, first aid, mountain medicine, and rescue techniques.

Figure 3.2 Wind-sculptured snow, called "sastrugi," may be soft and skiable, or icy and dangerous. The dangerous variety should be avoided by inexperienced skiers.

The most vicious Wasatch storm in recent history occurred late in January 1965. It resulted from the meeting of a southwardly descending cold arctic airmass with a southeastwardly flow of low pressure moisture from the Pacific. The storm lasted seven days and deposited 109 inches (9 feet!) of snow at Alta. Avalanche conditions became so severe at the resort that all guests and non-essential employees were evacuated by snowcat to the valley.

Ski touring during a storm is generally discouraged. Visibility during a mountain blizzard is marginal at best, and avalanche conditions are often at their worst.[2]

Wind. Wind creates a number of problems for the tourer. The movement of large quantities of snow (as will be detailed in the next chapter) contributes greatly to the hazard of avalanches. Wind can

---

[2] A very small, but growing number of highly competent ski mountaineers enjoy the challenge of touring near the end of a snowstorm. There is, after all, virtually no competition for the terrain, the helicopters are grounded, and the powder snow is usually light and limitless.

NATURAL HAZARDS 73

Figure 3.3   Wasatch Mountain Club tourers Karin Caldwell (*left*) and Dennis and Karin Caldwell and Rolf Doebbeling (*right*) remain well clear of snow cornices overhanging steep slopes.

erode a thin, soft snowpack to expose rocks that a skier can scrape against or fall onto. Wind can pack snow into a dense, icy layer that is almost impossible to ski on. It can also sculpt the snowpack into a form known as "sastrugi" (Figure 3.2), which is sometimes soft and enjoyable, but may be crusty and unskiable. Skiers should approach sastrugi with caution, since it is often especially challenging to negotiate.

Wind also creates cornices (Figure 3.3) along mountain ridges. Tourers can fall off cornices, and cornices can collapse under, or onto, tourers. Cornices should be treated with utmost respect.

Perhaps the greatest hazard posed by wind is its ability to remove heat from the tourer's face, body, and extremities. This will be discussed in later sections on frostbite and hypothermia.

Rain. Rainstorms are relatively rare in the Wasatch during winter, but when they come, they can devastate a snowpack and generate severe and lingering hazards for the backcountry tourer. The contributory effect of rain to avalanche hazard will be discussed in the next chapter.

Rain is more effective than wind in transforming soft, skiable snow into a potentially lethal ice crust. While fatal accidents due to slippage on ice crusts are quite rare in the Wasatch backcountry, they are fairly common on ski packed slopes of local resorts. During the 1991-92 ski season, for example, three resort skiers were killed and several were seriously injured after sliding down ice-glazed ski runs.

Beginning tourers who intend to continue expanding their backcountry touring horizons to steeper and more challenging terrain will do themselves a great favor by learning techniques of self-arrest to be used during a slide. Even those well practiced in self-arrests generally prefer to avoid climbing or skiing along steep icy slopes.

Lightning. Lightning occasionally accompanies an intense frontal system and can be a hazard to ski tourers who venture out during a storm. Tourers should stay off exposed ridges and large open areas during periods of lightning. Taking shelter beneath tall trees is also not recommended. The best thing to do when caught in such an intense storm is to quickly descend to low elevations, preferably by way of a ravine or gully that is sheltered from lightning strikes.

Temperature. Areas in proximity of the Wasatch Range, such as the "Logan Sinks," are famous for their extraordinarily low nighttime temperatures, sometimes reaching $-70°F$. Such cold temperatures are usually associated with very clear nights, when a significant amount of heat can be radiated from the earth's surface.

Hazards Associated with Terrain

Several hazards related to the snowpack, water features, and topography have contributed to severe injuries and fatalities over the years.

Streams. Tourers should be aware that Wasatch streams flow throughout the winter. During early snowfalls their channels are easily visible, but as the snowpack deepens sections of stream can become bridged. With continuing accumulation of snow through the winter, large areas of stream become covered and difficult to discern. Distributed over the length of skis, the weight of a cross-country skier is usually insufficient to collapse the covering mantle. During the coldest periods of winter, when streamflows are at their minimum, collapse of a snow bridge beneath a tourer usually results, at worst, in wet ski boots.

Snowcovered streams are most dangerous during springtime when flow volumes are high and currents are swift. Worse yet, the rushing waters may have undercut the snowcover to a thickness of only a few inches. A fall into such a swollen stream may result in a thorough soaking and subsequent hypothermia. Swift currents have been known to kill backcountry recreationists by sweeping them downstream and

Figure 3.4 *Top:* Early in the season, when flow volumes are low, streams can be crossed easily and safely. Westminster College student Bertha Washington demonstrates one easy technique. *Bottom:* Dave Hanscom uses an imaginative (and not recommended) technique to cross Little Cottonwood Creek. Mountain streams are most dangerous during spring, when flow volumes are high and currents are swift.

trapping them beneath the snowpack.[3]

Stream channel hazards are most serious along the bottoms of major drainages, where numerous small tributaries have joined to form a sizable stream. Ironically, these same canyon bottoms provide much of the terrain used by beginning tourers. It is essential to be *very* careful

---

[3]During the 1993 spring runoff, the stream in Little Cottonwood Canyon claimed four lives, none related to ski touring.

76   CHAPTER 3. MOUNTAIN HAZARDS

Figure 3.5 "Glide cracks" form as gravity pulls the snowpack downward along smooth, steeply-dipping slopes. Such cracks indicate instability of the snow layer and should be avoided.

in the vicinity of stream beds, especially during the warm weather of spring. Danger is lowest early in the morning after the snow has frozen at night; snow bridges are less likely to hold the weight of a tourer as the sun softens them during the day.

Lakes. The snowpack that covers Wasatch mountain lakes can be deceptively dangerous. Early season freezing spells, followed quickly by a deep snowfall, may result in the deadly combination of a thin ice crust camouflaged by a deep layer of soft powder snow. Tourers should always give a good measure of consideration before crossing any lake during winter.

Crevasses. *Crevasse* is a French word for a deep crack or fissure. The word is most frequently applied to glaciers, where the flow of ice over convex surfaces causes the ice to crack and the cracks to spread. In motion pictures, glacial crevasses serve as a tidy means to dispose of evildoers: During pursuit by the forces of good, the villain's escape is thwarted by a wide-open crevasse. He spies a nearby snowbridge spanning it, and with a sneer at his pursuers starts across. Midway over, the bridge collapses under him, and he spirals screaming into the dark void. *Finis!*

NATURAL HAZARDS   77

Figure 3.6   Rock/snow interface fissures often develop wherever the snowpack meets outcroppings of rock. They can be dangerous if deep and covered with a thin layer of fresh snow.

Since there are no glaciers in Utah the *term* crevasse has become associated with any kind of crack, fissure, or undercut in a snowpack. Three types of fissures are common in Utah: glide cracks, rock/snow interface fissures, and waterfall fissures.

Glide Cracks. A crevasse created by the slow movement of the snowpack downslope is correctly called a "glide crack." Glide cracks, according to the *Avalanche Handbook*, are an indicator of the snowpack's instability. The slope exhibiting such cracks, as well as proximate slopes, should be avoided under most circumstances. Figure 3.5 illustrates a major system of glide cracks in Big Cottonwood Canyon's Broads Fork. Note a barely discernible—and very ill-advised—footpath of a hiker between the upper and lower crack systems.

Rock/Snow Interface Fissures. The most common Utah crevasse (Figure 3.6) is formed by the slow creep of the snowpack away from a rock wall or outcropping. The fissure thus created can be quite dangerous to someone unaware of its presence. The opening of such a fissure can be camouflaged with a thin bridge of freshly-drifted snow that can

Figure 3.7 Waterfall fissures and glide cracks can form on gently-sloped terrain as well as on slopes that are steep.

easily collapse under the weight of a tourer. Because snow accumulations are often deeper at the base of cliff bands than on flat terrain (due to drifting, etc.), the interface fissures can reach lethal depths. Tourers should suspect the presence of a fissure whenever approaching a rock/snow interface. Probing a suspicious area with a ski pole can help determine the presence of a crevasse.

Waterfall Fissures. A fissure created by a waterfall is the most lethal of the crevasses to be found in the Wasatch. Waterfall fissures usually occur at the base of cliffs—or dipping rock formations—that have a stream flowing or cascading over them. Waterfall fissures are similar to rock/snow interface fissures, but due to the melting effect of the rushing water they are usually much broader and deeper than the dry variety. The presence of great amounts of flowing cold water, and the spray associated with its fall, make this variety of crevasse especially dangerous.

The waterfall fissure located adjacent to the popular Primrose Cirque hiking trail on Mount Timpanogos, has a well-earned reputation as the most lethal fissure in Utah. The most statistically unusual sequence of fatal events occurred there in 1980. On Sunday, June 8th, a 26-year old hiker from Portland, Oregon, tumbled into a 50-foot deep hole in the snowpack at the base of the trailside waterfall. His body was recovered on Monday. Some hours after conclusion of the recovery, a 25-year old hiker from nearby Orem was killed when he fell into the same fissure.

NATURAL HAZARDS

Figure 3.8 Selecting routes beneath and among cliff bands exposes tourers to multiple dangers and generally should be avoided.

Waterfall fissures can also form along the gentlest-sloping rock surfaces. Midway up Maybird Gulch, as an example, the stream riffles over some smooth, gently-sloping bedrock. During early winter the bedrock surface and the riffles are easily visible, but as winter progresses, both soon disappear beneath a blanket of white. Should an unsuspecting skier fall through to the smooth surface of the bedrock, he would likely slide down the wet surface to become wedged in the narrow crevice between rock and snow.

- It is vital that tourers study their skiing terrain during summer and use exceptional caution along stream channels during winter.

Cliffs. Cliffs are the most notorious killers of unsuspecting summertime hikers. Most cliff-related fatalities occur in the rugged western flank of the Wasatch adjacent to population centers. During winter, cliff and rock outcropping related fatalities are more common among the commercial ski areas east of Salt Lake City than in the rugged backcountry. Most resort fatalities have resulted from people skiing beyond their control, skiing onto dangerous areas that are either unmarked or poorly marked for hazard, or entering areas marked closed to skiing. Only two cliff-related backcountry fatalities have recently occurred during winter. In both cases the victims started sliding on an ice-crusted slope, were unable to regain control, and slid or fell onto rock piles.

Ski touring among cliffs presents several dangers. Touring beneath a cliff exposes the tourer to possible rockfalls or avalanches from above. Touring above a cliff exposes the tourer to the possibility of falling off

Figure 3.9 Due to their steepness, couloirs should be avoided whenever possible. Couloirs that terminate at cliffs have the added hazard of rockfall; couloirs that terminate at ridges may have overhanging cornices at their summit. The photo at right, taken along the north flank of Mount Olympus, shows what may be the steepest and narrowest couloir in the Wasatch.

it. Touring on "hanging" snowfields between cliff bands, such as the one illustrated in Figure 3.8, exposes the tourer to both hazards.

Most beginner touring routes will not expose participants to cliff hazards as severe as those described. But to a novice skier careening on the edge of control along a smoothly packed roadway, even a road cut or a steep embankment can become a menace worth avoiding.

- Tourers should develop the habit of keeping a mental record of possible hazards during the ascent so that they may be avoided on the way down.

Couloirs. *Couloir* is the French word for a steep gully. Alta's "Baldy Chute" is probably Utah's most famous couloir. The highest and longest Wasatch couloirs descend southward from the summit of Mount Timpanogos into Provo Canyon; some of the narrowest and steepest are found on Mount Olympus. Two common varieties of couloir are illustrated in Figure 3.9. One type terminates at cliffs or other rock outcroppings; the other remains open to its summit.

Due to their steepness couloirs are often used by experienced tourers and mountaineers to quickly gain elevation. A beginning tourer's

NATURAL HAZARDS 81

Figure 3.10 Dave Hanscom observes a small deer herd (individual animals circled) from a distance to avoid spooking them to flight. Since the conversion of most foothill winter range to housing developments, large wildlife species have been forced to winter along higher, more snowcovered terrain.

encounter with one of these steep gullies, however, too often leads to trouble. Its ability to trap snow, as well as its steep profile, make the couloir an ideal place for avalanche. Their steepness—especially during icy snow conditions—may turn a skier's casual slip or misstep into a "slide for life." A cliff-terminated couloir adds the hazard of rockfall to its other dangers.

Hazards Associated with Wildlife

As more and more tourers venture into the mountains, an increasing number of them visit the low-elevation foothills generally used by wildlife as winter range and during springtime as areas for calving. If proper etiquette is observed, an unexpected trailside encounter with a deer, a moose, or an elk can be one of the more sublime experiences in backcountry touring. Even a close sighting of a lowly porcupine, rabbit, or squirrel can be surprising and exciting. Interspecies etiquette during such a meeting, however, is not a well developed subject. The following ideas and experiences will serve as a starting point for ski tour discussions.

From the animal's perspective you are an uninvited guest in its bedroom, kitchen, and pantry. Due to previous encounters with mankind, the wildlife species you've just stumbled onto views you with considerable suspicion. The snow that blankets the ground makes its foraging difficult; presence of an alien species may be considered an act of attempted food robbery. Being a peace-loving creature, it will most likely avoid confrontation by simply moving away in the hope that you will do likewise. Some animals may encourage your departure by a variety of warning motions, including a charge. If you've stumbled onto a family unit, you may be in the presence of a yearling. Being good parents, the animals may be especially protective of their offspring.

What should a touring party do when coming face-to-face with a furry four-legged creature standing in or near the trail?

- *Make no sudden moves or noises that spook the creature to flight.* During summer and autumn, foothill mammals have accumulated a layer of fat that helps them survive winter. Sudden flight unnecessarily depletes that food store. During an especially severe winter the animals are in a physiologically stressed condition, and that one flight may mean the difference between the creature's survival and a lingering death by starvation.
- *Make a detour.* It is not that difficult for tourers to take a wide path around an animal or group of animals. When two moose settled next to a groomed cross country race course in West Yellowstone in the winter of 1992, officials decreed that all racers who failed to detour around the twosome would be disqualified. Most racers were delighted to comply; none were disqualified.
- *Plan an escape route in case the animal gets upset.* When a moose charged one Salt Lake tourer in the Tetons, he quickly learned to climb a tree *while wearing his skis.*

MAN-MADE HAZARDS

It's not enough that tourers have to confront hazards created by Nature; they're also required to deal with some pretty devilish hazards created by Man. Man-made dangers include remnants of a once-thriving mining industry, as well as elements of the most modern of technologies, the snowmobile, the helicopter, and the bomb. Even man's best friend, under certain backcountry circumstances, may become the tourer's worst enemy.

Don't Get Shafted!

Some seventy years of active mining in the Wasatch have left a legacy of rustic—and rusting—boilers, collapsed and partially-collapsed cabins,

MAN-MADE HAZARDS

Figure 3.11 Equipment abandoned during the demise of Utah's mining era may present special dangers when covered by snow.

buildings, tramways, and numerous tunnels, shafts, and air vents. While such remnants of a bygone era provide summer visitors with endless opportunities for rummaging and exploration, for the winter recreationist they pose a significant element of risk.

Tourers can be easily tripped by snow-covered anchor bolts extending from foundations and piers that once supported massive structures. Early in the season, ankles can be sprained and legs broken as tourers' skis slide beneath discarded cables while their torsos pass above. As the snowpack deepens, abandoned telephone and power lines, once strung high among treetops, become an obstacle to avoid. Tourers can be pierced by plumbing and gouged by sheets of galvanized metal. They can tumble into deep, unmarked mine shafts or into narrow, tortuous air vents. Impalement on upthrust rails and timbers lying just inches below the surface of the snow is also a discomfort to be shunned.

How can such drastic misfortunes be avoided?

With respect to the hazard of mining remnants, Fortune smiles on the novice tourer. Because beginners generally confine their activities to roadways, flatlands, and gentle terrain not likely to contain abandoned machinery, it is probable they'll avoid such mishaps. Since novices also ski more slowly and with less abandon than their more advanced com-

Figure 3.12 Only a small percentage of the open mine shafts and air vents scattered throughout the Wasatch Mountains has been rendered harmless by Utah's mine reclamation effort. Larry Swanson examines a 200-foot deep shaft (in a popular Big Cottonwood Canyon touring drainage) that has been covered with a metal grating. Clipping courtesy of the *Deseret News*.

rades, they are less apt to become seriously injured in event of contact with mining implements.

The State of Utah has recently initiated "reclamation" of mining areas, and a few of the most dangerous shafts have been filled or covered. As the November 3, 1991 clipping (reproduced partially in Figure 3.12) attests, however, their efforts have not always been successful. In an area laced with thousands of mine shafts, elimination of hazard is a Herculean effort that requires a considerable commitment of public funds.

There is only one certain way to avoid injury by artifact: *know the territory!* Exploratory summer outings to prospective touring areas will have immeasurable value. The U.S. Geological Survey's topographical maps are also an excellent source of information. Such maps often show concentrations of abandoned mining works. Vertical shafts are depicted by the symbol (■). The topo maps' only drawback is incompleteness. Not all shafts are included; vents and other vertical pits are not indicated at all.

- Skiing slowly and under full control is the best method to minimize injury in event of an encounter with the ghosts of Utah's once-booming mining industry.

MAN-MADE HAZARDS

Figure 3.13 While enjoying a ski tour near Daniels Summit, Brett Hanscom stops to chat with the Bo Bahoravitch family from Pleasant Grove. Because they enjoy the same public lands for their recreations, snowmobile operators and ski tourers have a common interest in protecting those lands from excessive commercial exploitation.

Interactions with Snowmobiles

"Snowmobile use can be expected in many areas," the Uinta National Forest officials advise tourers in their *Recreational Opportunities* map. "Many forest areas are used by skiers and snowshoers," they warn snowmobile operators. Each group of users, the officials plead, should "respect other recreationists' enjoyment of the winter environment." The warning and plea applies equally in the Wasatch-Cache National Forest.

When snowmobiles first came onto the winter recreation scene in the 1960's, they quickly earned a reputation as backcountry terrorists: Arrogance Through Power! Two decades later, most snowmobilers have learned to respect backcountry skiers and their sport. The authors have encountered numerous snow machine operators who've indicated admiration for tourers' abilities to do something they, themselves, are incapable of doing. Generally interested in the peace and quiet of mountain solitude, tourers have also learned to adapt their outings to the habits of machine operators. Snowmobilers, they've discovered, rarely commence their outings before ten in the morning, and usually confine their activities to gentle terrain such as jeep roads and open flatlands.

The potential for tourer/snowmobile *collisions* exists along narrow roadways used by both. Gently sloping and flat terrain allows machine operators to drive at wide-open throttle. Blind curves along roadways present the greatest hazard. Tourers should approach such curves along the outside edge, where they are most visible to the operator and the machine is most visible to the tourer. The most dangerous time is near and after sunset, when people are fatigued and their guard is down, when visibility is poor, and when everyone is hurrying home.

Snowmobile operators and backcountry skiers have a major interest in common: both utilize public forest lands for their recreation. Both groups should therefore be interested in opposing commercial developments that would limit or curtail their particular activities. Stopping to socialize with snowmobile operators provides opportunities for exchange of vital information of interest to participants of both activities. It also builds good will and trust, which should result in a more pleasant experience for all.

Man's Best Friend?

"Dogs can be a nuisance to others and may fatally harass wildlife," Uinta National Forest officials admonish tourers. *"If you do take a dog on your tour, keep it under control."*

Early in the 1992-93 ski season, University of Utah student Monique Carlson discovered just what a nuisance dogs on a ski tour can be. She was descending a trail in Salt Lake's Millcreek Canyon when a dog darted "out of nowhere" and grabbed the back of her leg. Although no blood was drawn, Ms. Carlson was left with a sizable bruise. "I wasn't doing anything to provoke it," she later explained to *Salt Lake Tribune's* Brett Prettyman. "If the dog was on a leash, it never would have happened. People need to be more responsible with their dogs."

The issue of dogs in the canyons goes back to the mid-1970's, when Salt Lake Mayor/Water Commissioner Jake Garn convinced the City Commission to pass an ordinance outlawing dogs in the city's watershed canyons (Big and Little Cottonwood, Parleys, and Lambs). Fecal coliform counts (a means of monitoring water pollution) were increasing in those areas and dogs were considered a contributory factor.[4]

With the major Salt Lake County canyons closed to dogs, most of the local dog traffic moved into the non-watershed Millcreek Canyon. As touring gained popularity during the next two decades, tourers returning from the canyon began sensing the unmistakable odor of dog feces along the bottoms of their skis and boots. The coating became

---

[4]Only "visitor" dogs were banned, however. Though the ordinance restricted somewhat their freedom to roam, the "resident" dogs—often owned by politically influential ski resort, property, and lodge owners—were still permitted in these canyons.

Figure 3.14 In Salt Lake's Millcreek Canyon, tourers Mike and Linda Palmer—and Kody—appear to be delighted with the "pack it out" philosophy initiated by forest and health officials.

known as "brown klister." Side stepping dog deposits during ascent became somewhat of a game; remaining upright while skiing down the narrow trail became an outright challenge. Dogless tourers were not the only individuals to get their noses out of joint; Board of Health officials also became alarmed over increasing levels of fecal coliform.

In mid-November 1992, after having warned dog-accompanied tourers that unless they "packed it out," dogs might soon be banned from the canyon, the City-County Board of Health and the Forest Service erected an informational station near the end of the canyon's paved roadway. *"Take responsibility for your dogs,"* the sign urged tourers, *". . . and dispose of your dog waste."* A "doggie bag" dispenser loaded with plastic bags and a waste disposal container were attached to the sign's supports. Based on the first season of usage, the Forest Service declared the educational/collection program a great success. At least one, and frequently two, 55-gallon containers of dog litter were removed from the popular trailhead weekly. A praiseworthy solution to a very sticky problem!

Tourers who take their dogs should pay special attention to Utah State Wildlife Provision *U.C.A.* ¶*18-1-3*. Enacted in 1973, the provision states that "any person may kill a dog while it is attacking, chasing, or worrying any domestic animal having a commercial value, or any species of hooved, protected wildlife. . ." Since most ski touring occurs on public lands, it's worthwhile to keep informed of dog-related regulations promulgated by the various land administering agencies. Posted restrictions should always be respected.

- Most dogs have an irresistible impulse to confront porcupines. A muzzle full of painful quills is the usual outcome of such an encounter. Knowledgeable tourers who ski with their animals carry a pair of pliers/cutters to be used for extracting quills from their pet's soft tissues.

Aeronautical Hazards

Commercial helicopter skiing recreation is authorized by the U.S. Forest Service on lands under its jurisdiction. On application, and payment of a (usually small) fee, Special Use Permits are granted to concessionaires for permission to operate their businesses on the National Forest. The permit system is intended to assure that permittees operate safely, responsibly, and with proper training, equipment, insurance, etc. If the number of written complaints to local officials of the Forest Service is any indication, not all helicopter skiing operations in the Wasatch may be operating safely and responsibly.

Two commercial heli-skiing businesses are based in the Wasatch Mountains. Wasatch Powderbird Guides pursue their business mostly in the Central Wasatch; their special use permit also allows them to operate as far north as the Francis Peak area above Farmington, as far south as Springville's Hobble Creek Canyon, and as far east as the Uinta mountains. Diamond Peak Heli-Ski Adventures operated on private lands in the mountains east of Ogden until the January 1993 helicopter crash that killed one of its owners.

Compared to heli-skiing in the Canadian Rockies, where approximately 50 patrons and personnel have been killed while heli-skiing since the early 1970's,[5] Wasatch Powderbird Guides appear to be operating a relatively safe business for their clientele. The company has been involved in only one serious (non-injury) helicopter crash and three—what they consider "serious"—avalanche accidents since commencement of business in 1973.

Some non-permitted area helicopter charters have transported skiers and Very Important Persons to mountain summits along the Wasatch. Such unauthorized flights and landings are illegal and prosecutable, and

---

[5]The "approximately 50 patrons and personnel" killed includes about 40 avalanche fatalities. The remainder of the victims either collided with trees or rocks, fell into "tree wells," or died in helicopter crashes.

pilots involved in these activities are known as "renegades." Unauthorized heli-skiing landings are not limited to renegades; on at least one occasion forest officials reprimanded operators of Powderbird Guides for similar infractions.

The remainder of this section outlines touring hazards that the authors, several avalanche professionals, and numerous backcountry tourers believe have been created by activities associated with helicopter skiing. Based on content of numerous letters of complaint, official "for the record" memoranda, and other public communications,[6] hazards that may be initiated by heli-skiing fall into three clearly defined categories: direct heli-hazards, indirect heli-hazards, and latent heli-hazards. Central Wasatch areas that may have potential for exposure to such hazards are plotted in Figure 3.15.

Direct Heli-hazards. Direct heli-hazards include flying or landing of helicopters above tourers, skiing above tourers, and setting off explosives while conducting avalanche control work.

Salt Lake backcountry skier Lori Webb described the following incident: "As much as possible we carefully choose a safe route away from avalanche paths. Another party of skiers were making a higher traverse in the same area. My partner and I were halfway up the slope when a helicopter flew through the pass just barely above the top of the pass. The reverberation of the helicopter blades set off three avalanches. The other ski party shouted to us 'Avalanche!' We skied down and out of the path of the slide . . . the incident certainly points out the conflicts that will continually arise when helicopter skiing is permitted in areas frequented by winter mountaineers."

Craig W. Beasley, Salt Lake, described an incident that especially concerned him: "Four people, including myself, were just below the ridge removing our climbing skins in preparation for a descent into Days Fork. While doing so, a Powderbird Guides helicopter attempted three landings directly above us during exceedingly windy conditions. The helicopter was unable to stabilize and could not land until the fourth attempt." Because Mr. Beasley had worked on a mountain rescue team for four years, he was very aware of hazards associated with operation of helicopters in windy and high altitude conditions. "All four of us felt that the helicopter hovering overhead jeopardized our safety."

---

[6]The helicopter and subsequent explosives hazards sections are based on extensive examination of numerous Forest Service documents obtained through the Freedom of Information Act and by other means. In addition, the authors have received, over the years, many copies of complaints submitted to the Forest Service and to the Flight Standards office of the Federal Aviation Administration.

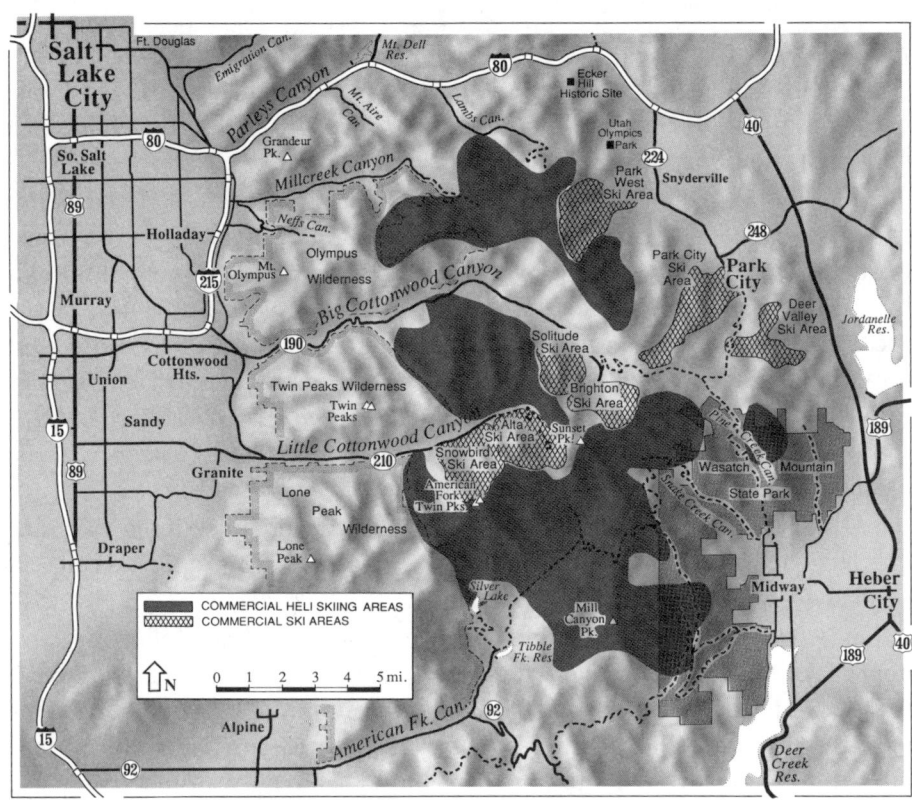

Figure 3.15 Darkened areas (based on U.S. Forest Service heli-skiing map) indicate areas of possible endangerment by heli-skiing operations in the Tri-canyons/American Fork Canyon area of the Central Wasatch.

On a Saturday in mid-December 1992, Victor Heilweil, his wife Ann, and two friends were touring in the upper regions of Big Cottonwood Canyon's Silver Fork when they were subjected to a very unpleasant and dangerous encounter with a group of heli-skiers. In a complaint to the Federal Aviation Administration (FAA), Mr. Heilweil described the incident:

> "My wife and I were traversing along the ridge towards Flagstaff Peak when a helicopter landed right between us, easily within 30 feet of each of us. It was so close that the intense wind and blast of snow that it created nearly knocked me over. . . . As I passed one of the guides, he asked me how I was doing in a pleasant manner, and I responded that I thought it was unnecessarily dangerous for the helicopter to land so close to us. He then completely changed his tone of voice and stated that he had authority

from the Alta Sheriff's Department to have me arrested for obstructing the landing of the helicopter, and threatened to physically force me into the helicopter and transport me down to the Sheriff's Office. He also asked for my name so that he could call up 'the authorities' on his walky-talky."

Mr. Heilweil suggested to the FAA that the heli-ski concession should abide by "some sort of safety code while operating aircraft on public lands where other people are present" and that the heli-ski operators "have more flexibility in their flight plans, so that if they see other backcountry users, they are able to land elsewhere and avoid this type of confrontation."[7]

Thankfully, no reported examples exist showing that backcountry tourers were endangered by avalanches released above them by explosive charges thrown from the heli-ski aircraft. The topic, however, continues to be the subject of frequent discussions and "for the record" memoranda by independent avalanche professionals and Forest Service avalanche hazard evaluators.

"I write this to protest the actions and philosophy with which WPG [Wasatch Powderbird Guides] uses explosives in the backcountry," a very agitated Utah Avalanche Forecast Center hazard forecaster Brad Meiklejohn wrote in a "for the record" memo early in 1991. "My sense is that WPG likes to throw explosives and likes to see avalanches run." To emphasize his point Meiklejohn ennumerated one special use permit violation "wherein they produced avalanches . . . in an area they do not ski" and several examples of excessive bombardment episodes. "As an individual and a professional," he concluded his letter, "I am indignant."

In a January, 1990 letter urging officials of the Wasatch/Cache National Forest to curtail or to limit the heli-ski operation's use of explosives, American Avalanche Institute's president Rod Newcomb expressed concern for the safety of backcountry tourers: "When Powderbird Guides began using explosive testing for stability evaluation, the density of skiers in the Wasatch was low. As the years have gone by, the numbers of backcountry skiers has increased. . . I feel it is only a matter of time before one of the triggered avalanches encounters a person hidden in the trees below an avalanche path. This will not only be an avoidable accident, it will very likely result in restrictions for other

---

[7]Victor Heilweil's letter is not the only complaint describing intimidation. In another instance a heli-ski pilot is reported to have used his aircraft to chase a backcountry tourer.

permittees, such as myself, in the use of explosives."
- The Special Use Permit granted the heli-ski concession directs blasters to overfly and "canvass" the proximity of the target for tourers and winter campers. *All explosives work is to be concluded by 9:00 a.m.*

Indirect Heli-Hazards. Though "indirect" heli-hazards may be somewhat more subtle than the direct variety, because of their relationship to avalanche bombing they may be equally dangerous.

Sympathetic Avalanche Releases. Any time an avalanche starts to run down a slope or a chute, the air and ground vibrations it generates may trigger avalanches in adjacent—or nearby—slopes or gullies. Such avalanche releases are called *sympathetic releases.* Forest Service manuals frequently warn avalanche workers to be especially cautious of such releases when firing artillery to stabilize slopes. Sympathetic snowslides have occurred even on slopes along *the opposite side* of a canyon from the target slopes. A classic case of sympathetic release was observed during artillery control work at Alta's Greely Hill; its description in the Forest Service's *Snowy Torrents,* is worth repeating:

> "Shots then fired on the Greely Hill slopes released slides from adjacent hillsides. The fracturing continued to propagate clear around Albion Basin, releasing the Sugarloaf and Devil's Castle slides, and eventually releasing two small slides on the southwest face of Mount Wolverine, across the valley from the original target."

Wise backcountry skiers should not be ignorant of a possible sympathetic release avalanche hazard when they tour in areas used by helicopter skiers.
- When tourers hear the loud reports of nearby explosives detonating, they should make certain they are not standing on or at the base of an avalanche slope.

Post-Control Releases. "If an explosive fails to release an avalanche," international avalanche authority Ron Perla writes, "it may in fact *weaken*[8] rather than stabilize a slope." Perla explains that explosive control is most effective on slopes that are heavily skied, and hence compacted such that underlying layers offer solid support. "This is usually the case within developed ski areas. In the back-country, this is usually not the case. Any snow slab, over a weak base, that fails to release when bombed, may be made into a hair trigger trap to be set off by a ski tourer. This is true irrespective of the explosive size."

---

[8]Emphasis Perla's.

MAN-MADE HAZARDS

Post-control release is another hazard that may be associated with the heli-ski concession's use of explosives. At least one of their three "serious" avalanche incidents occurred on a slope that had been tested with explosives before being declared to be safe for skiing. Forest Service case histories also document numerous instances of post-control avalanches that have entrapped and injured skiers even though the slopes had been blasted *and* skied.

- Whenever tourers come onto a slope pock-marked with the black powder marks that result from explosives detonations they should not presume the slope is safe to cross. The safety-conscious tourer will treat any slope capable of avalanching with the greatest caution *even if it has been blasted and skied.*

"DANGER—Explosives On The Mountain"

An explosive device that fails to detonate is called a *dud.* The youngest of children become familiar with duds when the fuse they've lighted on their 4th of July rocket or firecracker fizzles and fails to set off the propellant or gunpowder. Attempts to relight fuses have all too frequently resulted in explosively amputated fingers and blinded eyes. Emergency services personnel at local, county, and state government levels work ceaselessly to have such pyrotechnic devices declared illegal.

Explosive charges used in avalanche control work can do considerably more damage than blinding or maiming. A 105-mm artillery or recoilless rifle round contains about 4 pounds of high explosive and can destroy a military tank or a building. The heli-ski concessions use hand-thrown bombs containing 2 or 4 pounds of explosive to "test" snow stability and to initiate avalanches. These can be nearly as destructive. To make matters worse, they're cast in the shape of large firecrackers.

Like the fireworks dud, explosives used in avalanche work may also fail to detonate. Since it's impractical for those shooting or throwing the explosives to immediately retrieve their duds, the armed charges are usually allowed to remain where they fall until spring or summer, when searchers are sent out to locate them for disposal. Not all duds are recovered, however, because they don't always remain where they land. A subsequent snowslide may sweep them a mile or more down a mountainside.

As early as the mid-1960's, at a time when use of explosives for avalanche control was limited only to the protection of highways and ski resorts, some Forest Service avalanche professionals began to discuss hazards posed by duds *on other forms* of forest recreation. In a letter

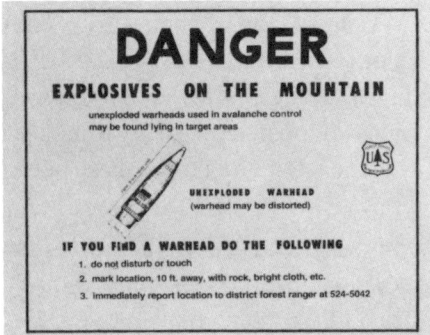

Figure 3.16 *Left:* An early (1960's) warning sign depicts a typical military artillery projectile used in avalanche control limited to resorts and highways. *Right:* A 1990's sign depicts three hardly-recognizable types of duds that now litter the canyons. *Bottom:* The typical high-explosive bombs thrown throughout the backcountry from helicopters resemble a large firecracker.

to the Supervisor of the Wasatch National Forest, Alta Snow Ranger Warren Baldsiefen was the first to describe the potential dangers:

> "The dud problem, particularly in a National Forest of heavy summer traffic, has grave overtones, and their accidental detonation by hapless hikers has been the source, more than once, of my waking in a nightmarish sweat. To have been the cause, though indirectly and through no negligence of mine, of some innocent person's death or injury, is more than I wish to live with. These feelings are shared by the others working here in winter."

The concern over duds so candidly expressed by the Snow Ranger worked its way through the federal bureaucracy, eventually to settle in the offices of the U.S. Attorney General. Enroute, the issue of public safety transformed to become an issue of public liability. In a late-December 1965 letter to local forest officials, U.S. Attorney T. Koskella strongly suggested that a lawsuit brought against the Forest Service in connection with an avalanche dud accident "probably would be indefensible in court."

Like the duds that now litter the canyons, the question of unexploded devices on recreational forest lands lay dormant for nearly a generation. During the 1980's, a few concerned tourers and hikers voiced informal "off the record" objections to escalation of heli-bombing in the local canyons, but their pleas were ignored by forest officials. Writing "for the record" in March 1991, snow ranger/avalanche forecaster Albert J. Soucie, described the situation: "They [the heli-ski concession] seem to be treating the backcountry as a ski area and instead of doing explosive testing they are performing avalanche control work on backcountry slopes." In another memo, avalanche forecaster Brad Meiklejohn suggested that in performing snow stability evaluation, "it takes brains, not bombs."

The use of explosives on National Forest lands "of heavy summer traffic" was permitted—and continues—to escalate. Today, the greatest concentration of undetonated explosive devices lost by the heli-ski concession is in three especially popular Big Cottonwood Canyon hiking drainages: Silver, Days, and Cardiff forks.

As a new version of the *Danger—Explosives on the Mountain* signs (Figure 3.16) began to appear near popular forest trailheads and picnic sites, still more concerns were raised. During a 1992 "illegal fireworks" amnesty program, organized by a local radio station to get dangerous fireworks out of the hands of residents, Salt Lake County fire officials were stunned to find that an avalanche control device had been turned in. "The ordnance is designed to be dropped out of a helicopter and to detonate on impact," county fire spokesman Capt. Dennis Steadman told the *Deseret News*. "It's an extremely dangerous device. . . . You would be surprised at the kinds of things people have in their basements."

Wasatch tourers and hikers would do themselves and their community a great service by becoming further informed of the heli-bombing issue and by actively participating in the soon-to-be-commenced revision of the Forest Service's "Land Use Plan" for the area.[9] An outline of the decision-making process appears in Chapter 7.

---

[9] The major organizations involved in the canyon urbanization and heli-skiing debates are the Citizens' Committee to Save Our Canyons, the Wasatch Mountain Club, and the Backcountry Skiers' Alliance. All organizations publish periodic newsletters that inform members of forthcoming public hearings and of other opportunities for public input. All groups are operated by dedicated volunteers and welcome contributions to defray costs of preparation and mailing.

HUMAN FACTORS

Although the human body has an incredible capacity to adapt to its surroundings, it is usually the weak link in the chain when it comes to a safe and enjoyable ski tour. It is susceptible to heat, cold, sun, wind, and altitude; the body also responds negatively to insufficient water or food. Winter mountain conditions can be extremely hostile and all efforts should be made to insure physical comfort and safety.

A number of physiological and psychological hazards are discussed in this section, along with ways to avoid and survive them. Physiological dangers are discussed in order of decreasing risk and likelihood of encounter. The most common and potentially lethal danger is hypothermia; it is followed by frostbite, sunburn, dehydration, and mountain sickness.[10] The section concludes with a discussion of hazards that may result from incorrect perceptions and evaluations of terrain and ski tour circumstances.

Hypothermia

The opening paragraphs of this chapter describe an incident in 1975 when a young winter camper died in Albion Basin, less than a mile from the ski area. The cause of his death was reported in the media as "exposure" brought on by "hypothermia." The *Oxford American Dictionary* defines hypothermia as "the condition of having a body temperature greatly below normal."

The normal temperature for a human being is approximately 98.6°F, and the body functions well only within a few degrees of that. The human brain contains a temperature regulator that senses when the body has become too hot or too cold and initiates appropriate physiological responses to return it to normal. When the body is too warm, the regulating mechanism initiates perspiration (which evaporates to cool the skin) and increases blood flow to the skin (where the blood cools). When the body's temperature drops, circulation near the surface of the skin is decreased and shivering (an involuntary muscular activity that produces heat) commences.

If the body's natural defense mechanisms are not able to maintain its core temperature at the proper level, hypothermia results. If the

---

[10]Dr. Howie Garber, Salt Lake ski tourer and emergency room physician, kindly reviewed this section, providing many helpful comments and suggestions. For detailed information on treating medical problems that may be encountered in the backcountry, he recommends *Management of Wilderness and Environmental Emergencies*, edited by Auerbach and Geehr, published by Mosby.

body's core temperature drops too low, the condition of a hypothermia victim quickly degenerates to a state from which it is very difficult to recover. Even worse, hypothermic individuals often do not realize that they have a problem until it is too late for them to help themselves.

Before discussing how hypothermia is recognized, prevented, and treated, it is necessary to understand how heat is generated and dissipated by the human body.

Generation of Heat. Body heat is generated principally by the metabolic process that converts food to energy. Of the energy produced by metabolism, only about 20% normally results in muscular work; the remainder is converted to heat. As the level of exertion increases during heavy exercise, more heat is generated. The body also obtains heat from external sources such as the sun, a warm stove, a hot bath, or a warm beverage.

Heat Loss. Loss of body heat occurs continually. The five primary mechanisms for this loss are radiation, conduction, convection, evaporation, and respiration.

Radiation. Heat is lost from any object if its surface temperature is higher than that of the surrounding medium. When the air is colder than the skin, heat is lost from any exposed body part, such as the face and head. Since the head has the best blood supply and is therefore often the warmest part of one's body, more heat may be radiated from it than from any other part. At an air temperature of 40°F an unprotected head may lose up to half of the body's total heat output; up to three-quarters of that output may be lost at 5°F.[11] The adage "when you begin to feel cold, put on your hat" makes sense.

Conduction. When two masses at different temperatures are in contact, heat will flow from the warmer mass to the colder one. When a person walks in cold snow or sits on a cold log, heat will transfer from his warm body to the snow or log. The more insulation one wears on body parts exposed to cold, the less heat will be lost. The ability of water to conduct heat is much greater than that of air; a wet garment will conduct heat away from the body hundreds of times as fast as a dry one. This quantifies—and underscores—the importance of having a layer of dry air close to the body in cold weather.

Convection. Convection occurs when heat is transferred from a warm object to a *moving* medium, such as air or water. Air is the most common medium in the convective heat losses experienced in winter

---

[11]This and other information in this section are derived from a pamphlet called *Hypothermia: Killer of the Unprepared* by Dr. Theodore G. Lathrop, published by the Mazamas in Portland, Oregon.

recreation. Since warmed air rises, the presence of wind is not necessary for convective heat loss to occur. Cool air comes in under our parkas, is warmed by our bodies, and rises to escape out the top. The heat exchange process is enhanced when air flow is increased by wind.

Evaporation. Just as evaporation of perspiration cools the body in warm weather, so it does in winter. Evaporation is an endothermic process, requiring heat to transform the liquid to its vapor. If the evaporating liquid is the perspiration on one's brow or back, much of the required heat is taken from the body.

The rate of evaporation is affected by air movement (convection) as well as its temperature. Moisture evaporates more rapidly in the presence of wind than it does in still air. The velocity of the wind, therefore, has as much—or more—effect on heat loss as does the air temperature. The mathematically-derived "Wind Chill Factor" shows what a body feels (as an equivalent *windless* temperature) for any combination of temperature and wind velocity. The concept of wind chill is illustrated graphically in Figure 3.17. Note two things in particular from this chart:

- *Wind has a greater effect at colder temperatures.* At an air temperature of 40°F, a 10 miles per hour (mph) wind only lowers the effective temperature by 10°, but it lowers it by 20° at an air temperature of 10°F.
- *The effect of changing wind is much greater at low wind velocities that it is at high velocities.* At an air temperature of 10°F an increase in wind velocity from 5 to 10 mph lowers the effective temperature by 15° (from +5°F to −10°F). An increase of wind velocity from 25 to 30 mph, however, has little incremental effect on the body.

Respiration. The act of breathing combines most of the previously mentioned heat loss processes. Cold air is inhaled, warmed by the lungs, then exhaled. The humidity is higher inside the lungs than outside, so moisture evaporates and is ejected during exhalation. The higher the rate of breathing, the greater the heat loss by respiration.

Symptoms of Hypothermia. As the body temperature drops below its normal level, a series of physiological responses occur. As blood circulation to the skin and the extremities is reduced, cold is sensed in the hands, feet, and ears. Continued cooling of the body usually causes moderate shivering, particularly if the victim isn't exercising too vigorously. Shivering intensifies as the body continues to chill.

When the body's core temperature drops below 95°F, the body and mind cease to function properly. Brain activity slows, affecting decision-making and the ability to perceive coldness; muscles stiffen and normal

	AIR TEMPERATURE (°F)							
	40	30	20	10	0	-10	-20	-30
5	35	25	15	5	-5	-15	-25	-35
10	30	15	5	-10	-20	-35	-45	-60
15	25	10	-5	-20	-30	-45	-60	-70
20	20	5	-10	-25	-35	-50	-65	-80
25	15	0	-15	-30	-45	-60	-75	-90
30	10	-5	-20	-35	-50	-65	-80	-95

WIND (mph)

Figure 3.17 The temperature that a person "feels" is determined by the velocity of the wind, as well as the actual temperature. This chart shows, for various combinations of cold and wind, the equivalent temperature in windless conditions. Since unprotected flesh can freeze in less than one minute at temperatures below −25°F, particular care should be taken to protect exposed skin even on a moderate 10° day when the wind exceeds 20 mph.

movements become awkward. As the temperature descends into the 80's, a person becomes irrational and may be unable to walk. Death usually occurs at about 80°F. The following table lists the body's responses at various core temperatures:

99 – 96°F	mild shivering, coldness in extremities
95 – 91°F	violent shivering, slowing of brain activity, apathy
90 – 86°F	stiff muscles, reduced mental capacity
85 – 81°F	confusion, lethargy, sometimes euphoria
80 – 78°F	unconsciousness
below 78°F	death

One of the reasons hypothermia is so dangerous is that its onset can be subtle, and victims may not notice the symptoms in themselves. They often become extremely apathetic, no longer noticing hunger, thirst, or cold. As their minds slow, it is common for people to do things that seem totally contradictory. Removal of clothing may be caused by decreased mental capacity coupled with a false sense of warmth that comes when the body's temperature drops below the range where shivering occurs. It is not uncommon for victims to experience hallucinations.[12]

---

[12] A Weber State University student reviewing this manuscript described the ex-

Prevention of Hypothermia. The four common factors that lead to this life-threatening condition are cold, wind, wetness, and a likely victim. A "likely victim" is one who doesn't eat and dress properly. Being alert to the warning symptoms in oneself and other members of the group is vital for safe backcountry outings at all times of year.

In order for body temperature to remain constant at 98.6°, the rate of heat generation must equal the rate of heat loss. Normal sources of heat are metabolism and physical activity. Heat generation can be increased by raising the level of exercise, which requires more consumption of food. Heat loss can be decreased by keeping inner layers of clothing dry (by removing them before perspiration starts) and by adding layers of dry clothing, particularly around the head, before one feels chilled.

The pace of the ski tour is an important consideration. Since vigorous exercise results in excess heat, one must choose a pace that will maintain the heat generation/loss balance, but will not result in fatigue or excessive perspiration. Fatigue reduces the capability of muscles to exert themselves and can cause a (sometimes sudden) loss of the body's ability to keep itself warm.

In order to sustain exercise for a prolonged period, the body must be provided with fuel. It is advisable to snack frequently and not wait until hunger is sensed. By the time a person feels hungry, he may be too tired to keep going at a pace that maintains warmth. The body *reacts* to a problem; only the mind can *predict* a problem.

In assembling food items to take on a ski tour, one should consider the amount of energy that may be gained and the rate at which that energy will be released. Fatty foods have more than twice the number of calories per gram as carbohydrates, but the energy from fats is generated much more slowly than that from carbohydrates. Some carbohydrates (such as common sugars) convert to energy very quickly; other carbohydrates (such as starches) are slower to metabolize. A peanut butter and jelly sandwich, as an example, provides quick energy from its jelly and slower energy from its peanuts. Candy bars containing nuts have a similar effect. A sandwich with meat or cheese will have a similar effect. Many commercial products, such as Exceed Bars and Power Bars are very compact and can be stored for long periods of time. A couple of

---

perience of her brother, whose snowmobile was stuck in deep snow during the winter of 1993. "While he and the other two snowmobilers were attempting to hike out, my brother thought he was sweating and so began removing his clothing. When his companions wouldn't allow him to go lay down by one of the several fires he saw, he became very irritable. To this day my brother still swears the fires were real; he just knows he wasn't hallucinating."

these in the bottom of a pack could save a life if a touring party is forced to stay out overnight.

Some tourers pre-load their bodies with carbohydrates during the 24 to 72 hour period before an outing. This technique, known as "carbo loading," is common among athletes who participate in sports that require prolonged muscular activity.

What about the use of alcohol in cold weather?

A common misconception suggests that a nip of brandy or some other alcoholic beverage warms the body. The effect of alcohol on the body is only to make the body *feel* warmer. Alcohol causes the arteries to dilate (become enlarged), which increases blood circulation to the skin. This makes the skin (and fingers and toes) warmer, but at the cost of accelerated cooling of the blood. Since one of the body's responses to cold is to decrease circulation to the skin and extremities (to slow the cooling of the blood), it is clear that alcohol actually counteracts this protective response and can accelerate the onset of hypothermia.

Treatment of Hypothermia. When early symptoms of hypothermia are observed in oneself or in a companion, it is important to act quickly to prevent further heat loss and to reestablish proper body temperature. When shivering starts, layers of clothing should be added and something hot ingested. Wet clothing should be replaced with clothing that's dry. Food that will quickly convert to energy should be consumed and vigorous exercise commenced. If shivering continues, a fire should be built. If the victim fails to recover within a reasonable period of time, rescue and evacuation to a medical facility should be initiated.

If symptoms of more advanced hypothermia are observed in a companion, and medical care is unavailable, it is vital to elevate his core temperature to normal as rapidly as possible. The choice of methods will depend on the state of the victim, as well as existing circumstances and available equipment.

The victim should be moved to as warm a place as can be found; a tent or a sheltered area is a good start, particularly if it can accommodate a fire. Dry clothing should be put on the victim, especially layers that will be next to the skin. To prevent further heat loss he can be placed into a warm sleeping bag or bundled in warm parkas.

At a certain stage of hypothermia the victim may not be able to generate enough heat to recover. One of the best ways to increase a person's core temperature is to place him in a warm sleeping bag with warmed water bottles in his armpits and groin, where blood continues to flow. (Be sure that the *outside* of each bottle is warm to the touch, but not hot.) If that is not possible, companions must provide external heat, usually from their own bodies. It may become necessary for someone to join the victim in the sleeping bag. A conscious victim should be given hot liquids with lots of sugar to serve the dual purpose of warming the body from within and providing it with fuel to start generating energy on its own. A victim of advanced hypothermia should receive medical attention as soon as he is able to be moved.

Other Physiological Hazards

A number of other physiological dangers may be encountered by backcountry skiers. Frostbite, sunburn, and dehydration are quite common, but seldom life-threatening. Mountain sickness is occasionally fatal, but less common. As with hypothermia, the key to preventing these maladies is to constantly *stay tuned to the messages sent by the body*.

Frostbite. A large percentage of the human body consists of tissue, blood, and various cellular and intercellular fluids. The freezing of these components is known as "frostbite." When freezing occurs, oxygen usually delivered by circulating blood is no longer available to affected tissues and some damage occurs. Frostbite damage may be minor, or it may be sufficiently severe to require surgical removal of dead tissues.

Symptoms of Frostbite. The first visible sign of frostbite is whiteness in the skin caused by lack of blood circulation and formation of ice crystals in the tissue. This symptom is commonly observed in cheeks or ears. As the severity of frostbite increases, the frozen area becomes hard and leathery, and some blistering may occur. In the most severe cases, the tissue dies and turns black.

Since frostbite often occurs in the hands or feet, which are not normally visible, one must rely on senses other than sight to detect the onset of the problem. Before a body part freezes, it usually feels very cold. After it is frozen, however, it becomes numb. Unless a person is conscious of the possibility of frostbite, the frozen—and numb—body part might seem quite normal. Frostbite can easily go unnoticed and become quite widespread.

Prevention of Frostbite. The most important preventative measure is to cover the ears, nose, and cheeks when the wind chill is low. Everyone should watch for white spots on other members of the touring party in cold weather, particularly early in a tour (before participants are warmed up) and late in a tour (when they are fatigued).

It is wise to wear several layers of insulation over fingers and toes. A rule of thumb is that mittens work better than gloves, since there is less surface area exposed to the cold, and the fingers can keep one another warm.

Fingers and toes should be worked constantly during a tour to maintain circulation. The wiggling of digits also increases the likelihood of detecting the onset of numbness. Any body parts that have previously suffered frostbite are more susceptible to the same problem, sometimes for several years after the initial injury. Recovered frostbite victims must pay particular attention to the state of their extremities; individuals with impaired circulation should also be especially careful.

If a member of a touring party with cold feet or hands isn't able to warm them by moving, rubbing or shaking, it may be necessary for someone else to help out. Hands can be warmed by putting them inside another person's parka or by periodically swapping mittens with someone whose hands aren't cold. Feet can be warmed by removing boots and placing the feet inside the jacket of a companion while another person warms the boots.

Preventative measures on cold days should also include drinking plenty of warm liquid before and during ski tours, and avoiding coffee. Caffeine is a vascular constrictor, which means that it decreases the blood supply to the fingers, ears, and toes and increases their susceptibility to frostbite.

Treatment of Frostbite. Minor frostbite can be treated immediately by placing a warm hand over the affected area. The pink color should return in a few moments, usually with little or no discomfort. It is best not to rub the area, since that may damage the tissue.

More severe cases require treatment by qualified medical personnel. If proper medical care is unavailable, the affected area should be thawed in 110°F circulating water until skin color returns; this typically takes 15-20 minutes. Dry heat, such as a campfire, is considered to be less safe as a warming method. Thawing is likely to be extremely painful, since surrounding tissues swell as the blood begins to circulate. *The frozen area should not be rubbed.* Rubbing pushes ice crystals into the injured (and surrounding) tissue and causes additional damage.

Some medical authorities suggest that if the victim must remain out in the cold, it may be better not to immediately thaw the frozen area. More damage is usually caused by thawing and refreezing than by leaving it frozen for a slightly longer time.

Dehydration. In order for the body to function properly, it must contain sufficient fluid to transport vital chemicals to the muscles and organs. The body should not be allowed to dehydrate, since its efficiency decreases drastically when the liquid content is much below the normal level. In addition to reducing the efficiency of muscular activity, dehydration increases susceptibility to hypothermia, frostbite, and fatigue.

Water is especially important on a ski tour. The low humidity of winter and the high rate of exertion during a tour combine to deplete the body's water. It is not uncommon for a tourer to lose one to three quarts of water in a day by transpiration through the skin and by respiration.

Symptoms of Dehydration. Fatigue and light headedness are the first signs of dehydration. Thirst is not always noticed until it's too late—yet another example of the body *reacting* to a problem. This is particularly true at high altitudes, where a person may also be experiencing mountain sickness. Headache, nausea, and muscular soreness may develop as the condition worsens, and the victim may find it difficult to continue. Recovery from this level of dehydration may take several hours.

Prevention of Dehydration. It is extremely important to drink regularly and not wait until one feels thirsty. Tourers should stop once or twice each hour and consume 6-12 ounces of liquid. Drinking regularly during the 12 hours preceding an outing also helps, since it allows the body to store as much liquid as possible. A prudent person may want to consume an entire bottle of water on the way to the start of a long tour.

An adult should drink at least two quarts of liquid during an all-day outing, but fluid requirements vary considerably among individuals. A major source of loss is hyperventilation (extremely deep breathing), so people who breathe harder often need to drink more. The best advice is to know *yourself* and err on the side of consuming too much liquid, rather than too little.

Water is preferred by many tourers, but some would rather have an energy drink or a concentrated solution of lemonade with plenty of sugar. Others carry a thermos of hot soup. Flowing water should be avoided due to the presence of Giardia and other water-borne contaminants. Eating snow should be done only as a last resort since it requires so much energy to melt.

Hot liquids help maintain body heat during a rest stop. In addition, the volume of liquid can be extended considerably by adding small quantities of snow. (One quart of near-boiling water mixed with 15°F snow will convert to over two quarts of cool water.) The recommended container for carrying hot liquid is a well-insulated, wide-mouth water bottle. An inexpensive polyethylene water bottle (and its lid) can be insulated by wrapping it with flexible foam and duct tape. It should be carried inside one's pack near the body to minimize heat loss.

Another means of preventing dehydration is to maintain a pace that minimizes perspiration and hyperventilation. The low humidity that pervades in Utah allows evaporation to occur at such a fast rate that people often don't notice how much liquid they are losing.

Treatment of Dehydration. Medical authorities recommend that the victim should slowly drink as much fluid as the stomach can comfortably accept, but no more than 32 ounces. Small quantities of liquid should then be consumed at regular intervals for two or three hours. A reasonable dose is 4-6 ounces every 15 minutes, but that should be reduced if feelings of nausea occur. Both dehydration and rehydration take considerable time. Water is probably the best liquid, but a dilute solution of an energy drink or fruit juice may be absorbed more quickly into the body and will also serve to re-energize the victim. In severe cases, a dehydrated person may have to lie down for an hour or two while the body recovers.

Sunburn. Sunburn is an inflammation of the skin caused by overexposure to solar radiation. The risks associated with too much sun have received increasing publicity in recent years. Sun exposure is linked to about 90% of all skin cancer, a disease that has been diagnosed in almost a million Americans.

Sunburn is a greater hazard to wintersports enthusiasts than to people involved in most other outdoor activities. Since less of the earth's atmosphere is available to protect a person from the sun's harmful rays at higher altitudes, it takes less exposure to exceed the body's normal level of tolerance. For each 1000 feet of elevation, the intensity of solar radiation increases about 4% above that found at sea level. Since Wasatch tourers often ski at elevations at or above 10,000 feet, their exposure to solar radiation can be as much as 50% higher than for individuals located at sea level.

The snow's high reflectance and the sun's inclination above the horizon also contribute to the sunburn hazard. Since snow reflects most of the sun's rays, the risk of sunburn is greater during winter than during other seasons. As the sunlight's angle of incidence increases during spring, the light passes through less atmosphere, is therefore less filtered, and consequently more dangerous than at other seasons. Tourers add additional risk by wearing less protective clothing during springtime,

Different individuals react differently to sunlight. Light skinned people often need very little exposure to become burned, while those with a dark complexion may have a much higher tolerance. The dark brown pigment that gives skin its color, called *melanin,* absorbs both visible and ultraviolet light and protects the surrounding tissue from damage.

It is important for everyone to know how their skin reacts to exposure to sun.

Symptoms of Sunburn. The first symptom of excessive sun exposure is a reddening of the skin, a sign not always noticeable on a bright day. The reddening can be detected by pressing on the skin with a finger. If a white spot remains when pressure is removed, sunburn has started. Severe sunburn results in blistering, but this may not occur until several hours after exposure. Sunburn is often extremely painful.

Long-term symptoms of excessive exposure to ultraviolet radiation are leathery appearance of the skin and various bumps, sores, or areas of discoloration. Any new growths, sores that don't heal, spots that bleed easily, or areas that change color should be brought to the attention of a physician.

Prevention of Sunburn. The harmful effects of sun can be prevented by covering the skin with either clothing or one of many commercially available sunscreen products.

Sunscreens are rated according to their ability to block ultraviolet B (UVB), the band of solar radiation thought to be most responsible for sunburn. The "Sun Protection Factor" (SPF) is a measure of how long an individual protected with a sunscreen can be exposed to UVB without experiencing burning, relative to the amount of time he can be exposed without any sunscreen. Covering the skin with a sunscreen rated SPF-25 allows one to remain in the sun 25 times longer than without sunscreen. For the average Caucasian at Wasatch touring altitudes, it takes less than 30 minutes for skin to begin to redden, so a screen rated SPF-15 or greater should be used. In springtime, when the sun is higher and its radiation is more intense, an SPF-30 preparation should be considered. If one perspires heavily, it is important to reapply sunscreen often, but a heavier dose does not increase the SPF.

Recent research indicates that the more dangerous type of radiation for humans is ultraviolet A (UVA). Many sunscreens do not block UVA effectively, and the SPF rating number does not measure protection against it. Some new products do claim to contain compounds that block UVA. A careful reading of the product's label is imperative.

Since the eyes are sensitive to the rays of the sun, they should also be protected. Corneal burns (sometimes called "snow blindness") can be prevented by a good pair of sunglasses. Be sure to purchase a model that provides protection from both UVA and UVB radiation.

Treatment of Sunburn. Many commercial products are available to ease the pain and promote healing. If the burn is so severe that the skin blisters, it should be kept clean and covered with sterile bandages to prevent infection. Especially severe sunburn may require medical treatment. In all cases, one should avoid the sun for a few days. Victims may have increased sensitivity to the sun's radiation for several months.

Mountain Sickness. Without the proper quantity of oxygen, the human body cannot function properly. Oxygen enters the lungs and diffuses through the tissue to be absorbed by red blood cells. The blood carries the oxygen to the rest of the body, where it is used to support muscular activity and food metabolism. If one tries to exercise at a level beyond the capability of the body to carry out this process, the normal reactions are an increase in rate of respiration and an increase in the heart rate. Brain activity is also reduced by a deficiency of oxygen.

Air at an elevation of 10,000 feet above sea level contains only two thirds the oxygen that air contains at sea level. Since the pressure of air is also less at higher altitudes, it is more difficult for oxygen to penetrate the walls of the lungs. Thus, a person must breathe more and exercise less as he climbs to higher altitudes.[13]

Extended periods at high altitudes may also lead to *mountain sickness* (sometimes called *Acute Mountain Sickness* or AMS). This condition is relatively common above 8,000 feet in non-acclimatized individuals. Incidence of AMS increases with altitude and rate of ascent. Surprisingly, well-conditioned athletes may be more susceptible to mountain sickness because they are capable of climbing much more rapidly. AMS is rarely life-threatening, although it may cause considerable discomfort.[14]

Most people in good health can enjoy themselves at altitude if they allow themselves enough time to acclimate. A person's rate of acclimatization is thought to be determined by genetic factors. Over a period of several days, the brain automatically programs the body to increase the respiration rate. Greater urine production is also commonly observed.

Symptoms of Mountain Sickness. The most common reactions to rapid ascent to high elevations are headache, shortness of breath, nausea, coughing, loss of appetite, and weakness. People coming from sea level may also experience insomnia. Only one or two of these symptoms may be present, with headache being the most common. The symptoms have a tendency to come on when a person is at rest, since the rate of

---

[13] Federal aviation regulations, in fact, require airplane crew members who fly at or above 12,500 feet for periods longer than thirty minutes to supplement their normal air intake with oxygen.

[14] An excellent reference on the effects of altitude on the human body is *Going Higher—The Story of Man and Altitude* by Charles S. Houston, M.D., published by Little Brown and Company.

respiration is lower at that time. An affected individual may be able to ski tour the next day without problems.

Two potentially fatal forms of high altitude illness affect a small number of people. *High Altitude Pulmonary Edema* (HAPE) is characterized by acute shortness of breath, anxiety, and frothy saliva or cough. Symptoms of *High Altitude Cerebral Edema* (HACE) are severe headache, loss of balance, and loss of coordination. Confusion and hallucinations are late symptoms of HACE. These problems may occur after two or three days at altitude and are not always preceded by the warning symptoms of AMS.

Prevention of Mountain Sickness. A high caloric diet (70%) for several days before altitude exposure is believed to decrease the severity of symptoms. Dehydration and alcohol consumption can make mountain sickness more likely. People coming from sea level to ski in the Wasatch, particularly if they have previously experienced problems with altitude, should spend a night at 6,000 to 8,000 feet before their first day of skiing. Someone with a history of repeated mountain sickness should talk to a physician about medication to prevent it.

Treatment of Mountain Sickness. Since the symptoms of mountain sickness may be quite similar to those of dehydration, it is sometimes possible to distinguish between the two conditions by briefly hyperventilating; if the problem is due to altitude, the symptoms often disappear.

Aspirin usually takes care of a minor headache associated with high elevation exercise. More serious cases may not respond to simple medications since headaches result in part from the increased flow of blood, which may cause a throbbing sensation in the brain. The feeling of listlessness and weakness is normally reduced by breathing more deeply, slowing the pace of the ski tour, and taking more frequent rest stops. It is important that other group members be aware when someone is experiencing difficulty so they will travel at a more comfortable pace.

If the above measures don't help, symptoms will often improve quite dramatically by a descent of only 500 to 1000 feet. If there is no change after resting for an hour or two at the same or lower elevation, it is advisable to descend farther. A person with mountain sickness should not be left alone or allowed to descend by themselves due to the possible subsequent development of pulmonary or cerebral edema.

A person with a severe headache at high elevation should be checked by other members of the skiing party for loss of balance (ability to walk a straight line, heel to toe). Anyone experiencing the symptoms of HAPE or HACE should be taken to lower altitude immediately. Medical attention could be life saving.

Psychological Hazards

A perusal of winter backcountry accidents leads to the conclusion that many mishaps are *initiated* by factors best described as "psychological." Poor decision-making in route selection, the taking of unnecessary risks, or carelessness during changes in weather are but three examples of such factors. While detailed evaluations of pre-accident circumstances exist for avalanche incidents,[15] the authors are unaware of similar evaluations of other types of backcountry misfortunes. In the *Avalanche Handbook,* as an example, only a few paragraphs are devoted to what may be considered psychological factors.

"There's a macho, omnipotent, 'not me' psychology among a lot of victims we've brought off the mountains," Richard Casto, Emergency Services Division Commander of the Utah County Sheriff's Department, replied to our inquiry. "There's a brash refusal to acknowledge the dangers that are out there," he added. "It's always going to be someone else that's going to be injured or killed."

Based on some thirty years' mountain rescue experience as ski patrolman at Solitude and Park West ski resorts, as well as mountaineering experience throughout the world, Larry Swanson offers some thought-provoking observations with respect to the psychological aspect of mountain hazards. "It's not on the bad, stormy, icy, and overcast days when accidents are most likely to occur," he states, "but on clear, sunny days with fresh snow and deep powder." He bases his conclusion on two interrelated human factors, *perceptions* and *confidence.*

"I believe that people are more motivated by their perception of conditions than by the reality of conditions," he continues. Given two identical hazard situations, one in good and the other in bad weather, Swanson feels that most backcountry recreationists will perceive the hazard differently. "Clear, sunny weather and good snow bring on a feeling of excitement and exuberance. These feelings influence hazard evaluation in a way that minimizes the hazard. On a good day we're hauling injured skiers off the mountain a lot more than on a bad day."

Swanson maintains that the individual's confidence level also plays an important role in pre-accident situations. "How deeply we expose ourselves to a hazard depends on our level of confidence. The more confidence we have at a moment, the more hazardous the situation we might become involved with." He returns to weather as an example. "When weather is good, we're confident. When weather is terrible,

---

[15] References and citations will appear in the next chapter, dealing with avalanche safety.

we're not as confident. During terrible weather we're apt to be less confident of ourselves and therefore choose to do things that are safer."

Confidence, according to the ski patrolman, also plays a significant role within a touring group. "As humans we tend to place trust in individuals who are confident. The most confident individual within a group, the strongest, the one with the most ability, usually emerges as the group's leader. Too often, he's not conscious that others in the group may be slower, less strong, and with less physical reserve than he." During a ski tour this factor may lead to separation of weaker members of the group from those who are stronger. "Such partitioning," Swanson warns, "frequently leads to backcountry accidents."

While evaluating hazards before or during a backcountry outing, Swanson urges members of the party to ask themselves two important questions: "Is this particular tour or route really safe, *or is our evaluation being influenced by our enthusiasm?*" "Does the individual who's assumed leadership of our group really know what he is doing, or are we following him simply because he *seems* to know what he's doing?"

Perception of a hazard may also be influenced by the distance between the hazard and the observer. Distant terrain features look smaller and seem less dangerous that they really are. It's important to keep this factor in mind when planning a touring route to an objective visible in the distance. Tourers who select a route from afar should avoid developing an early mindset over distant features; the hazard potential of terrain features is best evaluated from a closer distance.

But not from too near, since proximity of the observer also plays an important role in perception of the angle of a slope, a critical avalanche and rockfall hazard evaluation criterion. As one approaches a steep slope, the angle of view permits less of the slope to be visible, and the slope appears to be less steep. This illusional factor is illustrated in Figure 3.18, two photographs taken of Alta's High Rustler avalanche path from different perspectives.

"Force of habit" is another psychological factor that has lead to mountain accidents. Many Wasatch ski tours utilize common approach routes that include a variety of mountain hazards. Repetitious, safe use of such common routes leads to a sense of complacency on subsequent ski tours.

- Tourers should not take for granted the safety of a route based on previously safe passages. Each new day of touring should commence with a new evaluation of dangers.

Figure 3.18 The illusional effect of slope angle—and hazard—perception is shown in these photos of Alta's High Rustler avalanche slope as it appears from the highway and from its base.

EQUIPPING FOR SURVIVAL

In event of a serious backcountry accident, rescue by entities outside of the immediate touring party is chancy at best. In Utah, the resolution of emergency situations is delegated to county sheriff's departments. Mountain rescue response times, due to the large bureaucracies involved, too often have lead to body recoveries rather than live rescues. Several Wasatch Front counties have recently organized specialized rescue teams that have demonstrated somewhat improved response times in handling mountain emergencies.

News, medical, charter, and military helicopters have participated in several dramatic mountain rescues (and recoveries) over the years, but they are not always available and are generally grounded during bad weather. Wasatch Powderbird Guides, the heli-ski concession discussed previously, has a policy of responding immediately to all avalanche and injury-related backcountry accidents whenever their helicopters are operating in the area. Their guides are all trained in first aid and avalanche rescue, and their communications capabilities allow rapid mobilization and transportation of backup rescuers.[16]

Forest Service publications and signs posted at some Forest Service trailheads advise backcountry tourers to *Be Prepared for Self Rescue.*

Contents of a Day Pack

Self rescue is made easier, and an overnight bivouac is made more comfortable, when all members of a touring party carry within their packs basic survival equipment to be described in this section. Whatever the destination of a tour, the pack's contents should include extra clothing, food, ski repair materials, as well as avalanche, survival, and first aid equipment. Many experienced tourers assemble various items into small modules or kits that contain all the items in a particular class. Commercially assembled kits are also available.

Clothing. Gloves and socks become damp or wet very easily. It's a good idea to carry an extra set of glove liners and/or mittens and a pair of heavy socks. The extra socks also make an excellent shockproof wrapping for camera equipment and in an emergency can double as mittens or an extra layer next to one's skin to protect valuable body parts. A neck gaiter can give added protection during extreme weather conditions. A down or synthetically insulated vest or sweater can provide added protection for the torso. The inclusion of a windproof shell or cagoule should also be considered. A small foam pad is excellent for sitting or kneeling on during rest stops.

Repair Kit. A good repair kit can mean the difference between a pleasant outing or one that exposes participants to darkness, cold, and unnecessary stress. The components can easily fit into a small, nylon utility bag; a quality kit will contain the following items:

Extra ski pole basket.
Extra cable for cable binding or extra bale for 3-pin binding.
Different diameter steel wire.
Pliers. Special multi-purpose pliers designed for repair kits are commercially available.
Hacksaw blade. A short portion of a blade will suffice.

---

[16]Prospective rescuees should be advised that evacuation by helicopter may cost them dearly. On at least one occasion, W.P.G. invoiced the survivors of an avalanche whom they ferried off the mountain. In most places, victims are not required to pay for emergency services *rendered by governmental agencies.* That policy may soon change in Salt Lake County. As this book goes to press, the Salt Lake County Sheriff's department has proposed rescue fees that would be charged victims of backcountry accidents.

EQUIPPING FOR SURVIVAL

Screwdrivers. Short Posidrive or Phillips for screws sized to bindings. Some multi-purpose pliers incorporate screwdriver heads into their handles.

Glass filament and duct tape. Tapes are used to repair climbers, packs, and gloves and to seal rips in down garments.

Rope/cord. Cord can be used to tie skis together to form a rescue sled. 100 feet is not too much.

Razor or utility knife blades.

Steel wool. This can be used to fill screw holes that have enlarged or distorted.

Epoxy. Small vials of a quick-setting, general-purpose compound.

Assorted screws and rivets. Screws should be matched to bindings, etc.

Aluminum sheet. A small piece can be taped around a broken ski pole as a splint.

Spare ski tip.[17]

Avalanche Search and Rescue Equipment. Many beginner tours have little exposure to avalanche dangers. When routes are exposed to such hazards, however, each member of the party should carry—and know how to use—basic avalanche search and rescue equipment. (These are detailed in Chapter 4.)

First Aid Equipment. Because backcountry touring is a combination of two sports, skiing and hiking, injuries associated with each sport are possible during a ski tour. Speed associated with skiing on uncertain snow surfaces can lead to sprains, dislocations, and fractures. Abrasions, lacerations, and punctures are possible from encounters with trees or rocks. Frostnip and frostbite are common on cold and windy days, and sunburn can result from excessive exposure to sunlight. Snake bites, while possible during a late-spring ski tour, are unlikely on winter outings.

First aid procedures applicable to backcountry touring are limited to procedures covered by good samaritan laws and those recommended by the American Red Cross and the National Safety Council's First Aid Institute. Tourers should consider participating in basic first aid courses—or specialized winter or backcountry first aid courses—taught by certified instructors.

Commercially-assembled first aid kits that meet basic first aid requirements are available at most outdoor recreation outlets. Tourers

---

[17]Ski tips, adjustable for skis of different widths, were common when all touring was done on wooden skis. With use of metal and fiberglass skis, they're much less common (except among tourers who continue to use wooden skis).

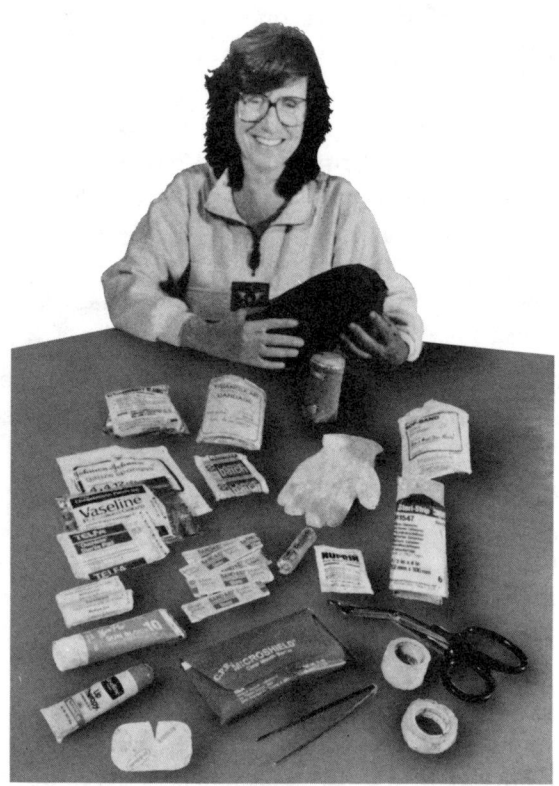

Figure 3.19 Park City Emergency Medical Technician Cheryl Soshnik exhibits the contents of a backcountry first aid kit she has assembled. Preassembled first aid kits are available commercially. Kits should contain an instruction booklet.

can also assemble personal first aid kits from components available over the counter. Items to be included, and their functions:

Instruments. Scissors for cutting away clothing, boot laces, etc. and for cutting bandage material; tweezers for removing splinters; Swiss Army Knife.

Bandaids. Assorted sizes, including steri-strips or butterfly bandaids to close gaping wounds before bandaging.

Dressings. Non-stick sterile telfa dressings to place over a wound before bandaging; 4 x 4 inch gauze dressings to clean or cover wounds.

Gauze rolled bandage. Used to secure splints or dressings.

Vaseline-coated gauze. Doubles as a napalm-like fire starter.

Elastic rolled bandage. To secure splints or dressings, and to supply some compression for injury-related swelling or bleeding.

Triangular bandage. Used to hold arm or other splints in place.

Adhesive tape. Provides support for a sprained ankle.

Eye patch. An over-the-counter eye patch is handy to protect the eye from further damage in the event of an injury or snow blindness.

Moleskin. Precut pieces help prevent blisters.

Second Skin. A soft cushion prevents further injury after a blister forms.

Sun/Wind screens. Sunburn creams and lip protection ointment.

Medicines. Over the counter pain and anti-inflammation medicines such as Aspirin, Tylenol, etc. and an antacid.

"Universal precaution" articles. Latex gloves provide a protective barrier between the person giving first aid and the blood or blood products of another person.

CPR microshield. This provides a protective barrier during mouth-to-mouth resuscitation.

Personal prescription medicines. Individuals on daily medication regimens should carry at least a day's supply of prescription medicines.

Emergency first aid pocket guide. A number of commercially available booklets summarize common first aid procedures.

Survival Equipment. No matter how experienced the tourer, a time may come when unforeseen circumstances necessitate spending a night in the mountains. Such a forced encampment, called a *bivouac*, can result from accident, illness, major equipment failure, loss of route, bad weather, or separation of some members of a touring party from others. A bivouac may also become necessary when a touring party comes across a group that's in trouble. Nighttime temperatures in the Wasatch mountains can easily descend below zero; accompanying winds can push the chill factor to $-50°F$ or even lower.

Keeping one's head is the most important element of mountain survival; next in importance is the ability to improvise under adverse conditions. Since loss of body heat can lead to hypothermia and affect the ability to think clearly and to solve problems, *keeping warm becomes the most fundamental element of mountain survival.*

Most knowledgeable backcountry recreationists—both summer and winter—carry with them materials and implements best described as survival equipment. Many purchase commercial "storm kits." Some tourers assemble their own survival kits. Whether one chooses to purchase or to assemble, the tourer should carry most—if not all—of the following items:

Matches. Special wind-proof or water-proof matches are available for use in survival kits. Matches should be kept in a waterproof container. Some waterproof match containers are equipped with a piece of flint that can be used to strike sparks. (Butane lighters may not always work at low temperatures).

Candle(s). Candles are used to ignite kindling when building a fire. As described previously, a candle can be kept lighted under one's cagoule, and it can provide considerable heat in a well-constructed shelter. After purchasing a batch of candles, it is important to test one for burn time; slower burning varieties are better in an emergency situation.

Lighting fluid. Some tourers prefer to carry a small vial of charcoal lighting fluid to be used for quickly starting a fire.

Tube tent. A tube tent is a continuous cylinder of thin plastic that can be stretched between two trees to form a small "tent."

Thermal blanket. Thermal blankets are straight out of the space-age. Developed initially to insulate the interiors of space capsules, they are designed to reflect the body's radiant heat back onto itself. Thermal blankets occupy only a few cubic inches of space when folded properly.

Plastic garbage sacks. Thin plastic garbage sacks are useful for many purposes. With holes cut for arms and neck they provide excellent protection for the torso. For sitting on snow, they can provide a waterproof barrier between buttocks and snow. They're excellent for wrapping extra clothing to be carried on a tour.

Flashlight or headlamp. In addition to its normal use as a light source, a flashlight makes an excellent signaling device.

Signal mirror. Signal mirrors can be used to attract the attention of search parties on the ground or in the air. To be effective a signal mirror must be aimed properly, so practice is essential. Military-style glass mirrors come with instructions printed on the back. Metal mirrors are also available.

Whistle. This can be an important signalling device. Three blasts is a widely-accepted distress signal.

Snow shovel. A snow shovel is a necessary component for serious backcountry touring. It is generally carried as part of avalanche rescue equipment by every member of a party. Shovels are equally important in a bivouac situation, where they can be used to dig a snow cave or to construct an igloo.

Wire saw. A wire saw is a braided metal wire impregnated with carborundum particles. It can be used for cutting branches from trees for use as firewood.

Map/compass. These are excellent items for passing the night. Better still, they can help the touring party stay on its intended route and eliminate the need for a bivouac.

Survival food. Energy bars or candy bars with high caloric value will help maintain body heat. Bullion cubes, powdered lemonade, tea packets can be used to make hot drinks.

Water purification tablets. Mountain water should not be consumed without purification due to the omnipresence of contaminants. A palatable alternative to tablets is Betadine, an iodine solution; adding 8 drops to a quart of water will kill Giardia in less than 30 minutes.

Metal container. A metal can with a lid can be used to hold the survival equipment. It may also be used as a pot for melting snow and heating water for the bullion, lemonade, or tea.

Après-tour Equipment

When a ski tour terminates successfully at the car, the tourer is usually damp and cool, sometimes nearing a hypothermic condition. The dampness is generally due to frequent tumbles into snow and to perspiration caused by overdressing. The coolness is due to low-angle evening sun or to its total absence. The sudden cessation of activity—and thus cessation of rapid heat-producing metabolism—also contributes to cooling.

Wisdom suggests assembly of an after-tour kit. In addition to a towel, such a kit would include a complete set of dry clothing to change into: socks, insulated boots, turtleneck, hooded sweat-shirt, sweatpants. A dry vest or parka adds comfort during the warm-up of the car's heater. A thermos of hot soup or hot coffee warms one from within.

Capitalizing On Calamity

When an alpine adventure inverts into an alpine misadventure, the first consideration should be the continued well being of the participants. Once survival is assured, and everyone has returned safely, most misadventurers will withdraw in shame. A few enterprising individuals will seize the opportunity to market their misfortune. Gleaned from previously profitable mountaineering films and survival documentaries, five critical elements emerge as essential for successful conversion of cold calamity to cold cash.

Cast of Characters. What should the party makeup be for optimum marketability?

The cast of *White Tower*, a popular 1950 mountaineering melodrama, may provide a clue. A self-effacing American bomber pilot joins a highly-motivated, pushy woman driven to complete a first ascent that claimed her father. She is joined by a dissipated, alcoholic, has-been writer, an effete English "intellectual," a competent-and-confident, coming-out-of-retirement guide, and an arrogant young Nazi.

During the Renaissance of cross-country skiing in the 1960's, nearly every touring party was an assembly of colorful eccentrics, since touring at that time was a pastime of the unorthodox. Today, with the mass popularization of the sport, uncommonality among members of a party may be somewhat difficult to realize.

Developing a Theme. All successful entertainment productions contain clear-cut themes. Drive, self-sacrifice, and cooperation are the primary themes in *White Tower*. The beautifully photographed 1956 film *The Mountain* interweaves inter-generational jealousy and unfettered greed. "A boy matures, the British play fair" is the gist of Disney's *Third Man on the Mountain*. "Motherhood—a traditional American family value" may underscore the forthcoming docu-drama depicting Mrs. Jennifer Stolpa's and her infant son's week-long ordeal surviving a January 1993 blizzard in the Sierra Nevada.

In view of current Congressional disdain for sex and violence on television, these themes may not be as marketable tomorrow as they were in the past. Wasatch tourers should not be concerned that so many excellent motifs have already been utilized. Utah's uniquely colorful culture may provide themes that are well beyond the limits of Hollywood's most imaginative screen writer.

Villainy, Conflict, and Retribution. Constantly voicing the phrase "to rest is not to conquer," the arrogant Nazi in *White Tower* quickly assumes the role of villain. He soon discovers that being a bad egg, and rejecting an outthrust, solid, American helping hand while balanced on an uncertain foothold, are the conditions for retribution; he plummets screaming into a white void. After festooning himself with cameras, watches, and jewelry removed from the dead of an airplane crash, Robert Wagner (in *The Mountain*) meets a similar fate in a glacial crevasse. Not all resolutions of conflict require such dramatics, but the more dramatic appear to be the more marketable.

Prolonging the Suffering. In February 1993, unforeseen circumstances, exceptionally severe weather, and numerous errors in judgment joined forces to prolong the suffering of a touring party presumed lost in the mountains of Colorado. For nearly a week, not a newscast went by without coverage of search and speculation. Equally suspenseful was the March 1993 coverage of a large group of Michigan tourers who had become unaccounted for in the Great Smoky Mountains during an intense blizzard. The group's preparedness and competence in winter survival prevented suffering. The reader can guess which group will be depicted in made-for-television productions.

Keeping a Journal. Scripting will be made easier if screen writers can rely on journals maintained by a misadventure's participants. The immortal last words of a very mortal Robert F. Scott have been quoted and requoted ceaselessly since he penned them during his fatal South Pole expedition in 1912. They have inspired a symphony and have concluded many a documentary dealing with the Antarctic. "I do not regret this journey," one of his final entries states. "We took risks, we knew we took them, things have come out against us, therefore we have no cause for complaint."

The marketing of one's misery is best accomplished with the aid of a literary agent specializing in the field. Several are listed in the book *Literary Agents of North America*. The use of a press agent skilled in depicting a survivor's frozen toes (each separated from the other by sterile gauze) in the nation's newspapers will help immensely.

Adhering to the principles discussed and finding the appropriate agents are but two facets of reaping dollars from disaster. Assuring prolonged marketability requires additional considerations. Such long-lived survival epics as the Donner Party's debacle (nearly 150 years of marketability) and the South American epic of an Andes mountains air-crash (21 years' marketability includes two movies, several books and television productions) suggest the inescapable conclusion: in considering commercial longevity, one should not discount the possibilities offered by cannibalism.

Even with the intensive control procedures utilized at mountain communities, life-threatening snowslides still occur. The arrow points to Alta's avalanche-destroyed chapel. Most backcountry touring is done in areas with no avalanche control. Photographs by A. Kelner and L. Swanson.

Chapter 4

AVALANCHE SAFETY

New Years Eve, 1972. At 3:00 pm near the community of Furnace Creek, two 13 year old boys decided to enjoy the calm at the end of a series of snowstorms that had added eight to twelve inches of snow to a layer already a foot deep. The boys liked to play snow games in a nearby ravine. They especially delighted in kicking small cornices off the hillside and watching the blocks of snow roll downward, disintegrating along the way. As they were kicking a cornice, a small avalanche released, sweeping the boys downslope and burying them completely. Both died of suffocation.

Surprisingly, Furnace Creek is located in up-state New York where one would not expect deep snowfalls and avalanche danger. In Utah, the combination of sudden and violent winter storms, extended periods of high wind, and snow depths that often exceed 10 feet frequently results in very treacherous avalanche conditions.

Thousands of snow avalanches occur naturally in the Wasatch Mountains every winter and spring. Since the days of the pioneers, avalanche burials have been common in Utah. Over 170 deaths were attributed to this cause during Utah's mining era. Since then most avalanche incidents have been associated with downhill and cross country skiing. In the past 50 years more than 30 skiers have perished in snow slides in the Wasatch canyons.

Unlike the mining days, when avalanches involved persons who spent their lives in the mountains and who knew the dangers they faced, today's victims are often unsuspecting winter travelers who venture into the nearby mountains for recreation. A research forester snowmobiling in the foothills above Farmington was buried during the winter of 1965. In 1967, two young hikers were killed by a snow slide in Pharoahs Glen, just two miles from the Mount Olympus subdivision on Salt Lake City's east bench. The next winter another avalanche killed a Boy Scout on an outing in Rock Canyon near Provo. In 1986, a snowboarder died in an avalanche near Brighton; an early winter hiker suffered the same fate at Alta that year.

Even commercial ski areas, where the snow is meticulously "controlled" by professional ski patrols, have had their share of avalanche fatalities. Alta has lost three of its paying customers over the years; the most recent loss occurred in 1986. Two people have been killed in Park City on novice runs after other skiers released avalanches above them. Park West lost a ski instructor in 1973, and a Snowbird skier suffered a similar fate a few years later. Figure 4.1 tabulates avalanche fatalities that have occurred in the Wasatch in recent years.

With the continually increasing growth of winter sports such as snowboarding, snowmobiling, snowshoeing, and ski touring, it is important that Wasatch Front residents become aware of the avalanche dangers that exist in the mountains so near their homes. This chapter deals with these dangers in general terms. It covers the conditions that may lead to avalanches, describes ways to avoid them, and discusses the tactics that one should employ to increase chances of survival if caught in moving snow.

AVALANCHE INFORMATION

A novice cross country skier is not expected to immediately learn all of the avalanche evaluation criteria discussed in this book. The information here must be supplemented with personal observations, repeated practice, and continued avalanche education.

Becoming informed about avalanches and using good judgment during outings appear to be the best preventive measures. Wasatch tourers are especially fortunate in the amount and quality of avalanche prevention information available to them. Backcountry users are urged to extend their avalanche awareness process by attending one of several local avalanche classes.

Avalanche Instruction

As recently as the early 1970's, the only instructional programs dealing with avalanches were convened for the benefit of professionals working in the field of hazard evaluation and control. Today, numerous avalanche

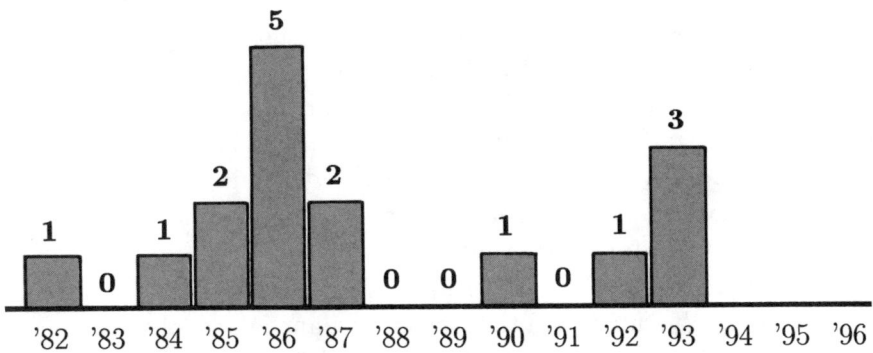

Figure 4.1 Annual avalanche fatalities along the Wasatch Front. Data courtesy of the *Utah Avalanche Forecast Center*.

instruction alternatives are offered specifically for backcountry recreationists. These are usually held during the touring season.

Northern Wasatch Area. The best opportunities for avalanche education are offered by area universities. Logan, Ogden, and Brigham City's mountaineering and ski stores should be contacted periodically to see if any avalanche seminars are held locally.

Utah State University. The Department of Forest Resources often lists a Watershed Science avalanche snow class that is available for students *and* nonstudents. The course consists of approximately ten 2-hour class sessions and three Saturday field trips.

Central Wasatch Area. Salt Lake City is the home of the Utah Avalanche Forecast Center (to be discussed later), several active outing groups, and the state's major university. Several commercial enterprises are also involved in avalanche education.

Wasatch Mountain Club. The Wasatch Mountain Club, a cooperative organization of local outdoorspersons, has been active in backcountry winter recreation since the 1920's. During the early 1970's, they convened Utah's first introductory avalanche class geared specifically for the backcountry recreationist. The popular day-long class is held once yearly, usually during January. The morning is spent viewing avalanche instruction films and discussing hazards specific to the Wasatch; the afternoon session consists of an avalanche rescue practice conducted in one of the nearby canyons. The class is open to the public; a small donation is encouraged to offset costs of preparation.

Sierra Club (Salt Lake Group). The local Sierra Club group has an active touring program that includes a day-long introductory avalanche class similar to that described above.

University Of Utah. The Division of Continuing Education, the Department of Geography, and the Department of Recreation & Leisure carry both credit and non-credit classes and seminars dealing with avalanches. Class availability changes yearly, so individual departments should be contacted for current information.

Commercial Avalanche Instruction. The American Avalanche Institute of Wilson, Wyoming, and the Alaska Avalanche School occasionally provide avalanche classes and workshops in Utah. These are very intensive and can be quite expensive. Information regarding them can be obtained from the Utah Avalanche Forecast Center and from local backcountry equipment dealers.

Your Personal Avalanche Guru. "The Wasatch range," it has been written, "contains more avalanche professionals per square mile than any other place in the world." Several of the experts have achieved near-legendary status; some offer group and individual tutoring in the physics—and metaphysics—of avalanches.

Southern Wasatch. Until recently, residents of Utah Valley have enjoyed a full and varied life of avalanche apathy. With establishment of Hansen Mountaineering Co. in Orem, the scene has changed. Area tourers should visit the store often to keep informed of avalanche (or backcountry recreation) classes or seminars the staff either organizes or publicizes.

Brigham Young University has offered no classes in avalanche mechanics or safety in recent years.

Publications

Another means of preparing for a safe season of backcountry recreation is to become familiar with other people's avalanche misfortunes. Enough burials have occurred in the United States to warrant compilation and publication (by the U.S. Forest Service) of three volumes of avalanche case histories. The books are entitled *The Snowy Torrents—Avalanche Accidents in the United States.* Volume I covers 1910-1966; Volume II describes 1967-1971; and Volume III includes 1972-1979. Some of the discussed incidents involved backcountry skiers; other incidents occurred at major ski areas.

Two other publications that provide valuable information are the U.S. Forest Service's *Avalanche Handbook,* by R. I. Perla and M. Martinelli, and *The ABC's of Avalanche Safety*, by E. R. LaChapelle. All of these authors are internationally recognized avalanche authorities. While the *Avalanche Handbook*[1] primarily discusses techniques and procedures to be followed by professional avalanche control personnel, it also includes information about hazard formation and evaluation. Chapter 8 of that book deals with backcountry avalanches, the statistics of survival, route selection, rescue, and first aid; hence, it is must reading for the ski tourer.

The video tape, *Avalanche Awareness—A Question of Balance*, covers the subject well. It was produced in 1988 under the sponsorship of the American Association of Avalanche Professionals and the Colorado Mountain Club Foundation. Much of the footage and several interviews were done in Utah.

The Utah Avalanche Forecast Center

Avalanche education in Utah has a long and illustrious history. It commenced, in principle, with the employment of the first Forest Service Snow Ranger at Alta in 1941. The Alta Avalanche Study Center was organized after World War II to formally study the phenomena of avalanches. A part of its mission involved the semi-annual convening of an intensive avalanche training course for Forest Service, ski area, and highway maintenance personnel concerned with snow safety. M. M. Atwater, E. R. LaChapelle, and R. I. Perla served as the center's directors and while there achieved national and international scientific recognition.

The Utah Avalanche Forecast Center came into being in 1980 as a cooperative effort between the Wasatch-Cache National Forest and the National Weather Service. It was established to disseminate accurate mountain weather and avalanche condition reports and to provide an avalanche education service to the general public.

Today, under the direction of Bruce Tremper, and operating generally on a "budgetary crisis" level,[2] the Forecast Center maintains telephone recordings in various locations around the state that contain cur-

---

[1] The Perla/Martinelli *Avalanche Handbook*, published by the U.S. Forest Service, is out of print, but look for it in local or university libraries. *Think twice before purchasing the expensive, commercially-published book that has the same title.*

[2] In response to declining public funding, a non-profit corporation, Friends of the Utah Avalanche Forecast Center, was organized in 1991 to solicit private (tax-deductible) contributions for the Center. Your donations are critical to the continued existence of this valuable service and should be sent to 337 N. 2370 W., Salt Lake City, 84116.

rent avalanche condition information. These are updated on at least a daily basis. The Center also provides avalanche and mountain weather reports to local media. When conditions are especially hazardous special *Avalanche Warning* bulletins are immediately broadcast.

The Utah Avalanche Forecast Center's telephone numbers are listed on the inside front cover. Tourers are urged to call one of these recordings before commencing any winter outing. Skiers who frequent the more hazardous areas of the Wasatch should get into the habit of calling *daily* so that they may stay abreast of evolving conditions within the snow pack.[3]

The Cold Facts of Avalanches

Compounding the actual danger of snow slides are many misconceptions harbored by people whose only exposure to avalanches is occasional mention of the word in the media. "The Greatest Snow on Earth" herald the advertisers. Practically from birth, Utahns are taught to adulate deep powder and its pleasures. Vast fortunes are spent to promote winter sports in the Wasatch Mountains. The message is clear: "Powder snow—it's light, it's fluffy, it's fun." "It's harmless" is the implication.

When an avalanche occurs, particularly if it involves a fatality, public apathy is shaken, but only momentarily. Headlines and television vignettes speak of "huge walls of snow", of "giant snow slides", and of "freak winter conditions". Such exaggerations create the false impression that unusual conditions are necessary or responsible for fatalities, that large avalanches are usually the killers, and that avalanche victims just happened to be in the wrong place at the wrong time.

Another misconception perpetuated by news coverage of avalanche accidents is a false belief that most victims come out unscathed. A fatality is usually covered by the press in one brief article or news clip; there is, after all, no opportunity to interview the victim. On the occasions when an avalanche victim miraculously survives, he immediately becomes a celebrity, complete with feature articles and lengthy personal interviews about his entombment.

What are the facts concerning avalanches that every tourer should know?

- *After 15 minutes of burial, a victim's chance of survival is only about 50%.* This fact should be kept in mind by the members of a ski touring party when one of their companions is buried by

---

[3]Like any public service, this one is funded partly on the basis of how much it is used—one more reason to call often.

a slide. They must consider the victim's decreased chances for survival if they send someone to bring help.

- *Fewer than 20% of the victims who are completely buried—with no trace showing—have been found alive.* This leads to the conclusion that a victim's best chance for survival is to thrust an arm, a leg, or a ski out of the snow as he comes to rest.
- *About two thirds of avalanche fatalities are due to suffocation.* This fact negates the popular misconception that a lot of air is present in the snow for a victim to breathe. In actuality, the snow packs so tightly around the victim's throat and chest that respiratory failure occurs very rapidly.
- *Most of the remaining fatalities result from serious injuries.* It is not uncommon for a victim to be swept through rocks and/or trees.
- *Small avalanches can be as fatal as large ones.* About 50% of fatal accidents have involved slides which ran less than 300 feet. One doesn't have to be on a huge open slope to be in danger.[4]
- *About 95% of all avalanche accidents occur when the victim— or someone in the same group—triggers the slide.* Staying off a hazardous slope is the best protection against entrapment by an avalanche.
- *Even professional avalanche forecasters cannot always tell when snow is unstable enough to slide.* The science of snow physics is extremely complex. Many factors influence the stability of the snowpack, and it is impossible to predict instability with 100% certainty.
- *Anyone can be caught in a snow slide.* As the group of Scouts learned in Rock Canyon, and as the Farmington snowmobiler discovered, avalanches can happen to almost anyone who ventures into the mountains in winter.

TYPES OF AVALANCHES

In order for an avalanche to occur, three conditions must exist: there must be snow, a slope on which that snow can slide, and a failure of the snow to support itself. Some form of external disturbance may set the

---

[4] A tragedy occurred in downtown Toronto, Canada, where two girls, tobogganing in a city park, were killed by an avalanche that was only 6 feet wide and several hundred feet long. The volume of snow in which they were buried was approximately equal to that of a large city bus.

Figure 4.2 Started by an explosive charge detonated in the backcountry above Alta, a relatively small, loose-snow avalanche gathers speed on its descent into the valley below.

snow in motion, but a release can also be initiated by gradual changes within the snow.

The snowpack consists of a number of layers that form throughout the winter. The layers may be held together very tightly or they may be poorly bonded. Two opposing forces act on each layer. Gravity pulls it downward, and underlying snow layers (or the ground) hold it up.

Snow can be set in motion in a number of ways. A weak layer may collapse from the weight of new snow deposited on it or occasionally from a ski tourer moving along its surface. Alternatively, a strong layer on the surface may start to slide when it is cut by the passage of a skier, or when it is disturbed by the shock waves from an explosive device or a helicopter's rotor blades.

There are two basic types of avalanche, *loose-snow* and *slab*. Loose-snow avalanches are characterized by surface layers that are poorly bonded; small versions of loose-snow avalanches are known as "sluffs." Figure 4.2 depicts a typical loose-snow avalanche. Slab avalanches occur when a *cohesive layer* of snow is set into motion. The layer, or slab, typically consists of very densely-packed snow, although it may be soft enough to ski in. Figure 4.3 shows the aftermath of a classic slab avalanche. The causes and behavior of both types of avalanche depend

TYPES OF AVALANCHES

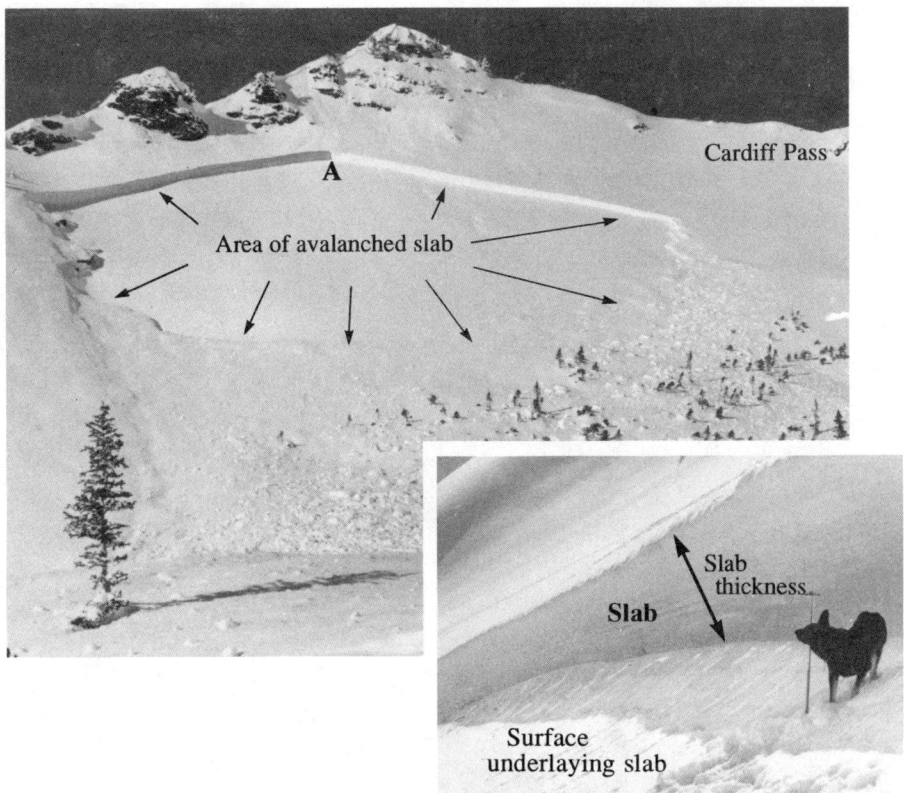

Figure 4.3 Aftermath of a classic slab avalanche near Alta's Cardiff Pass. The inset was photographed at point A, at the base of the slab's fracture surface. The Alta Avalanche Studies Center's renowned ski mountaineering canine, Dogowitz, helps gauge the slab's thickness. "When a slab breaks loose and slides down a mountainside," R. I. Perla states in the *Avalanche Handbook*, "it may bring down 100 times the initially released amount of snow." Photos courtesy of Dr. R. I. Perla.

on a number of factors, such as moisture content, temperature, density, and structure of the snow crystals.

Loose-snow avalanches usually occur during or soon after a snowfall. Typically, loose-snow avalanches start from a point and spread out as they flow down the mountain. Only the surface layer is generally involved in such slides. The danger of this type of avalanche decreases with time as the new snow stabilizes by consolidation. The lower the ambient temperature, however, the slower the stabilization process. Consolidation may require only a few days at 20 degrees, but could take well over a week at subzero temperatures. This is one reason why cold north-facing slopes present such a great danger in the Wasatch;

Figure 4.4 Wet snow avalanches generally occur during spring, as the warm sun loosens snow clinging to rocks. It is not uncommon for the entire depth of the snowpack to slide down the mountain.

storms often occur every few days, leaving insufficient time for one snow layer to consolidate before a new layer is added.

Loose-snow avalanches also occur when warm temperatures soften the snow and saturate it with water, thus weakening the internal bonds between individual snow crystals. Rain can quickly increase the weight of the top layers of the snow pack. Wet snow avalanches usually occur in spring, but they have been observed during mid-winter thaws. Due to the excessive weight of water-saturated snow, they are often the most destructive. The avalanches depicted in Figure 4.4 and the photographs at the beginning of this chapter were wet snow avalanches.

Due to their unpredictability, slab avalanches present the greatest threat to backcountry skiers. Slabs may remain in place for many days without sliding, then suddenly become unstable and prone to slide. Two

TO TOUR OR NOT TO TOUR?

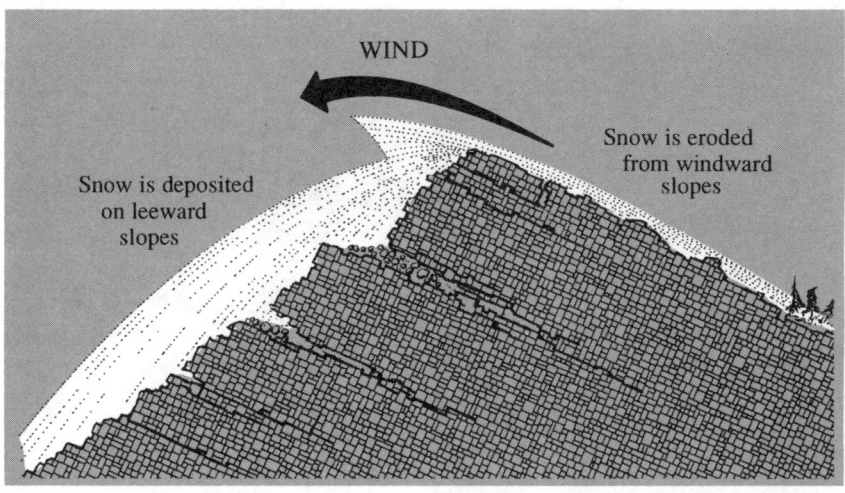

Figure 4.5 Wind can transport great amounts of snow, frequently creating severe avalanche hazards on leeward slopes where heavy deposition occurs. While windward slopes are generally safer, tourers should watch out for isolated pockets of deep snow in these areas as well.

conditions lead to destabilization: (1) Due to fresh snowfall or drifting, as illustrated in Figure 4.5, more snow can be added onto the slab, increasing its weight beyond the ability of the underlayer to support it. (2) An underlayer may become weakened by internal changes brought on by variations in temperature, humidity, and other factors.

Slab avalanches are usually characterized by a clearly defined fracture line that may be many yards in length. Slab hazards can remain in place for weeks or months, particularly in mid-winter when temperatures are cold.

TO TOUR OR NOT TO TOUR?

Each weekend from November through May, backcountry recreationists struggle with the decision of whether or not to initiate an outing. An examination of recreational tracks made by heli-skiers, ski tourers, and snowmobile operators along the Wasatch reveals that too many backcountry visitors are either ignorant of—or purposefully ignore—safe travel practices while in avalanche country. Taken during a March 1992 airplane flight, the two photographs in Figure 4.6 illustrate the point. Both photos show ski or snowmobile tracks entering clearly dangerous avalanche-prone terrain. Both shots show avalanches that had released at—or after—the time the tracks were made.

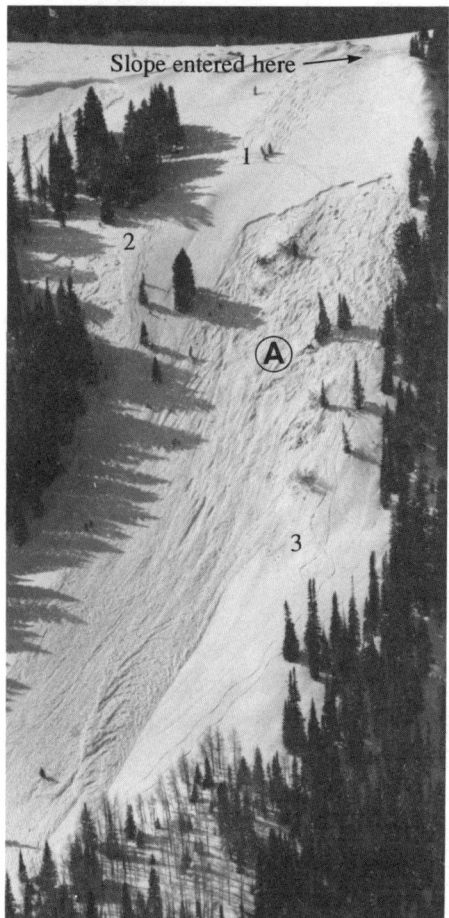
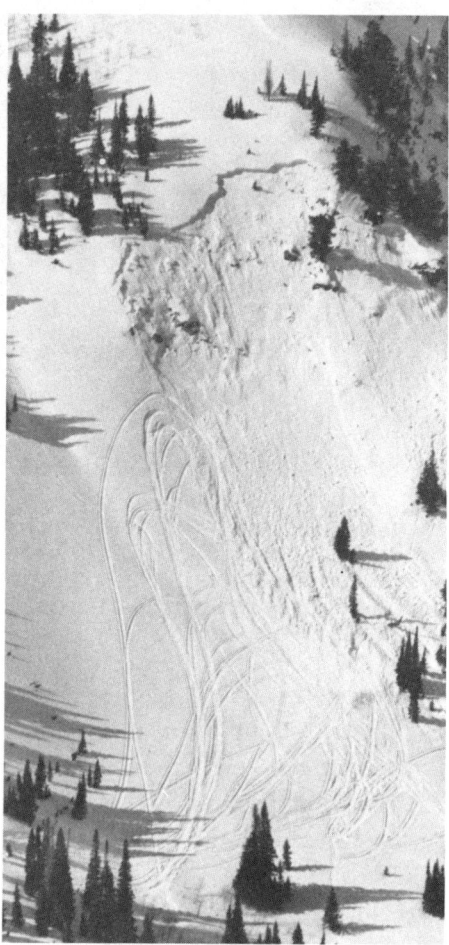

Figure 4.6 *The tracks tell the story! Left:* Ten ski tracks enter an avalanche path from the ridge. It appears that the group assembled near two small trees at 1; most of the group chose to continue their descent adjacent to dense timber at 2. Two skiers traversed into the middle of the avalanche slope A; both tracks come out at the bottom of the slope at 3. It is impossible, from the photo, to determine if the two skiers who traversed onto the slope triggered the moderately large slide. *Right:* It is common for snowmobile operators to ascend steep hillsides at high speed and then, as power is lost, to turn sharply downhill. Such maneuvers can undercut a slab and set it in motion. Note the large size of the avalanche that has released above the snowmobile tracks.

Backcountry users should consider three basic types of information before commencing a winter outing in the Wasatch: the history of the snowpack throughout the season, terrain features in the area to be visited, and the capabilities of the touring party.

TO TOUR OR NOT TO TOUR?

History of the Snowpack

An avalanche-conscientious tourer maintains familiarity with weather and snow patterns throughout the season. The best way for a weekend skier to keep abreast of the constantly changing snowpack is to call the Utah Avalanche Forecast Center on a regular basis. Careful observations should also be made during each outing.

A few generalities can be made about the snowpack during different parts of the touring season:

- In late fall and early winter, before irregularities in the terrain are obliterated by deep snow, conditions can be quite safe on slopes which have trees, stumps, bushes, and large rocks that can hold the snow in place. The skiing is often excellent at that time of year, but the tourer must be careful to avoid obstacles under the surface.
- Instabilities are most likely to develop in early to mid-winter. A weak layer that forms deep within the snowpack may exist for extended periods due to cold temperatures. As the weight of the snow increases with new snowfalls, conditions can become extremely hazardous.
- The best time for backcountry skiing is usually during late winter. The sun is higher and ambient temperatures rise, so weak layers usually stabilize faster.
- Spring is a mixed bag. Corn snow can be heavenly in the morning, but extended melting during a warm day can turn it to mush and cause deadly wet snow avalanches in the afternoon.

Early Season Snow Storms. In the Wasatch Mountains, early season snowstorms often lead to severe avalanche conditions that may last throughout much of the winter. Late September and October storms frequently deposit shallow layers of snow at high elevations. These snow accumulations usually melt from south and west-facing slopes, but remain on north and east exposures. If the unmelted accumulations are exposed to prolonged cold weather between additional storms, individual snow flakes can undergo dramatic physical change. As illustrated in Figure 4.7, branched, interlocked, star-like crystals transform into smoother granules commonly called *depth hoar*.[5] Hoar granules feel like sugar. Since there is little bonding between the granules, the layer is very weak. Subsequent snowfalls do not strengthen the

---

[5]Depth hoar is most likely to form when there is a large difference between the temperature below the layer (the ground usually stays at about 32°F) and that above it (the air gets extremely cold at night).

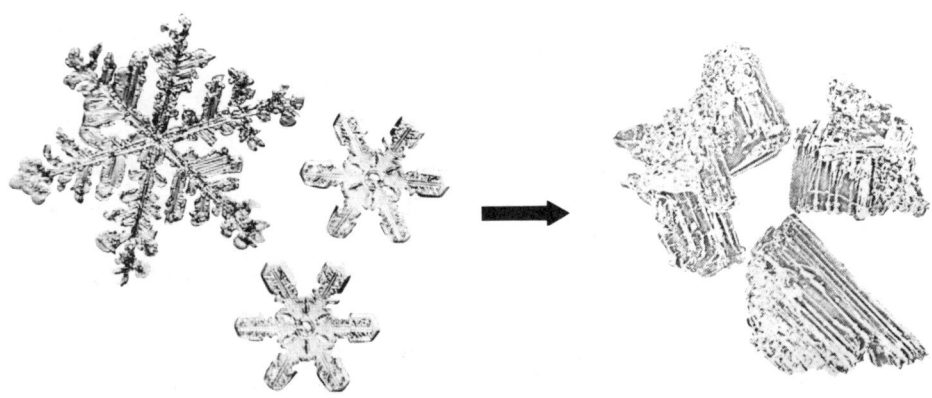

Figure 4.7 Periods of cold weather, aided by heat from the earth, can transform "regular" snowflakes, as shown at left, into larger, more rounded granules known as "depth hoar." A layer of such particles can cause avalanche hazards that may persist for months.

layer of depth hoar—they just camouflage it. If the winter starts out with few snow storms and long periods of cold weather between them, watch out!

Prolonged Cold Spells. As mentioned previously, prolonged cold may cause formation of depth hoar early in the season. Long cold spells without new snow can also cause similar transformations in the crystals of the surface layer. Large flat crystals, called *surface hoar*, form on top. Surface hoar can result in a weak layer after more snow is deposited.

One other danger of an extended period of cold weather is that *any unstable condition may linger indefinitely.* For example, a depth hoar layer, or a surface slab that is not bonded well to the underlying snow, is unlikely to improve when temperatures remain below 0°F.

Prolonged Warm Spells. A prolonged period of relatively mild weather (25 − 35°F) in mid-winter usually stabilizes the snow pack by causing the hoar granules to bond into a cohesive mass. It is common in Utah to have a warm period in late January which allows the snow to settle and improves its stability. If the temperature is much above freezing, however, a long warm spell can have the opposite effect. This situation can lead to the release of large "climax" avalanches, slides that take all of the snow down to the ground.

Temperature inversions, which often last for periods of many days, are common in the Wasatch. It is not unusual for temperatures to be above freezing at 10,000 feet when the valley is cold and smoggy. In this situation, tours on north and east slopes which have not melted may be more inviting.

TO TOUR OR NOT TO TOUR? 135

Figure 4.8   A deep snowfall onto an ice crusted base can transform the gentlest slope into a deathtrap. This photo was taken in an area considered by many tourers to be free of avalanches.

Large Snow Accumulations. The Wasatch Mountains often receive 30 to 60 inches of snowfall during one storm. Such deep accumulations in a short time should be regarded with extreme caution, and touring should not be attempted until several days (or even weeks) have passed to allow natural consolidation of the snow.

Wind. High wind often accompanies and/or follows a snow storm. Even when the air is calm in Salt Lake Valley, snow plumes can often be observed coming off the nearby summits. Since wind contributes to slab formation, these plumes are warning signals to watch for on days preceding a tour.

Surface Under the Last Snowfall. Two kinds of surface conditions result in weak layers when covered with more snow. One of these, mentioned previously, is the surface hoar that forms during periods of cold clear weather. The other is an ice crust which may result from warm temperatures, rain, or from the late-winter sun beating on a south facing slope. If cold snow falls on an ice crust, it will not bond to it well. Figure 4.8 illustrates a dramatic set of avalanches that resulted when several feet of snow fell onto an ice-crusted slope. This unstable condition can last until the temperature again increases.

Rain. Cold temperatures following a rain may create a hard glass-like crust. Future snowfalls may or may not bond to the crust, depending on temperature conditions before and during the storm. Rain can also cause wet snow avalanches when the water percolates through the snow and destroys its cohesion.

Late Season Snow Storms. Heavy snowfalls are common in the Wasatch Mountains during spring; April is often one of the heaviest snow months. Even if a spring storm deposits only a few inches of snow, extremely hazardous conditions will result if it falls on a surface crust.

Characteristics of the Terrain

The physical characteristics of the area to be traveled during a ski tour are the next important considerations in the decision-making process. A number of factors are critical to proper analysis of ski touring terrain.

Surface. Early in the season, when terrain features cause irregularities in the snow surface, new accumulations are less likely to slide off. Later on, when the snow has filled the depressions and covered the rocks and small trees, avalanches are more common. It is helpful to know the nature of the ski touring terrain in the summertime, particularly if there are any smooth rock slabs or grassy slopes that have little ability to hold the snow in place.

Presence of Trees. Avalanches occur in timbered areas as well as on open slopes, but densely-forested hillsides can provide some degree of protection. A simple rule of thumb maintains that when trees are spaced just close enough to make ski travel through them difficult and annoying, they *may* provide "adequate" protection. Figure 4.9 illustrates another important consideration with respect to trees: avalanches can start above a tree band and run through it. Many avalanche victims sustain serious injuries on being "strained" through groves of fir or aspen even though they avoided burial.

Steepness. Generally, the steeper the terrain, the greater the hazard. Avalanches are most common on slopes of 30 to 45 degrees; the greatest number of slides occur on slopes of 35 to 40 degrees. Brad Meiklejohn, a former Utah Avalanche Forecast Center hazard forecaster, emphasizes that learning to estimate slope angle is probably the single most valuable skill a backcountry skier can develop. Unless underlayer conditions are especially unique, such as depicted in Figure 4.8, slides rarely occur on inclines less than 30 degrees. Tourers must remember that a rapidly moving mass of snow has sufficient momentum to carry it onto—or across—flat areas or even up the opposite hillsides. (This is clearly illustrated in Figure 4.13.)

Figure 4.9 The presence of a dense grove of trees *(left)* has done little to impede an avalanche released from above. The smallest avalanche can cause serious injuries to a skier who is pushed into a tree.

Exposure to Wind. Wind can move great amounts of snow from one area to another in a relatively short period of time. This results in formation of large cornices and regions of deep snow accumulation on the leeward sides of ridges. As illustrated in Figure 4.10, the deep accumulations can lead to severe avalanching. The prevailing wind in the Wasatch is from the south preceding a storm, then from the west or northwest as the storm passes. North and east-facing slopes often develop dangerous slab conditions. All of the avalanches illustrated in Figures 4.5 through 4.10 occurred on leeward slopes of northern or eastern orientation.

The fragile nature of snow cornices is another potential hazard to tourers. Cornices may collapse spontaneously—or under the weight of an unwary skier who ventures too close to the edge—and initiate an avalanche.

Exposure to Sun. A slope exposed to the warming rays of the sun for extended periods can form an icy crust. New snow falling on such a crust may avalanche easily due to lack of bonding.

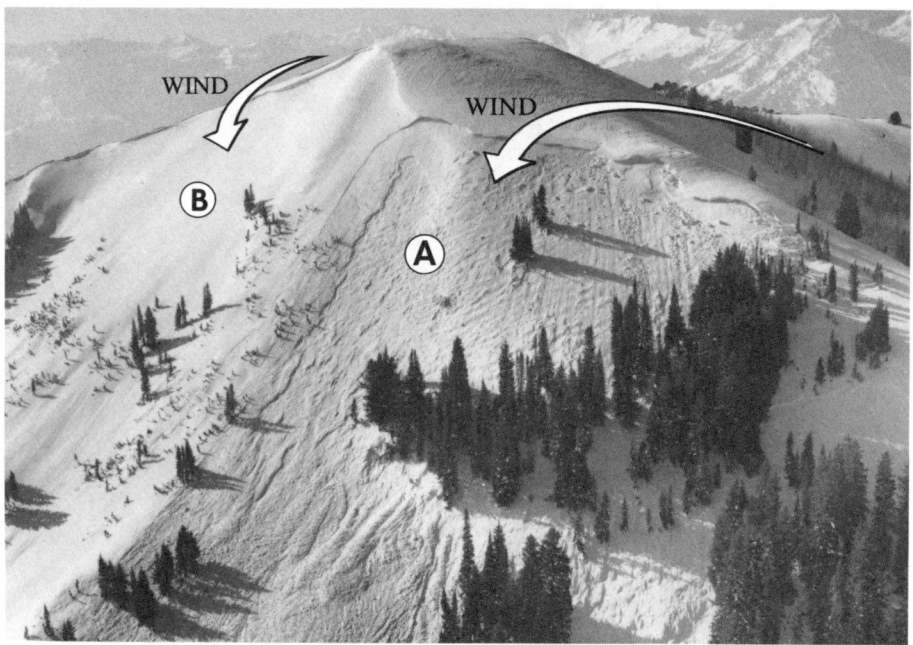

Figure 4.10 Prevailing winds (arrows) have deposited large quantities of snow on the leeward slope below the ridge. Slope A has avalanched, leaving an easily-visible fracture nearly two feet deep. Slope B has yet to slide.

Prolonged exposure to sun may also cause weakening of a snow layer by destroying its internal bonding. South-facing slopes soften most rapidly, especially during spring; west-facing areas are slower to soften, so they may be safe for an extra hour or two on a warm day. Freezing commences near sunset, and stability improves. The implication for spring skiers is obvious: be off the mountain by noon or take a very long summit siesta!

As mentioned previously, the sun does not always cause hazardous conditions. After a storm, for example, it can help to stabilize the snow. New powder consolidates more quickly on south and west-facing slopes where the temperatures are higher. As a result, north and east-facing slopes, usually the best for skiing, are the least stable during the cold periods of the winter.

Topological Features. The Wasatch Mountains possess some unusual topological features that can increase the avalanche danger along certain touring routes. In some areas of Big and Little Cottonwood canyons, for example, sheer slabs of rock have been thrust upward at quite a steep angle. These slabs are not sufficiently inclined to encourage the snow to slough off as it falls during a storm, so dangerous amounts

Figure 4.11   Rock slabs present special hazard during winter. The left photo shows a typical slab area as it appears during summer. The right photo shows a similar slab area covered with snow. Note the fracture line of a recent avalanche. Passing beneath such snow-laden slabs is an invitation to disaster.

of snow can accumulate on them. The photographs in Figure 4.11 show rock slab areas near the bottom of the Lake Blanche trail and high up in Cardiff Fork.

Steep, wide-open slopes that terminate in constricted ravines and gullies should be viewed with great suspicion. "Hanging valleys," whose floors are high above and not visible from the valley into which they descend, are also extremely dangerous. Bridal Veil Falls, in Provo Canyon, is an excellent example of a hanging valley. In January 1993, two sleeping ice climbers were abruptly awakened when their camper was overturned and crushed by an avalanche that came over the falls and into the parking area below. They didn't realize when they parked the truck that the unseen-from-below slopes of Cascade Peak avalanche frequently, sending cascades of snow over Bridal Veil Falls.

Gobblers Knob is an excellent example of avalanche slopes that terminate in narrow gullies. The Knob is a 10,246 foot peak on the dividing ridge between Big Cottonwood and Millcreek canyons. An immense north-facing avalanche slope channels snow into an ever-narrowing and deepening ravine that winds through dense timber toward the Porter

Figure 4.12 Snow from the north slope of Gobblers Knob frequently slides down the gully toward the cabins in Porter Fork.

Fork summer home area. Due to the dense timber all around, a casual tourer would never suspect the gully to be an avalanche deathtrap.

How wrong the tourer would be! In late February 1980, the entire slope beneath the summit avalanched, sending a thirty-foot high wall of snow into the narrow ravine. Large trees along the edge of the gully were snapped like matchsticks. The avalanche terminated just 100 yards short of Porter Fork's topmost summer home. Gobblers Knob, its face, and the avalanche's path are shown in Figure 4.12.

Elevation. Snow conditions can vary drastically as a function of elevation and location in the mountains. While it may be very warm at the 6,500 foot level, it may be well below freezing at 10,000 feet. On the other hand, temperature inversions are not uncommon in the local mountains, and it may be warmer at high elevations than low in the canyons. Totally different avalanche conditions should be expected at different elevations.

Capabilities of the Touring Party

Decisions about attempting a particular tour must depend on the degree of knowledge and experience of each participant. Outings in areas that have significant avalanche hazard should never be attempted by skiers without proper equipment and some practice in using it.

Physcal Condition and Experience of the Participants. An experienced backcountry skier can move quickly and confidently over all types of terrain encountered during a tour. If one member of a group is physically weaker or less competent than the others, he can cause delays in areas where speed is essential, or otherwise jeopardize group safety. A good tour leader will consider the ability of the group as a whole and choose a route that is safe and enjoyable for all.

The distance and elevation change of a ski tour directly affect the physical fatigue that is experienced by participants. Exhaustion inevitably leads to impaired judgement and decreased capability for handling any emergency that might occur.

Number of Tourers in the Party. As mentioned previously, an avalanche victim's chance of survival decreases very rapidly with burial time, dropping to less than 50% after 15 minutes. This suggests that a larger group could be more effective in a rescue. Too many people on a ski tour, however, can be difficult to keep together. This can lead to a situation where one portion of a touring party can expose others to avalanche hazard if they are higher up on a dangerous slope. Some Utah Avalanche Forecast Center staff members feel that a party of 3 or 4 persons is about optimum.[6]

Knowledge of the Terrain. A thorough understanding of terrain can help avoid avalanche incidents. A particular route may look safe to an unsuspecting tourer, but someone familiar with the surrounding terrain might realize that it is dangerous. A steep slab of snow or an overhanging cornice might be poised, ready to release, several hundred yards above the skiing party.

---

[6]Kelner feels that a larger group is better. If more than one person is entrapped by an avalanche, there may not be enough people left to mount an *effective* search and rescue. He prefers to ski tour with a party of 4 to 6.

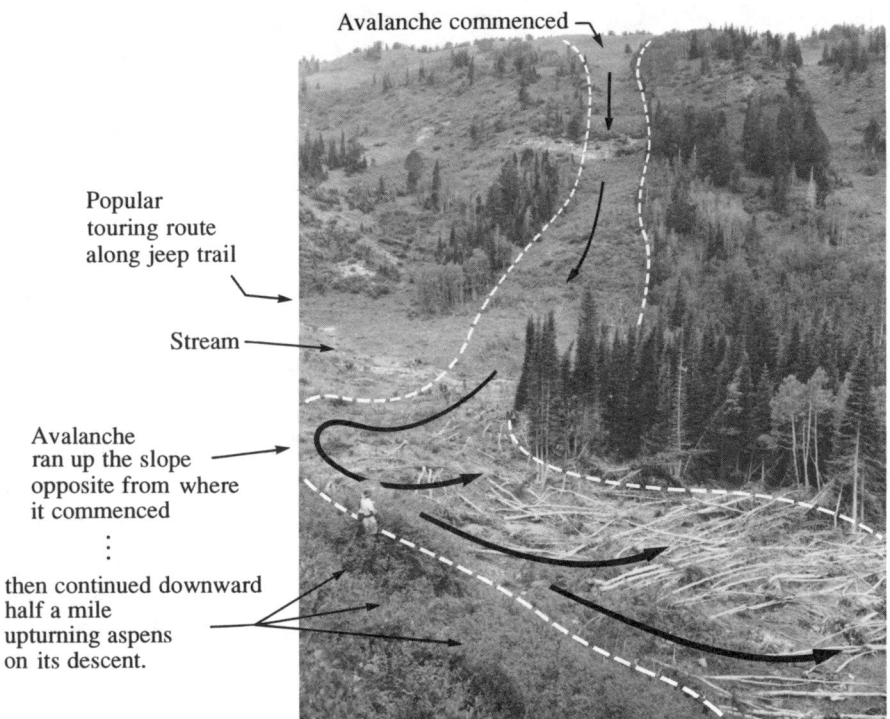

Figure 4.13 Knowledge of previous avalanche activity in an area can lead to better-informed route planning. In January 1993, a climactic avalanche in Silver Fork left an easily-visible trail nearly a mile in length.

Most of the intermediate and advanced ski tours in the Wasatch cross at least one known slide path. Some of these avalanche frequently, others only occasionally. Knowing the location of the most dangerous paths may prompt changes in a proposed tour, or, under extreme circumstances, cancellation of the outing. Figure 4.13, a photo taken in Silver Fork, illustrates the importance of knowing prior avalanche history in ski tour planning and route selection.

Party Enthusiasm. The level of excitement in a touring group can be a contributing factor in avalanche safety. Clear thinking must prevail in hazardous terrain. Here is what Perla and Martinelli, authors of the Forest Service *Avalanche Handbook* say about the subject:

> "Backcountry safety is first of all a matter of controlling enthusiasm. In the spirit of adventure, many incidents occur because even the most experienced ski mountaineer may take what he thinks is a small risk to reach his objective. This enthusiasm is reinforced by the psychological feeling of

group security that comes when several people push forward together—no single member of the group likes to admit concern and turn the party around prematurely."

ON WITH THE SKI TOUR

Once the decision to tour is made, a number of factors determine whether the participants return alive and well, or whether they are buried, injured, or killed by an avalanche.

- All members of the touring party must have the proper equipment and possess the knowledge to use it effectively.
- Safety depends on everyone's ability to handle themselves on slopes that have some degree of avalanche hazard, or on selection of an absolutely safe route.
- The group must have the ability to objectively evaluate all situations and to behave prudently as the tour progresses.

Avalanche Rescue Equipment

Equipment that should be taken on tours falls into four categories: avalanche rescue, first aid, survival, and miscellaneous (clothing, food, ski repair). Only avalanche rescue equipment will be considered here, since the others were discussed in earlier chapters. Figure 4.14 pictures equipment that should be carried on tours that involve avalanche-prone terrain.

Two vital ingredients of a successful avalanche rescue are a means of quickly locating the victim and—equally important—a means of extricating him from the snow as rapidly as possible.

It is mandatory for all members of a touring party to be equipped with an electronic avalanche beacon and a large, sturdy shovel. Other avalanche safety equipment that can be carried by each member of a touring party are avalanche probes and cords.

The beacon is a radio-like device that can transmit or receive an electromagnetic signal. *When used properly,* it is the most effective safety device yet invented for people who work or play in terrain exposed to avalanches. The principles of operation and search procedures by electronic means will be described later in the chapter.

Locating a victim does little good if he can't be dug out very quickly. *Skis do not work as shovels,* particularly in the consolidated debris of an avalanche. Despite having been located rapidly by a beacon, a number

Figure 4.14 Milt Hollander exhibits avalanche safety equipment: *a.* magnifying lens; *b.* slope angle indicator; *c.* collapsible probe; *d.* electronic beacon; *e.* avalanche cord; *f.* snow shovel. *Inset:* Tourers who ski with dogs may want to consider training them for avalanche rescue. Judy Markward ponders that option with Ajax and Sam.

of buried skiers have died because their companions could not dig them out in time. An ideal avalanche shovel should have a large scoop and a very sturdy handle. When purchasing a shovel, tourers should be wary of products made of breakable plastics.

An avalanche probe is either a collapsible metal tube that can be carried in a pack, or a pair of ski poles that are connected together at the handles. Once a buried avalanche victim's general location is ascertained using an electronic beacon, a probe is pushed into the snow to confirm his exact position to prevent wasted time digging in the wrong place. When tourers are not equipped with avalanche beacons, probes must be used to locate victims under the snow.

An avalanche cord is a long red nylon cord that is tied to a skier in the hope that some part of it will be visible to rescuers in event of burial. In 1968 avalanche cords were lauded in *Modern Avalanche Rescue* as "one unquestionably superior method" of locating a buried victim. By 1976, in the Perla/Martinelli *Avalanche Handbook*, avalanche cords were deemed "only partly reliable." Swiss Avalanche Institute research by then had indicated that in only 40 percent of complete burials could a victim expect to have part of his cord on the surface. The *Handbook*'s authors, however, comment that "using the cord may be worthwhile if it makes the tourer stop and reconsider his route selection and the possible danger."

Another item that should be carried on a ski tour is a slope angle indicator, which is a small rectangular piece of plastic with a string tied to one corner. A weight is attached to the string to make it hang vertically. When the bottom edge of the plastic is held parallel to a slope, the angle between the string and the edge of the indicator is the steepness of the slope. Markings on the plastic tell the user the number of degrees of the slope.

Finally, a 10 or 20 power magnifying lens comes in handy for analyzing the structure of the snow crystals at various levels in the snowpack.

Ski tourers who venture into the backcountry with their dogs should consider training them for avalanche rescue. In Switzerland, according to statistics published in the Forest Service *Handbook*, avalanche dogs participated in 305 rescues between 1945 and 1972. In only 36 of the rescues did the dogs fail to locate victims. Of those located, 45 were found alive and 224 victims were found dead. "The large number of dead recoveries is no reflection on the ability of the dogs," Perla and Martinelli conclude. "It is proof of the slim chance of survival of a buried victim." The two avalanche researchers describe a series of training exercises, as well as further references, for those who may want to convert their pets to avalanche professionals.

Route Finding

A number of touring routes in the Wasatch have little or no exposure to avalanches. Such routes are usually located in canyon bottoms, along gently sloping roads, or in heavily wooded areas. Many ridges may be toured in relative safety. Unless a route intersects the runout zones of higher avalanches, it can be considered safe if its slope is less than 20 degrees.

Much of the terrain suitable for beginners has little hazard. Nearly all of the locations available for intermediate and advanced touring, on the other hand, are exposed to some degree of avalanche hazard. Some intermediate routes include only an occasional, moderately dangerous area, while others may cross many consecutive slopes that are prone to slide. Most advanced terrain has considerable exposure to snowslide hazards.

With knowledge that some dangerous places will be traversed, it is the responsibility of the tour leader to select the safest possible route. Unfortunately, many tour leaders learned their route selection tech-

Figure 4.15 Gentle ridges like this one are usually suitable as routes for ski tourers and snowmobilers.

niques by following long-established patterns that have evolved over a period of time with little consideration for avalanche safety. Seeking the safest possible route is not always done with total objectivity. Like auto racing, backcountry skiing has its risks and its rewards. Too often the leader's judgement is slanted toward the reward side, with little or no consideration to the risks involved.

The following guidelines may be used for locating safe routes:

- Ridge tops, such as those illustrated in Figure 4.15 and canyon bottoms (far out from any avalanche runout zones) are generally preferred.
- The windward sides of ridges have the least snow depth and are usually safer than the leeward sides, which often contain dangerous slabs and have overhanging cornices that could break off and trigger a slide.
- Heavily wooded areas can offer some protection, but are not guaranteed safe, particularly if avalanche slopes lie above.
- Suspected avalanche slopes should be crossed as high as possible to increase the chance of ending up on the surface if a slide is released.
- When climbing fairly steep slopes, it is best to stay on small ridges or other prominences which could deflect or channel the snow away from a touring party.

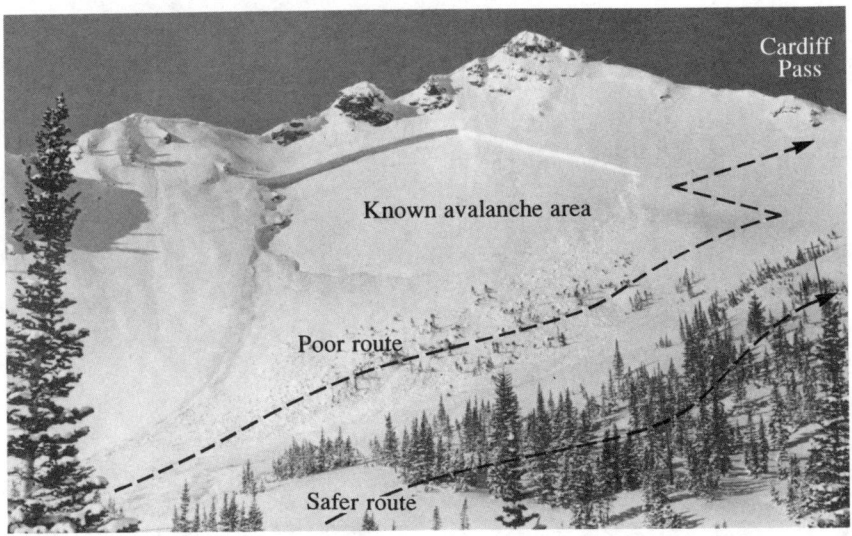

Figure 4.16 It is common practice for unwary tourers to follow the route depicted by the dotted line in the open slopes to reach Cardiff Pass. This route exposes them to a large avalanche path shown in the photograph. A safer route would lead them through the trees at the right. (Photo courtesy of Dr. R. I. Perla.)

- When ascending a known avalanche zone, a skier should keep to the flanks and edges, and climb straight up rather than traversing back and forth.

- Avalanche paths that end in ravines or gullies should be completely avoided. Large amounts of snow often pile up in these areas, and a victim could be buried deeply. Other terrain features to stay away from are slide paths that go over cliffs or other obstructions which could cause serious injury on impact.

Several more technical route planning guidelines are discussed in the Perla/Martinelli *Avalanche Handbook*, but will not be repeated here. Figure 4.16 illustrates a simple route selection problem on the Alta side of Cardiff Pass. Both *poor* (dotted line) and *safer* (solid line) alternatives are shown. The decision-making process in selecting a safe route on somewhat more complex terrain is illustrated in Figure 4.17.[7]

---

[7] The high resolution, low-altitude, oblique aerial photographs that appear throughout the three volumes of *Wasatch Tours* will give tour planners a birds-eye view of terrain features for most of the tours described. Hopefully, conscientious tourers will use the photographs to preview route options available for their outing.

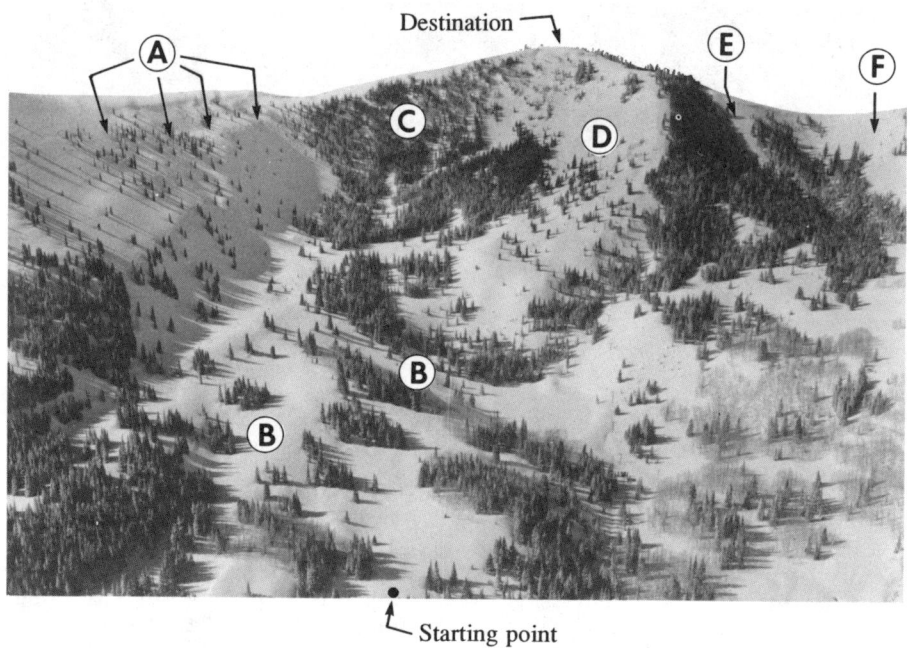

Figure 4.17 *Route planning analysis for an intermediate-level tour.* Slopes at A are large, steep, convex, and leeward. Sparse tree cover indicates active avalanching. Part of a fracture line is still visible near the summit ridge. *"Wow! We'll definitely avoid these."* Areas B are sparsely timbered flatlands, but are they possible outrun areas from the above-mentioned slide paths? *"If we have to cross one, we ought to do it quickly."* Although densely timbered, slope C has the same orientation and pitch as the slopes at A. *"Hmmmm. Better avoid that one!"* Steep sections, virtually free of trees, suggest active avalanching in area D. *"Better avoid these too."* Both E and F are leeward slopes. The narrow chute E has a cornice above it. *"Definite NO here."* Open slope F is fairly gentle, but with no cornice. *"But why no trees?"* Using the above process of elimination, the reader should now be able to plot a safe route between the starting point and the destination.

Important Observations

Just as knowledge of weather and snowpack history are important to the cross country skier, observations made *on the day of the tour* can provide information vital to a safe outing. Some observations may be made at home, while others must be made in the mountains.

Observations from Home. Weather, particularly temperature and wind conditions, is the first element to evaluate on the morning of a ski tour. The Utah Avalanche Forecast Center recording will provide much of this information. First consider whether or not there has been a temperature inversion in recent days. *Changes* in temperature should be

ON WITH THE SKI TOUR

Figure 4.18 Cones (or small mounds) of snow at the base of trees are indicators of a snowpack's consolidation and settlement.

noted; sudden warming or cooling often causes the snowpack to become unstable. Wind conditions are sometimes visible from the valley. If snow plumes are observed coming off the high peaks, it should be assumed that the wind is loading leeward slopes with snow.

Surface Snow Conditions. Once in the mountains, better information can be obtained. The depth and quality of the snow is one good indicator of potential instability. If a tourer is over his knees in powder immediately after a storm, loose snow avalanches might be expected. In the spring, when the snow becomes so soft that the skier sinks in over the top of the boots, it's time be out of the backcountry.

The process of consolidation of a fresh snow fall results in settlement. Snow cones at the base of trees are indicators of stability. Cones are sometimes created when snow near a tree begins to settle, while snow that's in contact with the tree clings to it. Figure 4.18 illustrates the result.

Slabs present the greatest hazard to Wasatch tourers. Cracks that suddenly propagate ahead of skis, and settling or "booming" sounds in the snowpack, are good indicators of instability. "When the snow talks to you," an old avalanche adage warns, "it's telling you to go home!" The left photo of Figure 4.19 shows an extremely dangerous slab condition.

Signs of Recent Avalanche Activity. Before approaching an area that is prone to avalanche, much can be learned by simply observing slopes of similar exposure. If recent avalanche activity is evident, care should be exercised. In spring conditions, a sign of potential danger is the formation of snowballs at the base of rocks that are warmed by the

Figure 4.19 Some signs of instability. *Left:* Cracks propagating in front of skis suggest the presence of a surface slab with a weak layer beneath. The width of the crack depicted in the photo, and extent of slab's displacement, indicates extreme danger. *Right:* Snowballs tend to form on spring days as rocks warm and new snow slides off. Such sloughing warns tourers to expect loose-snow avalanches.

sun. If these balls increase in size as they roll down the slope, or if they start small slides, watch out!

Underlying Snow Layers. The key to evaluating snowpack stability on a given day is to know what lies beneath the surface. Some information may be gained by simply thrusting an inverted ski pole deep into the snow. If the pole penetrates evenly with some resistance, then suddenly drops in with little or no resistance, a weak layer may be underneath. This method is limited, but provides useful information.

Professional avalanche workers and careful ski tourers dig pits in the snowpack to evaluate strength characteristics of individual layers. Pits are dug on slopes with the same exposure as the slopes to be skied on, but in a protected spot where an avalanche is unlikely. A good pit takes only a few minutes to dig, and is well worth the effort. The uphill wall of the pit is used to study the snow. If a granular layer is found under a slab, one can assume that it is only a matter of time before slopes of that aspect begin to slide. A thorough discussion of pits and snow layer evaluation is beyond the scope of this book, but the *Avalanche Handbook*, or a good avalanche class, will cover these subjects in detail.

ON WITH THE SKI TOUR

Figure 4.20 These tourers are tempting fate by exposing the entire group to potential danger as they cross a steep, avalanche-prone slope.

Precautions in Hazardous Terrain

In addition to being properly equipped with beacons, shovels, first aid kits, etc., there are several precautions that a touring party should take if it decides to cross or to descend an avalanche-prone slope.

Before entering the avalanche zone, clothing should be buttoned, parka hood pulled up, mittens and wind pants put on. These extra items of clothing will help protect a skier caught in an avalanche.

Wrists should be withdrawn from ski pole wrist loops, and ski safety straps should be removed from boots. If a victim's hands and feet are free, the chances of survival are increased. This will allow more freedom of movement during the victim's slide. Avalanche cords should be deployed at this time if they are being used.

In crossing dangerous avalanche terrain, only one person at a time should ever be exposed to the hazard. Others in the touring party should remain in safe locations from which they can watch the skier cross the slope. Each member should take his turn crossing, unlike the group shown in Figure 4.20.

It should never be assumed that the remainder of a group can safely

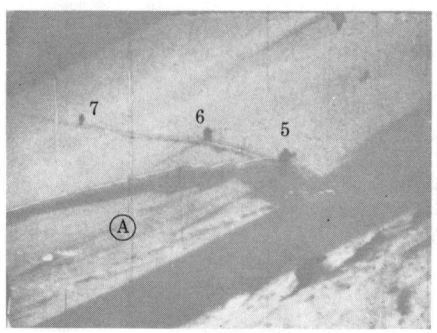
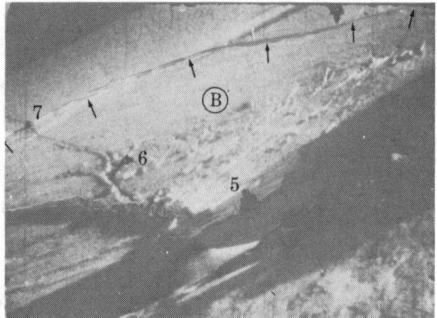

Figure 4.21 The photographer and three others had just crossed a known avalanche slope and were preparing to lunch atop "Cardiac Pass" near Alta. *Left:* As skiers 5, 6, and 7 approached the pass, a small avalanche A was triggered beneath the track of skier 5. The frame shows the large fracture that resulted from this slide. *Right:* As skier 5 hastily advanced to a safer location, a larger avalanche released, sweeping skiers 6 and 7 to the bottom of the slope some 1200 feet below. The arrows show the great extent of the second fracture line. The bottom photo, taken by tour participant Ron Weber after the victims had been extricated, shows the extent of the large slab avalanche.

ski on a slope because one, two, or three individuals have done so without incident. The first person may disturb the snow just enough so that an avalanche may be released by subsequent skiers.[8] Figure 4.21, which includes two frames from a spectacular 8mm motion picture sequence taken by Dave Hanscom during a 1972 ski tour, illustrates this.

The suggestions mentioned previously in the section on route finding should be followed. For obvious reasons, a skier should not linger on a

---

[8]Such avalanche releases, common in areas where explosive-related control work is practiced, have long been called "hang-fire" releases.

potential avalanche slope. Rapid movement is extremely important to minimize the time of exposure to the hazard.

Whenever the tourer is in an exposed location, he should be alert to possible escape routes. If an avalanche starts above him, or if he triggers one himself, a skier will not have time to search for ways to ski out of the path of the slide. It is important to always preplan the direction to go if the snow starts to move.

RUMBLE, ROAR, AND RESCUE

Some Utahns caught in avalanches have survived. Their experiences and their impressions at the "moment of truth" are revealing and instructive for would-be Wasatch tourers.

"I heard this rumble," recalls a 13-year-old scout involved in a fatal avalanche in Rock Canyon near Provo. "It was a big noise—pretty loud. I looked back of us and saw this big mass of snow coming. It was bumping and flying over the rocks higher above us." His troop's assistant scoutmaster, age 29, had a similar recollection of the incident. "I first heard a noise like a jet aircraft overhead but saw nothing. The next thing I felt was the snow engulfing me. I swam like crazy just trying to keep my arms and legs from being trapped." The assistant scoutmaster was buried to his chest in snow. One of his scouts was killed in this unfortunate accident.

Dr. R. I. Perla, at the time an Avalanche Hazard Forecaster for the Wasatch National Forest, recalls his miraculous escape as he was swept 1,500 feet down one of the Baldy chutes in a large avalanche at Alta.

"The cornice broke, and I was in the chute. I knew it was a large avalanche and I tried to make swimming motions to stay on top. The force of the snow against my face closed my eyes. The amount of time that I was in motion seemed to go by quickly, and I sensed coming to rest. I realized I was face up. I tried to place my left hand over my face, but the piling up snow pushed it away. Before the snow set up, I was successful in getting my right hand up through the snow. I knew my hand was out of the snow and that I had excellent chances. I then tried to conserve air awaiting rescue, but almost immediately blacked out."

Fortunately, his outstretched hand led several area skiers to him and he was dug out and revived in less than three minutes.

By studying and analyzing avalanche survivals such as these, researchers have evolved a number of suggestions that should become instinctive to every ski tourer and winter recreationist.

Actions by an Avalanche Victim

Although there is little—other than bidding farewell—a victim can do when caught in an extremely large avalanche, a number of actions have proven to be effective in improving chances for survival in smaller slides.

Skiing Out of the Moving Snow. If the avalanche occurs below his ski track (such as in the left frame of Figure 4.21), a skier should attempt to hold his position above the slide. When an avalanche starts around and above a skier, the best chance for survival is to quickly get out of it by skiing along with the moving snow and angling off to the side. Since avalanches quickly accelerate to high speeds, this reaction should be instinctive and instantaneous. It is vital to stay upright and to maintain as much control as possible.

Making Swimming Motions. If it is not possible to remain upright and to ski out of the avalanche or to stay above it, the victim should get rid of skis and poles[9] and make swimming motions to maintain an upright body position and to work his way to the side. In both the Rock Creek and the Baldy Chute incidents, as well as in many other avalanches that have been documented around the world, victims have avoided deep burial by using a swimming motion as they were being swept down in the snow. A breast stroke is recommended for victims being carried downhill head-first; a treading water motion works best for a feet-first descent.

Thrusting a Hand Upward. Many victims, like Dr. Perla, owe their lives to having a hand or other appendage visible above the snow. If the skier knows he is near the surface, he should push his hand upward at the moment the avalanche comes to rest. The thrust should be made quickly, since the snow sets up almost instantly.

Forming a Breathing Space. As the victim comes to rest, he should try to use one or both arms to form an "air pocket" in front of his face. This will enable him to breathe for a longer time while rescuers conduct the search. The snow sets up rapidly, so this must be done immediately. The snowmobiler mentioned in the introduction to this chapter may owe his life to an air pocket he was able to form with his arm. He beat the odds by surviving complete burial for four hours.

Conserving Oxygen. It is vital to relax and not to resist the sensation of blacking out. The victim should not waste energy struggling

---

[9]There has been some debate over whether or not one should also try to remove one's pack. "*Always* keep your pack on," Bruce Tremper, Director of the Utah Avalanche Forecast Center, says. "It will act as padding in case you bounce off trees and rocks and ensure that you have the supplies that you will need if you survive."

if he is not close enough to the surface to push the snow away from himself. Since sound is absorbed in the snow, shouting for help is *usually* futile until the rescuers are near. It is common for a buried victim to be able to hear his rescuers, but uncommon for them to hear him unless he is very close to the surface.

Search and Rescue Procedures

Once totally buried, the victim's chance for survival passes into the hands of his companions. His remaining longevity will be determined by how instinctively, how quickly, how expertly and confidently they perform the search and rescue. Effective behavior during an avalanche emergency does not come naturally; *it must be learned and practiced.*

Because the victim's best chance of survival is to be extricated in fifteen minutes or less, it may be inadvisable to send a messenger for help. In most backcountry locations in the Wasatch, it would take a competent skier at least 30 to 60 minutes to reach a telephone. If the touring party is small, every member may be better used at the accident site. Cases have been documented where a companion has left the scene of an avalanche and returned an hour or two later with an organized rescue party, only to find that the victim was already deceased, but with a portion of his body or a piece of his equipment clearly visible in the snow. Only if the group is particularly large, or if assistance is only a few minutes away, might it be worth sending someone for help immediately.

What should survivors do to locate a buried companion? Avalanche authorities recommend a number of quickly and efficiently performed steps.

Assessing Additional Danger. The danger from adjacent slopes should be analyzed immediately. Overzealous rescue parties have been buried by slides that occurred while they were searching for an avalanche victim. If further danger is perceived, an escape route should be planned and a lookout should be posted in a safe place to warn rescuers if more snow starts moving in their direction. In some circumstances, the remaining hazard may be so great that it is not advisable for the companions of a victim to even attempt a rescue.

Search Procedure. The point where a victim was initially caught in the avalanche should be marked with a ski or pole. Ski tracks or observations of witnesses can usually establish that location.

The "last seen point," the place where the victim was observed before finally disappearing beneath the snow, should also be marked. The

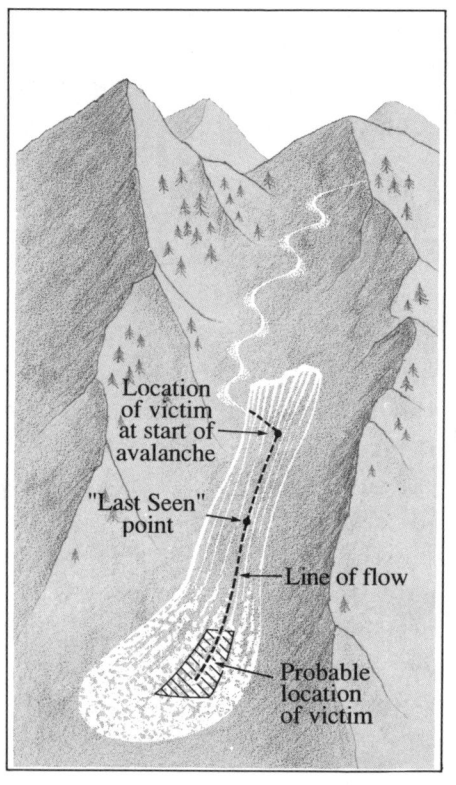 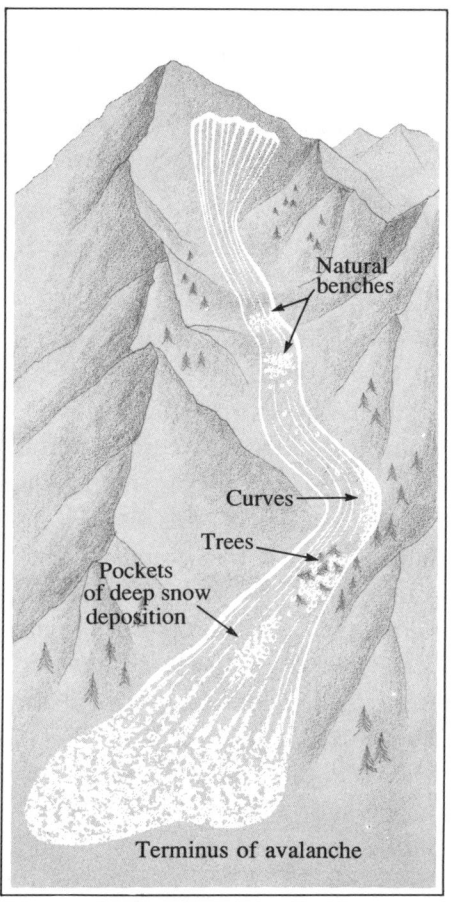

Figure 4.22 *Left:* If two points of a victim's trajectory can be established, a high probability exists that he will be near the downhill flow line passing through these points. *Right:* Most avalanche victims are carried to the area of greatest snow deposition, but the victim could also be located in other areas as shown by the arrows.

path followed by the victim will usually be an extension of the line between these two points, as illustrated in the left part of Figure 4.22. The regions of highest search priority can then be determined. Items of equipment may be visible along the line of descent and sometimes end up quite close to the burial point.

Other possible burial locations, as illustrated in the right part of Figure 4.22, are piles of deep snow debris (particularly at the terminus of the slide), areas around and among trees where the victim may have been caught, and snow depositions near natural "benches" or in curves of the avalanche path.

While making the above observations, all rescuers should be switching their beacons to the *Receive* mode in preparation for an electronic search. A detailed description of the steps that should be followed in this case are described in the next section. If the victim does not have an avalanche beacon, the rescuers should leave theirs in the *Transmit* mode in case a second avalanche occurs.

A rapid, but systematic search of the surface of the debris is then conducted in the regions of highest priority. All clues should be marked. The greatest probability of a live rescue is in this initial surface search, where a rescuer may spot some part of the victim or his equipment. If the surface search of the most probable areas fails to locate the victim, probing must be commenced. This procedure is also detailed in a later section.

During the search process, rescuers should make as little noise as possible to enable them to hear the victim if he shouts to them.

Rescue and First Aid. Digging should commence as soon as the victim's location is determined. Speed is critical, so there should be no concern about poking him with a shovel.

First aid procedures should be started immediately.[10] *Highest priority must be given to (a) clearing the airway and restoring breathing, and (b) stopping profuse bleeding.* It is common for an avalanche victim to have ceased breathing. If that is the case, the mouth should be cleared of snow or other matter and mouth-to-mouth resuscitation started as soon as the face has been exposed. This can continue while the digging is completed. If severe bleeding is discovered, it should be controlled with direct pressure to the wound. Minor cuts can be bandaged and suspected broken bones immobilized at a later time.

If the victim is able to ski out, he should be encouraged to do so immediately. If help is required, one or more members of the touring party can ski out to civilization and call for assistance. At least one person should remain with the victim to be sure that he is warm and comfortable. It is likely that he will be suffering from shock, so proper first aid should be administered.

Even if no injury occurs, the Utah Avalanche Forecast Center should be informed of backcountry avalanche incidents. The more complete their information, the better they can understand and predict snow stability.

---

[10] Backcountry users should take a class from the American Red Cross or another qualified organization to gain experience in this area.

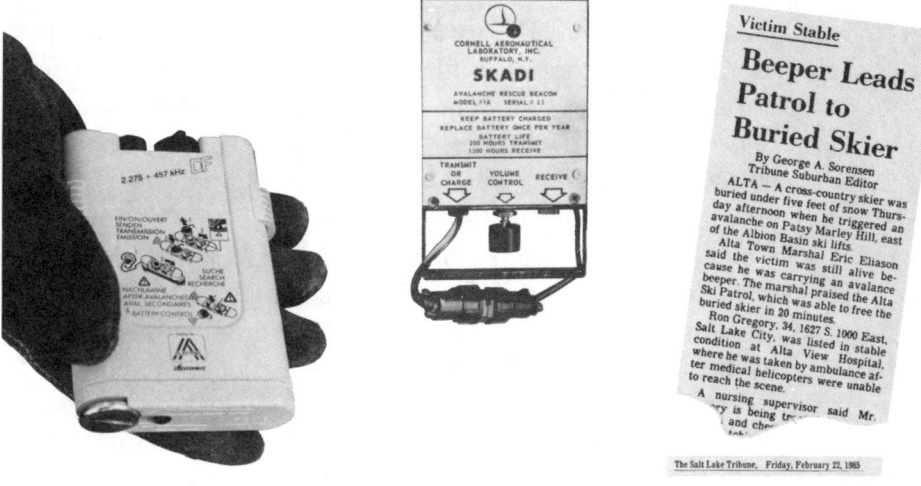

Figure 4.23 Modern avalanche rescue beacons have become mandatory items to be carried on tours in avalanche-prone terrain. This *SKADI* is an early prototype.

Avalanche Rescue Beacons

The avalanche rescue beacon is a battery-operated device that can either transmit or receive an electromagnetic signal. It was proposed as an avalanche detection system in the late 1960's by Dr. John G. Lawton, director of a research team at Cornell Aeronautical Laboratory in Buffalo, New York. The experimental and first production units were named *SKADI*, after the mistress of Ullr, the patron saint of skiing in Norse mythology. Working units were distributed for field testing to selected avalanche professionals during the winters of 1967 and '68. One of the early models of the *SKADI* is illustrated in Figure 4.23; a contemporary avalanche rescue beacon is shown also.

The principle of operation is basically quite simple: when the beacon is in the *Transmit* mode, it sends out a signal. When it is in the *Receive* mode, it picks up the signal of a nearby transmitting unit and converts it to an audible beep. . .beep. . .beep. The loudness of the beeps increases as the receiving unit approaches the unit that's transmitting. The beacon, it should be emphasized, measures only signal strength; *it does not indicate the direction the signal is coming from.*[11]

---

[11]It's quite possible that in the aftermath of the Cold War, as defense industries scramble to develop non-military markets, some weapons scientists will marry the non-directional avalanche beacons of today with microprocessors used in modern weaponry. Such a marriage could make possible the location of an avalanche victim with the precision of a "smart bomb" hitting an Iraqi outhouse.

The avalanche beacon enables a trained searcher to find someone buried in snow in a matter of minutes. The success rate of beacons in locating a victim is several orders of magnitude higher than that of the old method of probing with a metal probe.

Unfortunately, the availability of avalanche rescue beacons has added an element of false security to backcountry skiing. There is no doubt that a victim can be found in a fraction of the time that would have been required with probes, but the indisputable fact remains that a large percentage of those buried in snow slides do not survive. "A rescue beacon will not protect you," John Lawton warned. "It only speeds up locating a victim, dead or alive."

Beacon Frequencies. The beacons currently being used in the United States operate at a frequency of 2.275 kHz; the Europeans switched to the much higher frequency of 457 kHz several years ago. Avalanche professionals in America will use *dual* frequency beacons until 1995, at which time they will switch to the European version.[12] The time will soon come when commercially available beacons may no longer be compatible with ones currently being used.

Before the Avalanche. Like any electronic device, the avalanche beacon is somewhat fragile and must always be treated with care. It requires time and attention if the user expects it to perform properly in an emergency. A few precautions are highly recommended.[13]

- *The beacon should always have fresh alkaline batteries.* It is advisable to carry an extra set. For the occasional tourer, batteries may last an entire winter; someone who is fortunate enough to be out several times a week should change batteries regularly.

- *A beacon should be inspected and tested before each tour.* The range in both *Transmit* and *Receive* modes should be checked with touring partners. A decreasing range is a good sign that new batteries are needed. It is also wise to visually check for cracks and loose wires.

- *It is important to practice regularly with the beacon.* Using the device is not difficult, but performance improves with experience. Practice searches can be conducted at home by having someone hide a transmitting device in or under a piece of furniture. Lunch

---

[12]Research has shown the higher frequency to have a greater range and less susceptibility to external electrical noise sources, such as power lines. The new beacons also have a speaker instead of an ear plug, which seems to be more effective.

[13]Some of this information is based on a paper written by Mark Rasmussen of the Snowbird Ski Patrol.

breaks during tours also provide good opportunities for someone to bury one in the snow for others to find.

- *The beacon should be worn inside one's clothing.* This will keep it warm and will also assure that it is never separated from the tourer. It should never be carried in a pack or an open pocket. Packs are often ripped off an avalanche victim. Metal objects, such as a knife or shovel, should be kept at least four inches from a beacon. They can significantly decrease the range and battery life.
- *The beacon should be left on during the entire tour in Transmit mode*, even when avalanche hazard is not anticipated.
- *A beacon will be of little value without a shovel.* Everyone in the party should have one of each for maximum safety.

Search Procedure with a Rescue Beacon

The basic electronic search procedure to be followed after a member of a touring party is buried by an avalanche is to *first* ascertain the victim's approximate location and *second*, to pinpoint the location so that extrication can commence. The first phase of this process is commonly called the *Initial Search Procedure*; the second phase is known as the *Final Search Procedure*. Tourers who venture into avalanche-prone terrain should practice beacon searches sufficiently often to assure that both become instinctive.

Initial Search Procedure. The primary purpose of the initial search is to intercept the victim's electronic signal—which has a limited range—and thus to ascertain his approximate location in the avalanche's debris field. The specific pattern of search will depend on how many individuals are buried, on the number of searchers available, on whether the searchers are located above the suspected burial point or below it, on various characteristics of the slope, and on whether searchers are wearing skis.[14] Consciousness of time, unity of purpose, and disciplined action are the keys to a successful search.

For the discussion that follows, it is assumed that one person is buried and that one searcher (on skis) was located near the last seen point, but outside of the avalanche. One possible initial search pattern is diagrammed in Figure 4.24. In this and the subsequent illustration the outer rings around the buried victim represent the maximum range of

---

[14]In a backcountry touring avalanche situation, it's quite possible that members of the party may have lost skis during the avalanche.

RUMBLE, ROAR, AND RESCUE

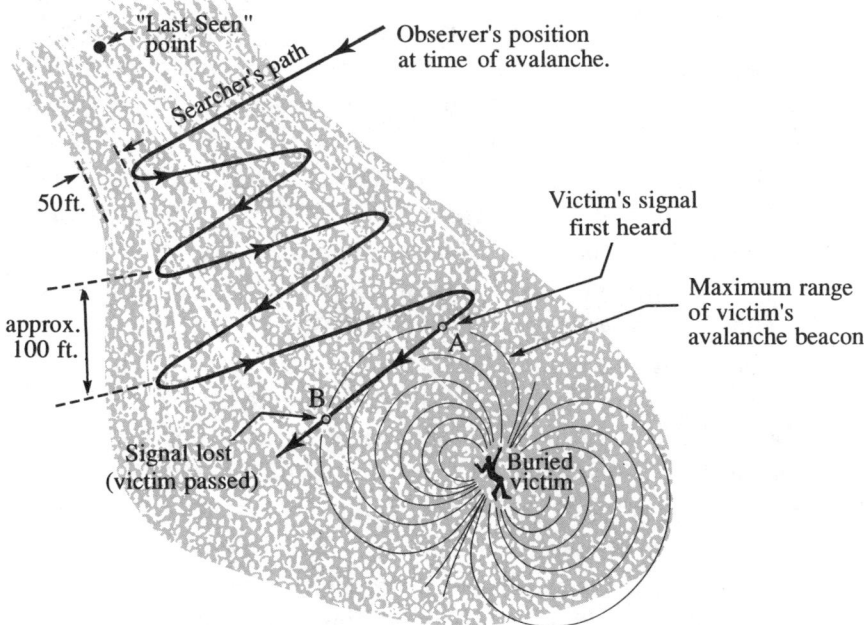

Figure 4.24 Hypothetical initial electronic beacon search pattern for one victim by a single searcher. Search patterns during an actual avalanche incident will vary according to terrain and personnel conditions.

the transmitted signal; the inner rings represent progressively stronger signals as they near the transmitting beacon.

- The moment an avalanche ceases movement the "last seen point" and possible trajectory of the victim are established. The searcher switches his beacon to the *Receive* mode and sets the volume at maximum. If the victim is out of range, only background noise will be heard.[15]

- The searcher starts at the top of the snow deposition in the area below the last seen point, then rapidly "zig-zags" down the debris field.[16] As he descends the slope, he should be especially watchful

---

[15] Earphones or an earplug speaker, if used, should be under one's hat and goggle strap for optimum audibility. If multiple searchers are involved, it is imperative that *all* searchers have turned their beacons to *Receive*. A digital watch on the wrist of the searcher's hand that is holding the beacon has also been known to send a false signal to the detector.

[16] Zig-zagging down a field of hard-packed avalanche debris is quite difficult and challenging even for a competent alpine skier wearing heavy-duty downhill skiing equipment. The average backcountry tourer on light to medium duty touring skis may spend more time falling and getting up than searching. It may be more prudent to remove skis and to conduct the initial search on foot.

for an upthrust hand or equipment laying along the surface. Each leg of the traverse should be separated by no more than 100 feet, and each traverse should go to within 50 feet of the deposition field's edge.
- When the searcher picks up the first faint signal of the victim's beacon (point A in Figures 4.24 and 4.25), he should pause and orient the beacon for maximum signal strength by twists and rotations of the wrist *best learned by practice*. The volume is then reduced to the least audible signal level.[17]
- Maintaining the same beacon orientation, the searcher continues to move forward slowly, reducing the volume as he moves, until the signal weakens rather than strengthens, indicating that the buried victim has been passed. This point, labeled B in the diagrams, is called the *first fade point*, and should be marked on the snow.

Final Search Procedure. The first fade point is where the final search procedure begins. The pattern for this phase of the search is based on a series of right angle scans illustrated in Figure 4.25. It has proven, according to the authors of the Forest Service *Avalanche Handbook*, to be the fastest way of finding a victim.

- Since point B is beyond the buried victim, the searcher must turn around. The beacon is reoriented for maximum signal strength, the volume is turned down to the lowest audible level, and the searcher proceeds to trace his path back toward point A.
- The signal increases and then decreases as the searcher moves forward. When signal strength has decreased to the level it was at the first fade point, the searcher stops and marks the point in the snow. This is called the *second fade point* and is labeled B' in the upper part of the figure.
- The searcher turns around again, then proceeds to the point C (approximately midway between B' and B), where he stops and turns 90 degrees to be perpendicular to the line between the two fade points.[18] The beacon is reoriented for maximum signal, and the volume is turned down to the minimum audible level.
- As the searcher moves away from point C, the received signal will either weaken or strengthen, depending on whether he is moving

---

[17]This is because the human ear detects *changes* in signal strength better at low volumes. When a signal is heard, all other searchers in the group should be notified. Total silence should be observed in case the victim shouts for help.

[18]Since the avalanche detection beacon is non-directional, the searcher will not know in which direction to make his 90 degree turn at the midway point. He will only know that the victim is somewhere along the perpendicular line.

RUMBLE, ROAR, AND RESCUE 163

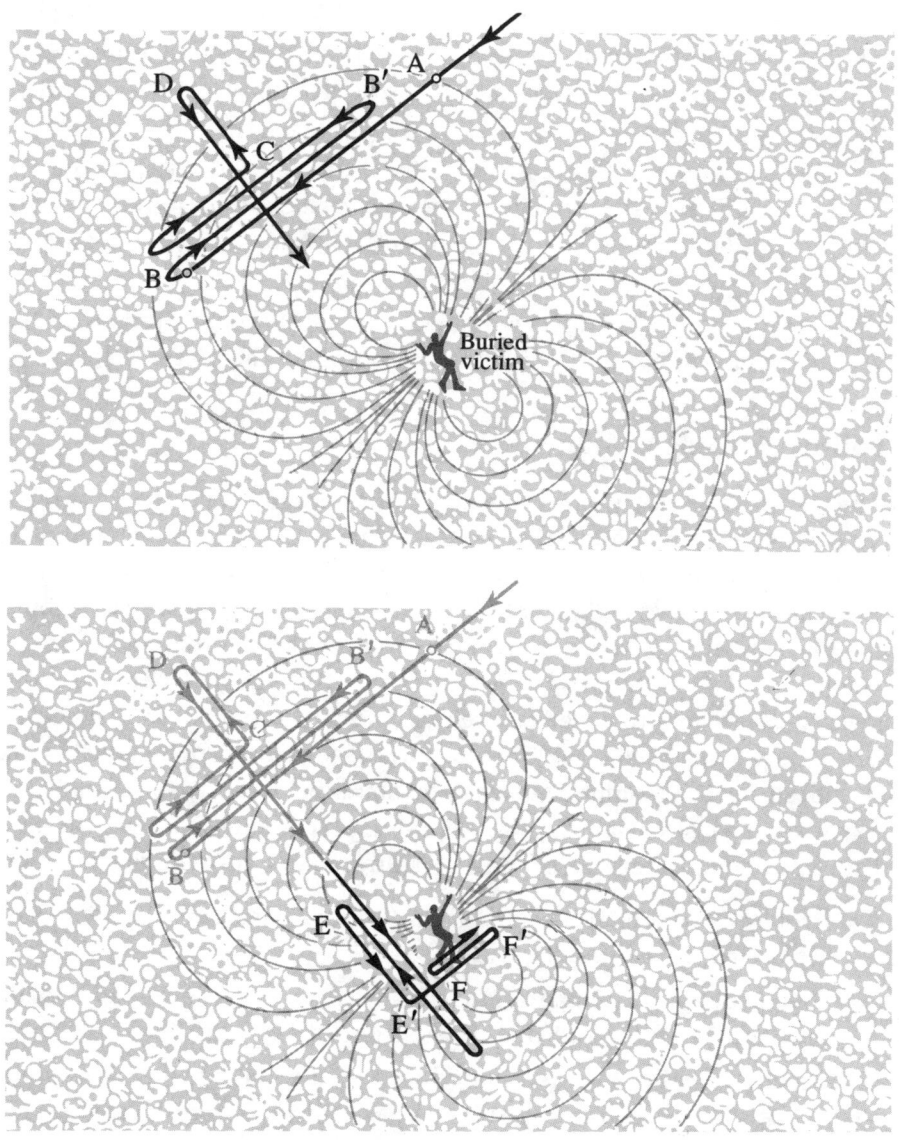

Figure 4.25 Final Search Pattern. *Top:* Establishing the first two fade points and perpendicular; *Bottom:* Establishing subsequent fade points and pinpointing the victim.

away from or toward the victim. If he's moving away, he will have to turn around, at point D in the diagram, reorient his beacon and proceed back along the perpendicular line toward the victim.

- As illustrated in the bottom part of Figure 4.25, two new fade

points, E and E', are established using the process just described.[19]
- Another perpendicular line is then established, and the process is repeated until the fade points F and F' are just a few feet apart.[20]
- At the place where the fade points are just a few feet apart, the beacon should be held at snow level and moved to the point of maximum signal strength. The victim should be found directly under that point—or hanging directly overhead from a branch of a tree!
- Digging should commence immediately. A ski pole or an avalanche probe can be used at this point to pinpoint the victim's location.

Probing for an Avalanche Victim

If the victim was not wearing an electronic beacon, and if the surface search fails to locate him, the next step in the rescue process should be to line up and to systematically probe the snow with collapsible avalanche probes, ski poles, or skis. There are two methods of probing for a buried skier, the *coarse probe* (poles inserted approximately every 30 inches) and the *fine probe* (poles inserted every foot). Coarse probing allows the searchers to cover an area more quickly and is used whenever there is any hope of finding the victim alive. This probing pattern is best suited for backcountry searches by small parties. It is preferable to make several passes using the coarse probing technique than to take time for fine probing. Figure 4.26 illustrates how coarse probing is executed.

- Probers line up at arms length (about 3 feet apart) with feet separated by a shoulder width.
- Two probe insertions are made in the snow, one to the left of the prober's left foot, and one to the right of the right foot.
- On command from a designated leader, the line advances one step, about 30 inches, and repeats the left and right probe insertions.
- If a possible "strike" of the victim is made, one person drops out of the line to investigate by digging or further probing. The remainder of the line keeps advancing and probing.

---

[19] *WARNING:* Since this line of search is perpendicular to the first line and intercepts a different part of the signal field, the pattern of the audible tone may differ slightly among different beacons. *It is extremely important for each tourer to practice with the device that will actually be used in the backcountry.*

[20] "Three or four criss-crosses," authors of the *Avalanche Handbook* state, "are usually sufficient." They also state that "it is possible to refine the fix [of the victim] to about one-fourth of the burial depth."

Figure 4.26 Although the coarse probe gives only about a 70% chance of finding the victim, its high speed maximizes the probability of finding him alive.

Strict discipline, clear and firm commands, and a comfortable probing rhythm are essential. Except for the leaders' commands, total silence should be observed by the probers to increase the chances that a victim's shouts might be heard.

CONCLUSION

The lessons to be learned by ski tourers are very simple: be informed about weather and snow conditions, and use a great deal of discretion as to when and where to tour. It is better to select a longer route, or to attempt a less-exposed ski tour, or even to stay at home, if there is any doubt about safety. An avalanche beacon around the neck doesn't guarantee survivability.

In the February 1991 issue of *Catalyst*, Bruce Tremper described an appropriate philosophy for touring on terrain exposed to avalanche hazards: "... *even when you're with your most trusted partner, pretend you're alone. Make decisions as if there's no one to dig you out.*"

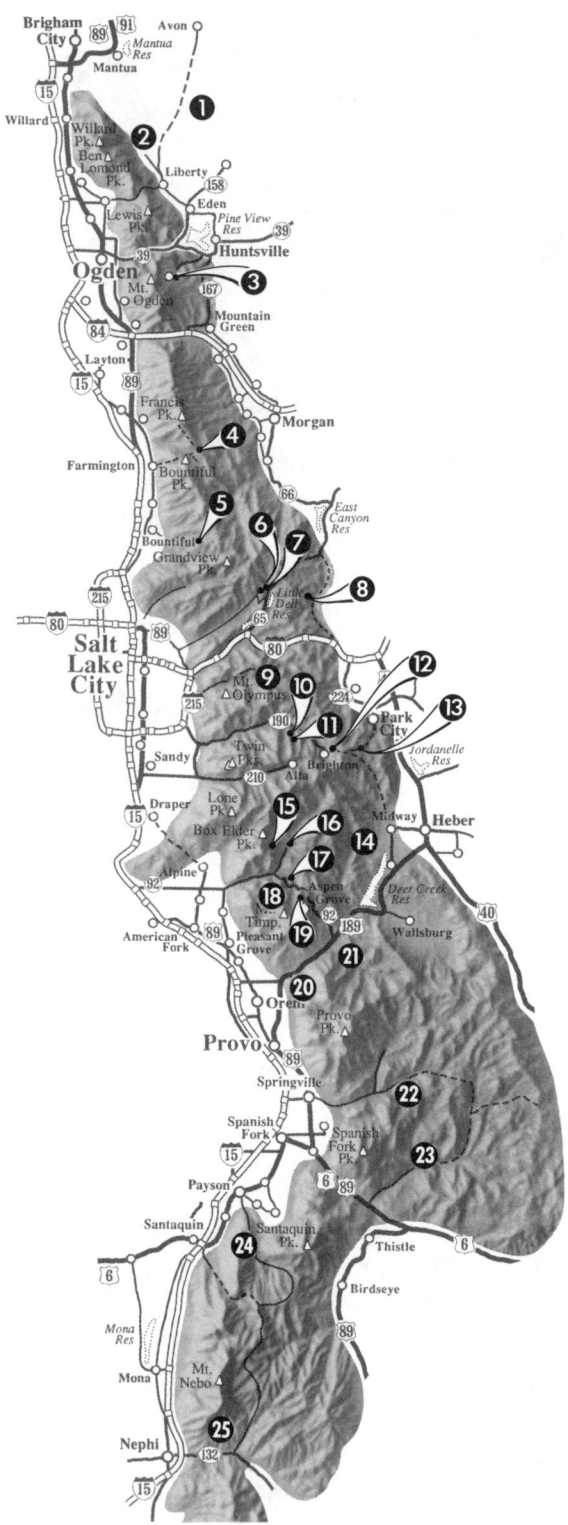

BEGINNER TOURS IN THE WASATCH

NORTHERN WASATCH

1. Liberty to Avon Road 181
2. North Fork Park 182
3. Snow Basin 184
4. Farmington Canyon 185
5. Mueller Park 186

CENTRAL WASATCH

6. Little Mountain Ridge ... 188
7. Mountain Dell Canyon ... 189
8. Little Emigration Can. ... 190
9. Millcreek Canyon 192
10. Spruces/Lower Cardiff ... 193
11. Lower Silver Fork 195
12. Guardsmans Pass
    (from Brighton) 196
13. Guardsmans Pass
    (from Park City) 197
14. Wasatch Mtn. St. Pk. 198
15. Granite Flat 200
16. Upper American Fork ... 202
17. Alpine Scenic Loop 202
18. Timpooneke 203
19. Aspen Grove 204

SOUTHERN WASATCH

20. Squaw Peak Trail 206
21. South Fork Provo River .. 207
22. Right Fork Hobble Cr. ... 209
23. Diamond Fork 210
24. Payson Canyon 211
25. Salt Creek Canyon 212

Chapter 5

WASATCH BEGINNER TOURS

Cross country skiing in the Wasatch Mountains is very different from that in many other parts of the country, where it is confined to machine-packed tracks and rolling terrain. Since most Wasatch touring routes are in canyons, skiers generally start their outings with a climb and end them with a downhill slide. Thus, tourers must learn to turn and stop their skis or confine themselves to flat areas found at touring centers, golf courses, or snowmobile roads.

Ski touring is made easier in the Wasatch by the large quantity of light powder snow. Its consistent texture enables novices to stay under control and helps them master skiing techniques. Many beginners are able to handle some of the intermediate tours by the end of their first season of touring. After reading the first chapters of this book, the beginner is probably too terrified of avalanches and other hazards to venture into the mountains. So where does he go to develop some confidence and skiing skills? Most of this chapter contains descriptions of places in the Wasatch Mountains that are suitable for novice skiers.

Throughout this and remaining chapters and volumes of *Wasatch Tours*, references to roads, highways, and touring routes will follow the convention:

Interstate Highways:	🛡80	I-80
U.S. Highways:	🛡40	US-40
Utah State Roads:	🛡150	SR-150
Ski tour routes:	⑤1	

Figure 5.1 Almost any gentle terrain is suitable for the beginning tourer. At the age of four, Eric Kelner took his first faltering ski steps in a Salt Lake City cemetery.

TIPS FOR THE BEGINNER

Beginners should start on flat terrain that is far from any hazard. If possible, they should take along an experienced tourer who can provide some guidance. As they gain the confidence to venture into more difficult terrain, novices can try skiing up a canyon until the terrain becomes too steep to enjoy, then turning around and sliding back down. It is important to remember that the condition of the snow can change very quickly due to snowfall, wind, and temperature. A pleasant climb on soft snow can turn into an icy bobsled run if the sun disappears below the hills or behind a cloud.

The physical condition of the tourer and the type of equipment being used are as important as the type of terrain in determining the difficulty of a tour. The elevation of the ski touring area can also make a significant difference. Many beginner areas that are described in this chapter start at elevations of about 6000 feet, where temperatures remain above freezing during all but the coldest weeks of the year. The best times to ski such places are mid-winter and/or mid-day in order to increase the likelihood of soft snow conditions.

Although danger of avalanches on most beginner tours is minimal, anyone venturing into the Wasatch Mountains in the winter must be

TIPS FOR THE BEGINNER

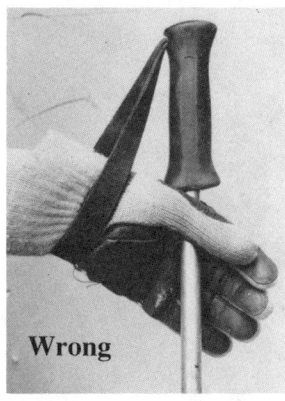 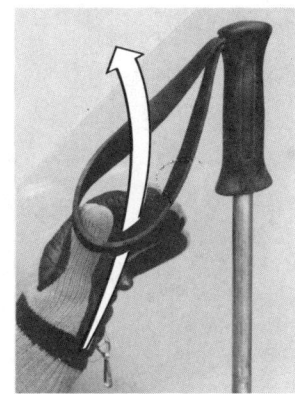 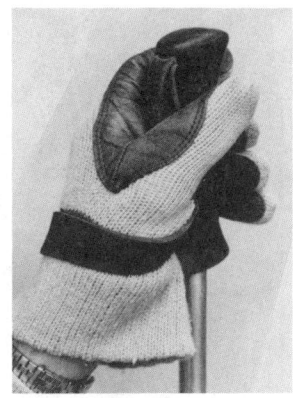

Figure 5.2 The correct means of grasping a ski pole is to push the hand *up* through the wrist loop so that the top of the handle and strap can be held in the palm.

aware of the surroundings at all times. A steep bank or a short slope above the trail can appear harmless, but the snow covering it might slide down upon a tourer. Other skiers high up on the side of the canyon could set off a major avalanche that could involve people on otherwise safe terrain below. One cannot be too careful or too enlightened on this subject.

Skiing techniques will not be discussed in this book, but a few suggestions might help the ski tourer make more effective use of equipment.

In order to push oneself efficiently along the snow, it is important to grip the ski poles correctly. Grasping the poles properly (as illustrated in Figure 5.2) will prevent fatigue or injury to the palm and will make forward propulsion easier.

A beginning skier should master the *kick-turn,* a quick means of turning around, before trying any tour that involves skiing along sloped terrain. Figure 5.3 illustrates this basic ski move. The kick-turn should be practiced on flat terrain (or on the lawn of one's back yard) before being attempted on a slope or in deep snow. Proficiency in kick-turning will assure a safe descent over almost any terrain via the "zig-zag method" of traversing across a slope, kick-turning, traversing back, kick-turning again, etc.

If a trail is too fast or too steep to ski straight down, and there is insufficient room for traversing back and forth, a couple of additional techniques might be useful. When the trail is well packed, but the snow beside it is soft, skiing with one ski in the powder and one in the track

 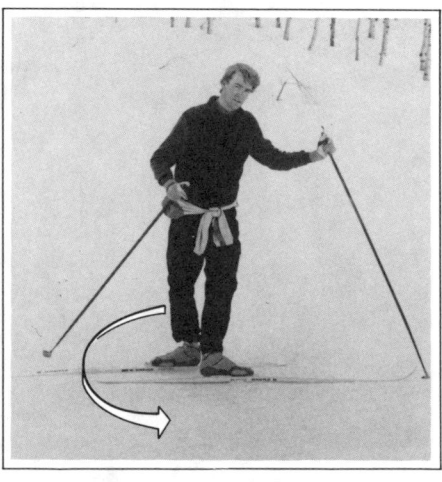

Figure 5.3 *Left:* The kick turn is accomplished by rotating one ski until it points in the opposite direction from the other ski. *Right:* At that point it is a simple matter to bring the unmoved ski around so both point in the same direction.

is helpful. Skiing with both skis in the deep snow works even better. Another alternative is to drag the ski poles along one's side or between one's legs as shown in Figure 5.4; as more pressure is applied to the poles, the braking effect increases. (This technique is not recommended for fiberglass poles except in cases of extreme panic.)

For most people, ski touring is much like walking. The powerful kicks and long glides that are seen on TV are usually racers skiing on groomed tracks. Even the average skier, however, can ski more efficiently by stretching out the stride and making use of the sliding properties of skis. By pushing one ski forward as much as is comfortable with each step, a faster pace can be maintained with little extra effort.

Ski poles allow one to use the arms to help propel the body forward. By pushing a little each time a pole is planted, the skis slide more. Side benefits of this poling motion are (a) it develops strength in the upper body, and (b) less kick wax is needed, so the skis slide and turn more easily.

Nothing is more frustrating than skis that slip backward during a climb. Skis adhere best to the snow when fully weighted, which means that they tend to slip at the end of each stride as the weight is being transferred from one ski to the other. Thus, it is important to support oneself with the poles between strides. This means that force is alternately being applied to the snow by a leg and an arm, but there is never a time when the skier is free to slip backwards.

Figure 5.4 Slowing down on hard snow can cause concern for the beginning tourer. If no room is available to ski into deep snow beside the track, the poles can be used as a brake.

GOLF COURSES AND PARKS

When covered by an adequate depth of snow, the relatively flat and wide-open terrain of local golf courses is ideal for the beginner tourer. Not all golf courses, however, welcome skiers; managers of some courses unreasonably associate the tranquil nordic tourer with such vegetation shredders as offroad vehicle and motorcycle operators. Managers of most public courses, fortunately, have a somewhat more enlightened view of tourers and have no objections to a few ski tracks on their fairways.

Most people know where the nearest courses are, so we won't attempt to list them here. The ones located in or at the mouths of canyons and along the east benches of the Wasatch Front have lots of rolling hills where a beginner can practice on easy ups and downs and try out different kinds of waxes without straying too far from the car.

Mount Ogden Park, east of Taylor Avenue between 30th and 33rd Streets in the city of Ogden, is especially friendly to ski tourers. In the mid-1980's, the Parks Department purchased a snowmobile with the intent of keeping a track set for residents. When snow conditions cooperate, a track can often be found there. Like many other foothills

Figure 5.5 *Left:* In Salt Lake City's Parleys Historic and Nature Park, Bob Woody pauses to contemplate masonry of a Salt Lake City aqueduct constructed in the early 1880's. *Right:* Westminster College field ecology students tour amidst streamside vegetation at Dimple Dell Regional Park in Sandy.

courses, Mount Ogden Park provides good rolling terrain for skiers even without a track.

Cross country skiers who prefer a packed trail should also consider Pioneer State Park, located across from the zoo on Sunnyside Avenue (about 800 South) at the mouth of Emigration Canyon in Salt Lake City. The Utah Division of Parks and Recreation maintains a track there when conditions allow. The elevation is quite low, so their season of operation is very short, but it is an extremely convenient area for many people.

Most parks located in urban areas along the Wasatch Front are skiable only during winters of exceptional snowfall. Two parks, both located along the eastern edge of Salt Lake Valley (and pictured in Figure 5.5), merit tourers' special attention.

Parleys Historic & Nature Park. It's ironic that one of the most urban of Salt Lake City's public parks (bordered by a major freeway and numerous residential areas) could be an island of backcountry tranquillity. The park is one of few areas *within* the City's boundary where tourers can occasionally exchange glances with deer and elk. It

GOLF COURSES AND PARKS

is an area where they can immerse themselves completely in Salt Lake Valley's colorful past.

Parleys Historic and Nature Park is located in the valley immediately west of I-215, where Parleys Stream emerges into Salt Lake Valley. The historic aspect of the park traces back to the earliest pioneers' use of Parleys Canyon as a major transportation corridor into Salt Lake Valley. It contains a well-preserved section of an 1880's stone aqueduct and a whiskey cellar, the only remnant of a brewery/distillery roadside rest stop established there in the mid-1860's.

The only practical ski tourers' entrance to the historic/nature park is located on Heritage Way (2760 South) and 2700 East. A small public parking lot is located a hundred feet west of 2700 East. At the terminal end of 2700 East, a large steel gate blocks unauthorized vehicular access to the roadway leading into the park. Alternatively, tourers can ski eastward along the north edge of the picnic pavilion (adjacent to the parking lot) to intercept the roadway. *Warning:* The first quarter mile of the roadway is steep and, due to several water seeps, often very icy. Its north shoulder is very steep and also rocky. Tourers, especially novices, should remove skis and *carefully* walk to the base of the park. Along the left edge of the roadway (about a hundred feet below the gate) is located an information station describing various roadways and trails within the park and depicting some of the area's unique history.[1]

Dimple Dell Regional Park. Dimple Dell Regional Park in Sandy offers Salt Lake County residents some very unusual ski touring opportunities. The park has the lowest elevation (about 4500 feet) of all the areas described in this volume. It is located in the heart of Utah's most rapidly growing urban area. When there is ample snow—as was the case in the winter of 1992-93—beginner touring there is excellent. A special bonus is that tours in Dimple Dell can commence from a shopping mall and terminate at a pizza parlor.

Dimple Dell Regional Park follows the depression that was formed by the glacial stream emanating from Bells Canyon, a moderately large canyon located immediately south of Little Cottonwood. Were it not for the efforts of many community activists, and a favorable vote by two Salt Lake County commissioners, Dimple Dell may have been yet another

---

[1] Establishment of Parleys Historic and Nature Park would not have been possible without the ceaseless efforts of the Canyon Rim Citizens' Association (joined by groups as diverse as Audubon Society, Sons of Utah Pioneers, and handicapped access proponents) and numerous park advocates. Some of the more dedicated community activists were John J. Nielsen, ElvaRene Plimpton, Clinton and Marion Mott, Barbara Woody, Dorothy Platt, Nancy vonAllmen, and Salt Lake Mayor Ted Wilson.

golf course.[2] The regional park is located within the area bounded by 3rd and 30th East, between 98th and 106th South. The upper region of the park (east of 1300 East Street) offers the best touring.

During the snowless seasons, Dimple Dell Regional Park is a popular equestrian area, so dogs in the park are not allowed. Not as many riders use the area in winter. When snow accumulates in the park, some neighborhood skinny skiers practically set a track along the park's roadways and among the dry streambed's meanders. Three excellent trailheads (with lavish parking during summer) provide access.

The "Wrangler" trailhead, located east of 13th East at 104th South (just south of a large shopping plaza) is an excellent starting point for tours. A steel gate blocks vehicular access to a jeep road that starts immediately south of the park's information station. From the gate, the road swings abruptly west, then makes a gradual, counterclockwise descent into the valley. Once in the valley, tourers can follow equestrian trails heading east or thread their way among treeless openings along the streambed. One excellent variation is to continue eastward along the bottom of the valley, turn north at some opportune point to ascend to the valley's rim, and return to the car along the rim.

Two other trailheads provide access to the park from its upper regions. The "Granite" trailhead (at about 98th South and 30th East) provides access at the northeast corner of the park; the "Southeast" trailhead is located on Dimple Dell Road at about 27th East.

CROSS COUNTRY SKI AREAS

The number and locations of commercial cross country ski operations in Utah seems to vary from year to year. Apparently the financial return from such ventures is somewhat marginal. The more established areas have full service ski shops with sales and rentals, as well as certified instructors to teach proper skiing technique to beginners and experts

---

[2]Long before Sandy City became a "growth industry," area community activist Norm Sims began efforts to protect Dry Creek's valley from development. Preservation efforts escalated when it became known that golf promoters were lobbying county officials to convert the valley into a golf course. Westminster College's biology professor Ty Harrison, Sandy pediatrician John Shakula, and John Fairchild joined the preservation effort. A citizens' lobbying group (Citizens for the Preservation of Dimple Dell Park) added voices of some 1500 area residents. Support of many horseback riders and several equestrian organizations was also mobilized. County Commission candidates Randy Horiuchi and James Bradley campaigned on behalf of preservation and on election to office fulfilled their promises.

alike. Others merely use a snowmobile to pack a track.[3] All of the touring centers that have existed over the years are described here, but tourers interested in patronizing one of them might want to consult a local specialty shop to be sure that the center is still in operation.

Sherwood Hills Resort

The Sherwood Hills Resort is in the Wellsville Mountains, the northern extension of the Wasatch. It was open for a couple of years in the mid-1980's, and recently reopened under new ownership. It is located on US-89 about 11 miles northeast of Brigham City. The trails are on a golf course that lies on the side of a hill among scrub oak trees. There are delightful views of the Cache Valley and the Bear River Range to the east and north. Skiers can enjoy a sauna and/or hot tub as part of the price of a day pass. Sherwood Hills is also a destination resort with a restaurant and rooms to rent for a weekend getaway.

Mountain Dell

Several unsuccessful attempts have been made to develop a ski touring center at the Mountain Dell Golf Course in Parleys Canyon. Since this location was designated as the site of the cross country events in Salt Lake City's bid for the 1998 Winter Olympics, snow making capabilities were designed into the most recent golf course expansion. Although Mountain Dell is listed as the cross country skiing site in the 2002 (and probably 2006, 2010, etc.) Olympic bid, insiders admit that another location is planned for actual events (should Salt Lake ever be selected). A formal touring center at Mountain Dell may never be realized. At present, cross country skiers will have to share the course with sledders, shredders, and tubers.

The Mountain Dell Golf Course is located just off I-80 about six miles up from the mouth of Parleys Canyon. Leave the freeway at the Emigration/East Canyon exit, head east toward the dam, and make an immediate right turn on the frontage road. The club house is less than a mile beyond the turnoff. The parking lot is plowed in winter, and the skiing can be delightful, particularly on weekdays when the fairways and nearby canyons are less crowded.

---

[3]The advantages of machine-packed tracks are smooth snow, which makes it easier to ski, and longer-lasting snow when temperatures rise above freezing.

Figure 5.6 The Mountain Dell Golf Course, recently expanded to 18 holes, provides access to Alexander Spring and the ridge overlooking the new Little Dell Reservoir.

Jeremy Ranch/Wilderness 910

Utah's first major cross country ski area was started in 1988 at Jeremy Ranch, a golf course/housing development located about three miles east of Parleys Summit. Unfortunately, the owners ran into financial difficulties in 1990. In an effort to support Utah's bid for the 1998 Winter Olympics, they agreed to host a World Cup cross country ski race. At the 11th hour, the Salt Lake City Olympic Bid Committee decided not to provide financial support, and the ski area went bankrupt. Shortly thereafter, the entire operation at Jeremy Ranch went into receivership for totally unrelated reasons.

When the ski area was in full operation, its headquarters was located at the golf course club house, but most of the trails were down

CROSS COUNTRY SKI AREAS 177

Figure 5.7 The terrain along East Canyon Creek is ideal for cross country skiing. The Wilderness 910 Company is currently developing an extensive network of ski trails in this area.

East Canyon Creek a couple of miles near an old homestead that was settled in the early 1860's. A wonderful variety of tracks of all levels of difficulty were maintained along the river and up the side canyons. Even a novice could have skied several miles from the trailhead among conifers and aspens without having to deal with the risks of being alone in the backcountry. As many as 20 miles of tracks were packed.

A cattle rancher purchased the undeveloped part of the property in 1992 and opened a minimal touring center there in the winter of 1993. The operation is called Wilderness 910 and includes the trails near the old homestead. As we go to press, more trails are being cleared and buildings constructed with the intent of having a more complete cross country ski area ready for the coming winter. Check the sports pages of the local papers for news on Jeremy/Wilderness 910.

To get to the trailhead, turn north from I-80 Exit 143 and drive over the hill by the Jeremy Ranch Golf Course club house. Continue on the same road for another 1.5 miles down the hill adjacent to the golf course and along the creek. Bear left through a gate to the touring center.

Figure 5.8 The farm along the west side of SR-224 north of Park City and the Park City Golf Course provide a variety of terrain for the White Pine Touring Center.

White Pine Touring Center

The White Pine Touring Center, located at the golf course in Park City, is Utah's oldest cross country skiing operation. The center includes a shop in the club house and one on Main Street in Park City. For many years the owners maintained only about five miles of packed tracks, most of which were essentially flat. In 1992, when Park City purchased a large part of the Osguthorpe ranch that borders the highway north of town, White Pine expanded its track onto that property, more than doubling the available terrain. Plans are underway to continue the track north all the way to the Bear Hollow Winter Sports Park near I-80.

The Park City Golf Course is an ideal place to learn about cross country skiing. The terrain is gentle, and the scenery is superb. A large part of Park City's water supply comes from a mine adjacent to the touring center, and it flows through several ponds on the golf course. Many ducks spend their winters there, so this is a particularly good place for kids to participate in winter outings. Touring at the farm north of town requires more effort, but it is a nice change for those interested in a longer workout with more hills.

CROSS COUNTRY SKI AREAS

The Homestead

The Homestead is a destination resort located in Midway, about four miles west of Heber City on SR-113. Their touring center was formerly located at the nearby Wasatch State Park golf course, but after park rules became unduly restrictive in recent years, the cross country skiing operation was moved to their own golf course. Midway is one of the most scenic spots in Utah, with spectacular Mount Timpanogos in the background and the Heber Valley below. The Homestead also has many other wintertime activities for the entire family, including an excellent restaurant. It's an ideal place for a multi-day outing, since overnight guests may swim in their hot pool.

Solitude Nordic Center

A location at the head of Big Cottonwood Canyon gives the Solitude Nordic Center a real backcountry flavor, despite the proximity of a road and two commercial ski areas. They have 11 miles of machine-packed trail. The terrain includes a loop around a meadow at Silver Lake near Brighton, with magnificent views of the surrounding alpine peaks, and loops around Redman Campground, which is nestled among aspens and conifers. The overall vertical drop of the track is about 500 feet. A popular touring option is to ski down from Brighton to Solitude, and then return via a previously arranged car shuttle or on a Utah Transit Authority (UTA) bus.

Due to the 8500 foot elevation, the Solitude Nordic Center offers the earliest and latest skiing—and usually the best snow—of any cross country ski area in Utah. The altitude, along with the steeper terrain, also makes this the most challenging of the commercial areas. The groomed tracks may be accessed from either Brighton at the top end, or from the Solitude Ski Area at the bottom. Ample parking is available at both locations. The Alpinist, a cross-country ski shop where one can rent equipment and arrange for lessons, is located near the upper end of the track. A similar facility is currently under construction adjacent to the ski track. The nearby Brighton Store serves excellent after-ski meals.

Sundance Resort

The Sundance Resort has recently added cross country skiing to its list of recreational opportunities. About six miles of track are set there, and a full service facility that includes a shop with rentals and lessons is

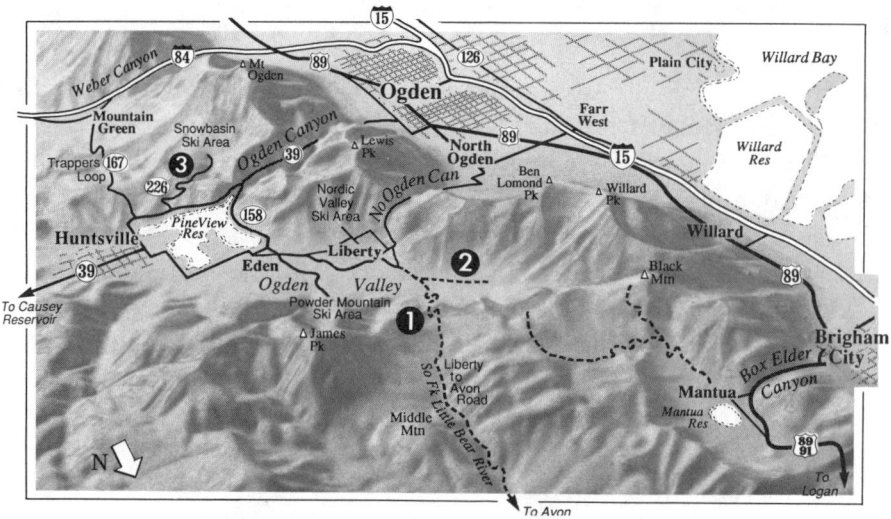

Figure 5.9 Few options exist for northern Wasatch beginning ski tourers. Most are on roads that are not plowed in winter.

available for patrons. The trails wind through Elk Meadow Preserve, a pristine tract of aspen groves and alpine meadows at the base of Mount Timpanogos.

NORTHERN WASATCH

Many of the northern Wasatch tours suitable for beginners are on roads that are popular among snowmobilers. Much of the land along these roads is private, so it is best to check with owners before wandering too far in search of solitude. Only Snow Basin is in the National Forest.

Ogden Valley

Most of the tours described in this section are in the Ogden River Valley, within a ten mile radius of Pineview Reservoir. Tourers who drive from areas located south of Weber Canyon should take I-84 east to Mountain Green, exit there onto SR-167 (the recently completed "Trappers Loop" road), then follow SR-167 to its junction with SR-39 near Pineview Reservoir. The starting points of several tours are near the communities of Eden and Liberty, north across the reservoir from the junction. They are easily reached by driving around the reservoir in either direction. Tourers who come from Ogden and its suburbs can reach the area via SR-39 through Ogden Canyon.

NORTHERN WASATCH

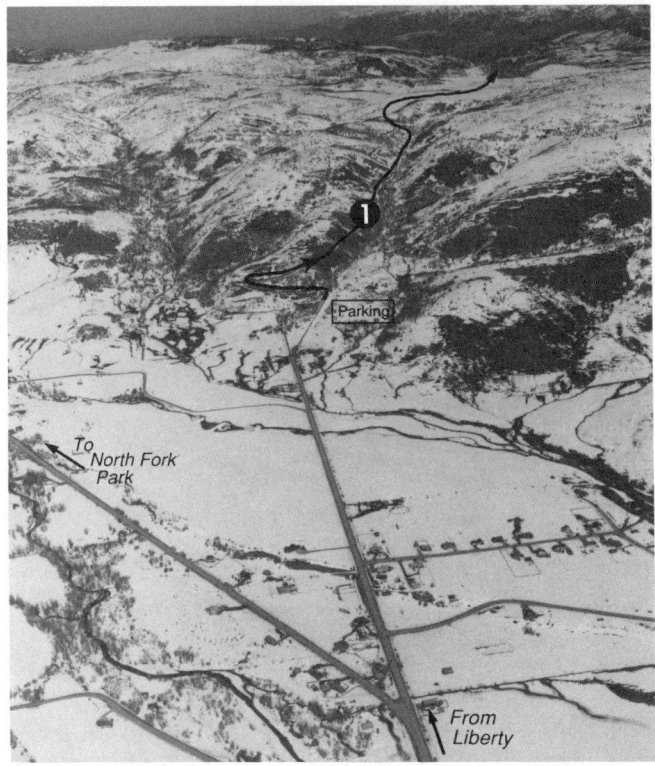

Figure 5.10 The northernmost beginner tour in the Wasatch leads to a pass that overlooks the Ogden River Valley to the south and Cache Valley to the north.

❶ Liberty to Avon Road. The road between Liberty and Avon provides access to a wonderful high plateau that overlooks the Ogden River Valley to the south and Cache Valley to the north. To get to the trailhead, follow SR-162 to Liberty, where the road turns sharply to the left (west) and heads for North Ogden Pass. Just outside of town, turn right and go north along the river. Stay right at the road fork about 1.5 miles beyond the town and continue to the end of the pavement where the snow plows turn around.

The elevation at this point is about 5400 feet, so the season for good skiing is quite limited. From there the road climbs 2.5 miles to a 6500 foot pass. This part of the tour is on terrain that faces south, so the snow may freeze in late afternoon and result in very difficult skiing conditions for the descent back to the car. Late and early in the winter, it may be possible to take a 4-wheel drive vehicle most of the way to the pass.

CHAPTER 5. WASATCH BEGINNER TOURS

Figure 5.11 North Fork Park, at the base of Ben Lomond, is owned by Weber County. In winter the site provides many alternatives for beginning tourers.

From the pass, the main road continues another 11 miles down the South Fork of the Little Bear River to the town of Avon, so this tour can be as long as the tourer wishes. There is a considerable amount of open terrain in all directions; several side roads may also be explored. One of the more interesting alternatives is to bear right at the summit and contour for several miles along the base of James Peak. Another road goes left about a quarter mile beyond the pass, eventually bending around to the northwest and overlooking the town of Mantua.

❷ **North Fork Park.** The North Fork of the Ogden River is one of the main tributaries of Pineview Reservoir. North Fork Park is a county-owned facility located about two miles north of Liberty. An attempt was made in 1988 to open a touring center at North Fork Park, but local residents and members of Ogden's Sierra Club protested to the Weber County Commission. North Fork Park is a superb location for touring. Several miles of unplowed roads wind along the base of Ben Lomond Peak in an area which seems totally isolated from civilization. The park is frequented by wildlife such as deer and moose. Tours range

Figure 5.12 The Snowbasin ski area is located on public forest lands administered by the Wasatch-Cache National Forest. A very controversial 1990 Forest Service decision authorized transfer of 700 acres of nearby public land to a real estate/resort developer. Until the transfer is "consummated," the area remains available for cross country skiing.

in elevation from 5500 to 6000 feet.

Access to this area is the same as to the Avon road, except one should bear left at the fork 1.5 miles north of Liberty. Two entrances, both marked with signs, provide access to the park. The first entrance is 1.0 mile up the road from the fork; the second is 1.9 miles beyond.

Either entrance is suitable for beginning cross country skiers. Skiers can drive about a mile into the park from the lower entrance and park near a gate. The second entrance is closed in winter, so skiers must park up the road near the Camp Utaba gate. A number of different loops can be taken along park roads that wind through wooded and open areas, across streams, and beside beaver ponds.

One particularly scenic route leaves the park and heads into the North Fork drainage, which rises gently for a mile or two before becoming too steep for beginners. Just follow the road from the upper entrance for about 0.7 mile to a junction. Turn right (north) and ski across Cutler Flats and up into the North Fork.

❸ **Snow Basin.** Much of the land associated with the Snowbasin Ski Area is located in Snow Basin, a broad forested depression that's part of the Wasatch-Cache National Forest. Due to a controversial Forest Service decision to transfer nearly 700 acres of public land to a destination resort and real estate developer, large portions of the Basin's terrain may soon become unavailable for tourers or other forest recreationists.[4]

Snow Basin is located on SR-226 south of Pineview Reservoir. Two options are available for novice tourers who would like to tour there. The Maples Campground is accessible from the lower Snowbasin parking lot and features a two mile loop road that winds through meadows and trees. The skier is treated with views of the Ogden River Valley and the surrounding Wasatch peaks from the upper parts of the campground. The elevation of this tour is about 6300 feet. When snow conditions are favorable, the adventurous powder hound may want to ski down the trail that follows Wheeler Creek along the ski area access road to the intersection of Art Nord Drive.

The second touring area is accessible from the upper Snowbasin parking lot by following the Forest Service road that goes southeast past a blockhouse. One can find many places to explore in the large expanse of open and lightly-timbered terrain south of the ski area. Several active

---

[4]The controversial land transfer will occur by means of a highly-debated land exchange approved in 1990. Sun Valley Corporation, owner of Snowbasin Ski Area and already owner of 7000 acres of land adjacent to the ski area, proposed to Forest Service officials that the agency transfer, via a land trade, 1300 acres of prime public forest lands near, and including, Snow Basin to the corporation for development of a four-season destination resort and private residences.

After a long and contested environmental impact process, Dale Bosworth, Supervisor of the Wasatch-Cache National Forest, approved an exchange of 220 acres to satisfy *only the public base facility needs* of the newly-proposed resort. With 7000 acres of private land only 1.5 miles away, he explained in his Record of Decision that he could not "in good conscience" dispose public land for the purpose of private residence development.

Sun Valley Corp., as well as numerous business, community, and environmental groups, appealed the Supervisor's decision to Regional Forester Stan Tixier. On March 13, 1990, standing before an assembly of the Ogden area's business, civic, and governmental officials, Senator Orrin Hatch condemned Bosworth's decision. "Stan," the Senator then said, fixing his gaze on Regional Forester Tixier, "Are you going to help us with this? I've never asked Stan to help us yet that he hasn't done it." Hatch then turned back to face his audience. "I hope that puts you on the spot, Stan."

No one knows whether Orrin Hatch's effusive personality or his having put the Regional Forester "on the spot" made the difference, but within six months of the one-sided conversation, "Stan" vacated Forest Supervisor Bosworth's 220-acre decision and instated a new decision approving a trade of 695 acres.

NORTHERN WASATCH

Figure 5.13 Quick access to high elevation terrain is afforded from the Wasatch Front via Farmington Canyon. The Farmington Flats area south of the road is ideal for novice cross country skiers.

beaver ponds can be found there in the summer, but winter wildlife is usually limited to birds and a few stray downhill skiers.

❹ Farmington Canyon

The Federal Aviation Administration plows the road to the Francis Peak radar towers throughout the winter, so Farmington area cross country skiers of all ability levels have quick access to good skiing terrain and spectacular views. The Wasatch Mountains are very narrow and steep in this area, so it seems that one could jump west into the Great Salt Lake or east into the town of Morgan from the top of the ridge. Quite a bit of flat terrain can be found along the ridge crest, however, so beginners can enjoy the snow and scenery.

The road up Farmington Canyon is a continuation of 100 East Street going north out of the town of Farmington. It is paved for 1.5 miles, then dirt for about seven more. The road is quite steep and extremely narrow in some places with severe dropoffs on the downhill side, so it is only recommended for four-wheel drive vehicles with good snow tires and attentive drivers. It is not for the faint of heart! The gate at the top of the canyon is usually kept closed in winter, so ski tours are described from there. The elevation at the gate is 7250 feet, which is high enough for several months of good powder snow.

The gate is located just beyond a road that turns off to the right (south) toward Bountiful Peak. This road forks after about 0.5 mile. The right fork goes south through a large group of privately owned cabins and then continues over Bountiful Peak and down to Bountiful. Beginners should not venture beyond the cabins.

The left fork leads to a Forest Service campground and then makes a 4-mile loop around Farmington Flat. It eventually intersects the Francis Peak road about 0.8 mile north of the gate, so skis might have to be removed for the walk back down to the car.

❺ Mueller Park

The closest touring area for Bountiful area tourers is the road leading through the Forest Service picnic areas at Mueller Park. This road is an extension of 1800 South Street in Bountiful, and it is gated to keep vehicles out. The elevation is very low, only 5100 feet, so the touring season is limited. The canyon is only skiable for about a mile or so, but this is a delightfully secluded area that is very close to the city. Mueller Park is also the gateway to the Sessions Mountains and Grandview Peak, which are more advanced areas seldom visited by skiers. Details on these tours are found in Volume 2 of *Wasatch Tours*.

CENTRAL WASATCH

Most of the cross country skiing terrain in the vicinity of Salt Lake City is quite steep and not suitable for beginning skiers. To make matters worse, many of the places that novices formerly enjoyed have been taken over by ski areas. The Forest Service's failure to recognize and acknowledge changing recreational demographics has led to a situation where cross country skiers must drive many miles to areas outside the Wasatch.

CENTRAL WASATCH

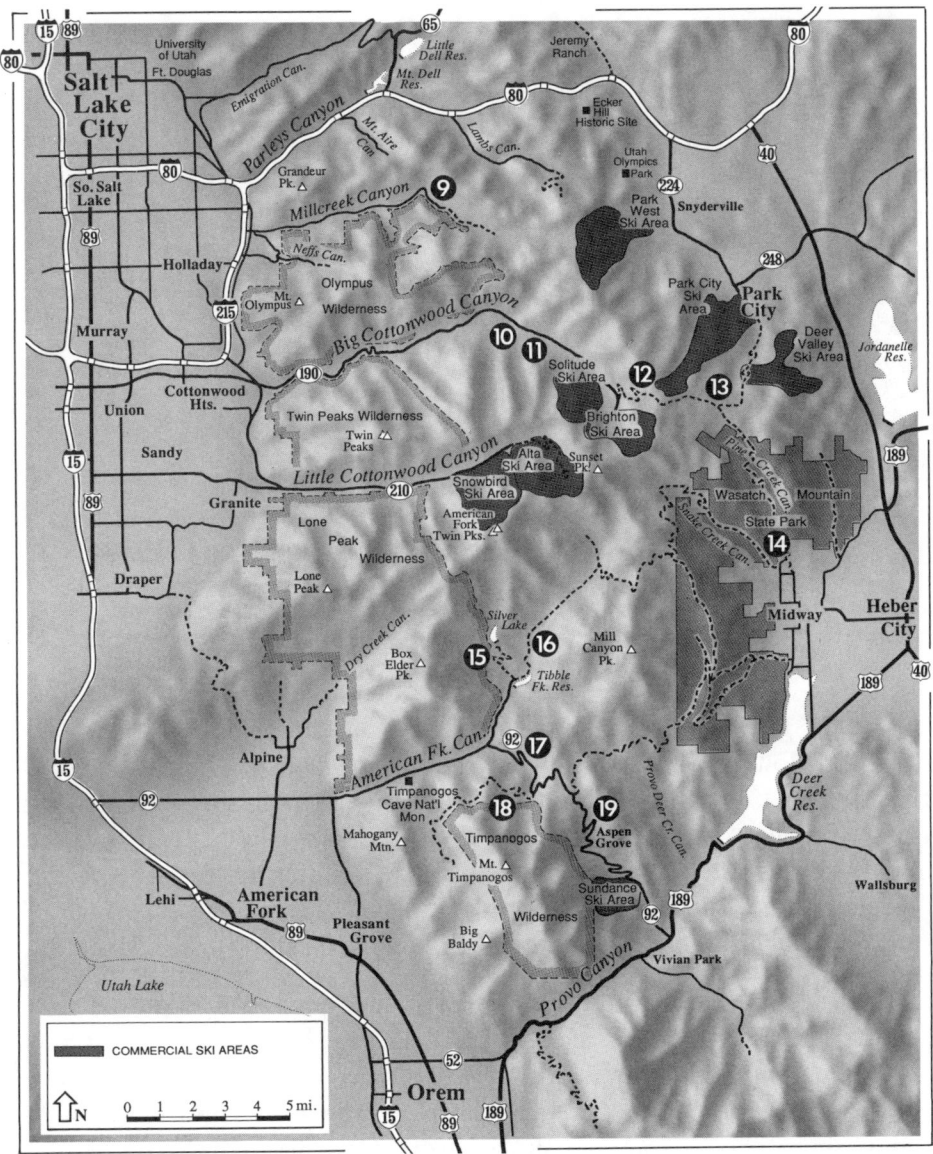

Figure 5.14   Due to severe competition for public land by ski area and real estate developers, few quality touring options remain for beginning cross country skiers in the central Wasatch Mountains.

Mountain Dell and East Canyons

Mountain Dell and East canyons have great historical significance in Utah because they contain the routes followed by the Donner Party and many early Mormon settlers. From the present site of the East Canyon

Figure 5.15 School buses were used to transport Salt Lake students to the Little Mountain ski area during winter months. National Archives photo.

Reservoir, both groups followed East Canyon Creek and then climbed over Big Mountain Pass via Little Emigration Canyon. From the pass, they dropped down into Mountain Dell Canyon to the site of Little Dell Reservoir, then climbed over Little Mountain Pass and descended to the Salt Lake Valley via Emigration Canyon. A number of monuments can be found along the highways commemorating these pioneers. Much of the route is suitable for cross country skiing almost 100 years later.

❻ **Little Mountain Ridge.** For many years, the ridge between Parleys and Emigration canyons was also a popular destination for Salt Lake downhill skiers. During the 1950's, Ray Watrous and Mel Henshaw operated a small ski area adjacent to the road known as "Little Mountain." The area had a couple of rope tows, lights for night skiing, and an eating establishment. The price of a tow ticket was only $.75 for an evening and $1.00 for a weekend day. An energetic person could ski for only a couple of pennies per ride—some difference from today, when the local areas will gladly take you for a ride for 50 times that much!

The Little Mountain ridge is still popular with skiers. Tourers can park at the pass, at an elevation of 6230 feet, and go in either direction for a scenic outing close to home. Beginning tourers will not want to venture more than a mile or so west of the pass, since the ridge soon steepens as it climbs to a 7376 foot peak. A longer outing is possible

CENTRAL WASATCH

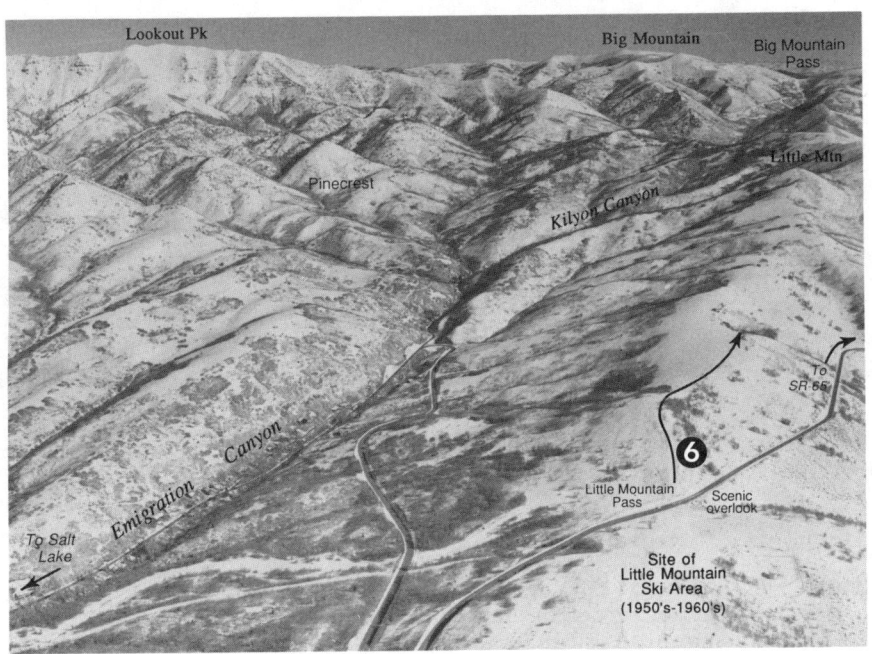

Figure 5.16 The ridge between Parleys and Emigration canyons is accessible by car and provides beautiful vistas in all directions.

to the east. A trail leaves the road and follows the ridge for about two miles to Little Mountain. Beginners can avoid most of the steeper sections by traversing around the high points of the ridge.

Little Mountain ridge may be accessed from Emigration or from Parleys Canyon. The road up Emigration Canyon is the eastward extension of Sunnyside Avenue (approximately 800 South). Little Mountain Pass is the highest point reached by the road. To access the pass from Parleys Canyon, take I-80 Exit 134 (Emigration/East Canyon) and follow the Emigration Canyon signs along SR-65.

❼ Mountain Dell Canyon. The road over Big Mountain Pass that leads to East Canyon Reservoir (SR-65) is not plowed in winter and is a convenient destination for Salt Lake cross country skiers and snowmobilers. The easiest access is from I-80 Exit 134 (Emigration/East Canyon). A gate (about three miles from the interstate) closes the road during the winter months.

The road climbs gradually from the gate for 2.0 miles to the Affleck Park picnic area, which is nestled along the stream among huge cottonwoods and imposing cliffs at an elevation of 6100 feet. There are

Figure 5.17 The road above the Little Dell Reservoir is closed to cars in winter. Beginning tourers can ski as far as Affleck Park for a picnic, or continue to Big Mountain summit when snow conditions permit. It is expected that trails for hikers and cross country skiers will soon be developed near the reservoir.

few prettier places for a lunch stop. Skiers can continue a little ways farther up Mountain Dell Canyon via a trail that passes through the picnic area.

At Affleck Park the highway bears to the right and climbs more steeply for 3.5 miles to Big Mountain Pass, overlooking East Canyon from an elevation of 7420 feet. Ambitious tourers can continue along the road down the other side of the pass, or turn right (south) and ski along the ridge. The latter option follows a jeep road that has superb views of the Wasatch peaks east of Salt Lake and the Oquirrhs to the west.

Volume 2 of *Wasatch Tours* contains more information on the skiing possibilities in upper Mountain Dell Canyon.

❽ Little Emigration Canyon (Pioneer Trail). The other drainage that terminates at Big Mountain Pass is Little Emigration Canyon, which commences in East Canyon just a few miles north of Jeremy Ranch. Little Emigration was the route followed by the Donner Party on their fateful journey in 1846, and the next year by the first company of Mormon pioneers as they trekked to the Valley of the Great Salt Lake. The canyon climbs very gently through scattered cottonwoods

Figure 5.18 In 1846 the ill-fated Donner party cleared a trail up Little Emigration Canyon that became the major route for Mormon emigrants to Salt Lake Valley.

and maples, gaining only 1200 vertical feet in about four miles. It's a great place to take the family.

The Mormon Pioneer Trail starts at Mormon Flat, which is between Jeremy Ranch and the East Canyon Reservoir. The gravel road along East Canyon Creek is kept open in the winter. To reach the trail head, take I-80 Exit 143 (Jeremy Ranch) and drive over the hill by the golf course club house. Continue on that road down East Canyon Creek to the large stone pillar on the left that marks Mormon Flat. The distance from the club house to the pillar is five miles.

Getting to the trail from the road is the most challenging part of this ski tour. The Utah Division of Parks and Recreation has built a fence around Mormon Flat to keep vehicles off the meadow and the trail. Two sets of steps have also been constructed to allow hikers and campers to enter the area. There is also a bridge over East Canyon Creek at that point. Tourers should climb over the first fence and cross the bridge. After crossing the bridge, go right (downstream) for about 50 feet and then left (upstream) on a trail through thick brush. The second set of steps is just beyond the bushes, about 200 yards from the bridge. The Mormon Pioneer Trail goes west up Little Emigration Canyon from there.

A couple of alternatives are available for beginning tourers in this area. One is to follow the canyon bottom to Big Mountain Pass with its spectacular view to the west. When the canyon widens near the top, a power line can be followed directly to the pass. Alternatively, to avoid the steeper area near the top, one can traverse to the right (north) from a power line and get on the highway that ascends to the pass from East Canyon Reservoir.

Another possibility is to turn right (north) on a road that intercepts Little Emigration Canyon about 2.4 miles from Mormon Flat. This road traverses up to a ridge and continues climbing for 2.1 miles to join the Big Mountain Pass road. The pass is another 1.6 miles up the road. The terrain on the ridge is more exposed to the sun than the bottom of the canyon, and it is steeper in spots, so the skiing is sometimes not as inviting for a beginner. Its advantages are the views of Big Mountain on the way up and of the Park City ski areas on the descent.

One other choice is available for skiers who don't mind a steeper climb. A road that commences about 2.1 miles from Mormon Flat bears left (southwest) and ascends a narrow canyon. It crosses a ridge and bends around to intersect the main trail just below Big Mountain Pass. A nice loop would be to go up this roadway, but to use the canyon trail for the descent.

Tri-Canyon Area

Officials of the Wasatch-Cache National Forest have labeled Millcreek, Big Cottonwood, and Little Cottonwood canyons as the "Tri-Canyon Area." Due to their proximity to about a million residents, these canyons are receiving extremely heavy use from all types of backcountry recreationists. Unfortunately, the Forest Service has failed to designate any significant amount of terrain in these canyons for beginning touring. Most of the gentle terrain has been permitted to be incorporated into downhill ski resorts. The few remaining areas are described here.

❾ **Millcreek Canyon.** Millcreek Canyon is the closest location to Salt Lake City that has consistent snow and good beginning terrain. The highway leading up the canyon is plowed to a gate about 0.7 mile beyond the Log Haven restaurant. A parking area is maintained at the end of the plowed roadway. Since snowmobiles are not permitted here, the area has become a favorite spot for tourers and walkers.

In 1993, Forest Service personnel decided to set a machine-packed track on the road as it continues upcanyon from the parking area. This provides an extremely convenient alternative for track skiers who want to exercise after work, but who don't have time to drive to Park City or Brighton.

The road ascends gradually to its end 4.5 miles from the parking area; the Millcreek drainage continues for another three miles. The upper reaches of the canyon are privately owned, so tourers are warned to respect trespass signs. Aside from an occasional cabin, this canyon has a most primitive atmosphere. Little vestige remains of the once-booming timber harvesting area that contained twenty sawmills processing lumber for residents of Salt Lake Valley.

The ski tours in and among the side gulches of Millcreek Canyon are described in Volume 2 of *Wasatch Tours*.

❿ Spruces Campground/Lower Cardiff Fork. Very few places exist where beginning tourers can enjoy the consistently light and deep powder that attracts tourists to Utah from all over the world. Such locations tend to be extremely busy, particularly on weekends. The Spruces Campground/Lower Cardiff Fork area in upper Big Cottonwood Canyon is one of those places.

Spruces Campground. The Spruces Campground is located about 9.5 miles up Big Cottonwood Canyon at an elevation of 7400 feet. Formerly called "Community Camp," this area was developed in the late 1930's as a winter recreation center. The top photo of Figure 5.19 depicts the wintersports area as it appeared at that time.

Today, Salt Lake County road maintenance crews plow the parking area at the campground for winter recreationists, and UDOT tries to keep the snow pushed back along the highway to make room for additional vehicles. The UTA bus that services Brighton and Solitude will usually stop to pick up or disembark cross country skiers.

Spruces Campground extends 0.7 mile up Big Cottonwood Canyon to an area of private cabins. Tourers can also venture down the canyon along the stream to the mouth of Cardiff Fork, which joins Big Cottonwood Canyon about a half mile downstream from the campground's entrance.

Lower Cardiff Fork. The flatland near the junction of Cardiff Fork and Big Cottonwood Canyon is a popular snowplay area that is of-

Figure 5.19 *Top:* The Community Camp winter sports center as it appeared at its dedication in 1937. Denuded by timber and mining interests, the hillside provided excellent terrain for all types of skiing. The ski jump takeoff visible above the crowd at right became known as Engen Hill. Photo courtesy of L. K. Irvine. *Bottom:* Tourers Joey Castillo *(l)*, Chris Maxwell, Monique and Ken Calder pause beneath the remains of Engen Hill on a warm spring morning.

ten overrun by tubers, walkers, and snowmobilers. The gentle terrain nearby, however, is less crowded and provides the novice tourer numerous opportunities to escape the crowds. The parking area for Cardiff Fork is about nine miles up from the paved parking complex at the mouth of Big Cottonwood Canyon.

An unplowed gravel roadway leads into Cardiff Fork. This road splits about 0.7 mile from the highway, and skiers should bear right across the stream.[5] A few places along the roadway might be too narrow and too steep for first-time tourers, so they should avoid venturing too far into the canyon. Cardiff Fork has been a center of mining activity since the turn of the century, and many signs of those operations are still visible along the way. Beginning tourers should avoid the upper reaches of the canyon, one of the most dangerous avalanche areas in the Wasatch.

⓫ Lower Silver Fork. Silver Fork (Figure 5.20) is one of several Wasatch Canyons that have challenging terrain at the top, but allow delightful beginner tours when approached from the bottom. As this book goes to press, the best starting point for a tour into Silver Fork is the lower parking lot of the Solitude ski area.[6] A road begins at the west end of the parking lot, goes around the bottom of the lower ski lift, and continues to the northwest through evergreens for about a mile to a summer cabin area. The road turns up the canyon just beyond a large building on the left that overlooks the highway. It's hard to believe that 100 years ago one could look down from this spot on the town of Silver Springs, a thriving mining community with a hotel, a post office, two stores, a smelter, several houses, and numerous homes.

A few hundred yards up the fork, the trail crosses the stream and remains along the right side of the drainage for the rest of the tour. The terrain steepens a mile or so up the canyon, so beginners will want to stop there. Just across the stream from that point are the tunnels of the old Alta mine, one of several rich silver lodes in the canyon. About the only activities in the area today are hiking and ski touring, with a bit of snowmobiling by residents of the nearby cabins.

Before attempting a tour into the lower part of Silver Fork, skiers should check the avalanche conditions. The photo in Figure 4.13 was taken in this canyon and illustrates why some beginner routes should be avoided when snow conditions are particularly unstable. Even though

---

[5]The other trail leads to Donut Falls, which is a popular hiking destination in the summer. This part of the canyon is very narrow with steep sides. A fatality occurred there in February 1981, when an avalanche dumped 10 feet of snow on three skiers who were walking up the gully.

[6]The Forest Service has discussed the possibility of building a new Silver Fork trailhead on the highway that will allow ski tourers and hikers to bypass the ski area entirely. It is not known at this time when funding will be available for the project.

Figure 5.20 The Silver Fork summer home area lies at the mouth of one of the most popular ski touring canyons in the Wasatch. Heliskiers and advanced skiers make use of the upper bowls, but beginners are urged to confine their outings to the lower mile or two of roadway.

the canyon bottom is relatively flat, it is possible for a skier or helicopter to send an avalanche down from a steeper slope above.

Lake Solitude (R.I.P.). Expansion of the Solitude ski area has eliminated this excellent tour.

Silver Lake/Redman Campground (R.I.P.). This area is still available for cross country skiing, but the terrain has been taken over by the Solitude Nordic Center. The general public may tour here only after purchasing a day pass.

⓬ Guardsmans Pass from Brighton. The road connecting Brighton to Park City and Midway is a popular spot for novice ski tourers and snowmobilers. The area can be accessed from any of the three communities, but the snow is usually best on the Brighton side due to the higher elevation. The Guardsmans Pass road branches from the Big Cottonwood Canyon highway about 0.4 mile below the Brighton Store. The road is plowed for less than a mile to the first switchback. Parking is limited, but is usually not a problem.

The Guardsmans Pass road climbs 800 vertical feet in 2.3 miles to the pass, where one is greeted with superb views of Heber Valley and the Uinta Mountains farther to the east. The elevation at the top is 9700 feet. Some sections of the road up from Brighton face to the south, so care must be taken during times of the year when the temperature rises above freezing during the middle of the day. A tour should be planned to avoid returning to the car after the snow surface has refrozen late in the afternoon.

Albion Basin (R.I.P.). Expansion of the Alta ski area has eliminated this tour during the winter months, but it is still a favorite for early and late season skiers. Park at the end of the plowed road and ski up the Albion Basin roadway from there.

Park City/Midway Area

All of the touring routes in the Park City/Midway area that are suitable for beginning cross country skiers either follow roads frequented by (and groomed for) snowmobiles or are located on private properties. A number of ski tours on public roadways are described here; tourers are advised to check with landowners before exploring other areas.

❽ Guardsmans Pass from Park City. (End.)[7] The second alternative for a ski tour to Guardsmans Pass is to drive through Park City and then follow SR-224 up Ontario Canyon to the end of the plowed road. Skiers may find parking to be a problem due to the popularity of the area. A couple of snowmobile rental operations are located there. The elevation at that point is 8000 feet.

From the parking area, the road ascends 800 vertical feet in 2.1 miles to a ridge overlooking Heber Valley and Deer Creek Reservoir. The superb view includes Mount Timpanogos and Provo Peak, making the climb well worth the effort. The area south of the ridge is called Bonanza Flat, in honor of the silver miners who acquired fortunes there around the turn of the century. In summer one can see the tailings of some of the largest mining operations in the Wasatch along this road. A couple of them are accessible on skis by taking a short side road off to the right (west) on the way up to Bonanza Flat.

A number of touring options become available at Bonanza Flat. The truly ambitious can continue up the road another 2.6 miles to Guards-

---

[7]This tour is designated as "Endangered" because the Deer Valley Ski Area is conducting a major expansion project as we go to press. Tourers may find it difficult—if not impossible—to get from Park City to Guardsmans Pass in the future.

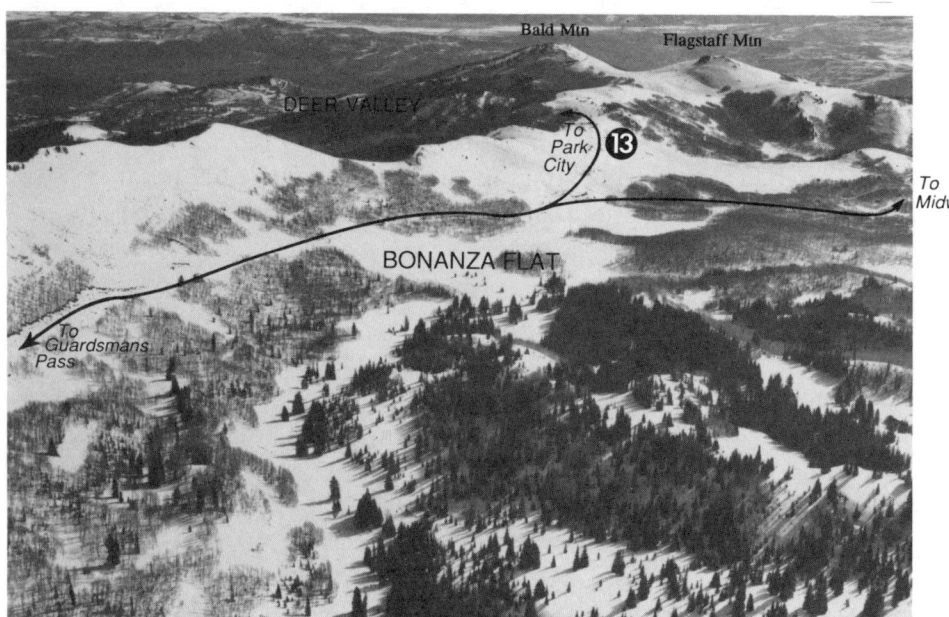

Figure 5.21 Few touring alternatives exist for beginners near Park City. The road to Guardsmans Pass is a favorite place for snowmobiles, but several side roads offer some opportunities for solitude.

mans Pass. This would be a total vertical climb of 1700 feet from the car, too much for most beginners. A more moderate alternative would be to explore Bonanza Flat and its rolling hills, without gaining or losing much elevation, before returning to Park City. Perhaps the most inviting prospect is to ski across Bonanza Flat and take the left turn that goes down Pine Creek to Midway, but this road is quite steep and is not recommended for beginning skiers. Also, some sections of the road face to the south, and the snow may freeze when the sun goes behind the mountains.

⑭ Wasatch Mountain State Park. The Utah Division of Parks and Recreation grooms many miles of snowmobile trails within the park. There are connections to the head of American Fork Canyon via Cascade Springs or Snake Creek, and to Guardsmans Pass via Pine Creek and Bonanza Flat. Skiers will find innumerable places to leave the main roads to ski through untracked powder. This area is all within sight of Mount Timpanogos, so the views are always spectacular.

Two of the park's major roads, those in Pine Creek and Snake Creek canyons, start in the northwest corner of the Midway valley. The park's Visitor Center can be found on Homestead Drive at the south end of the

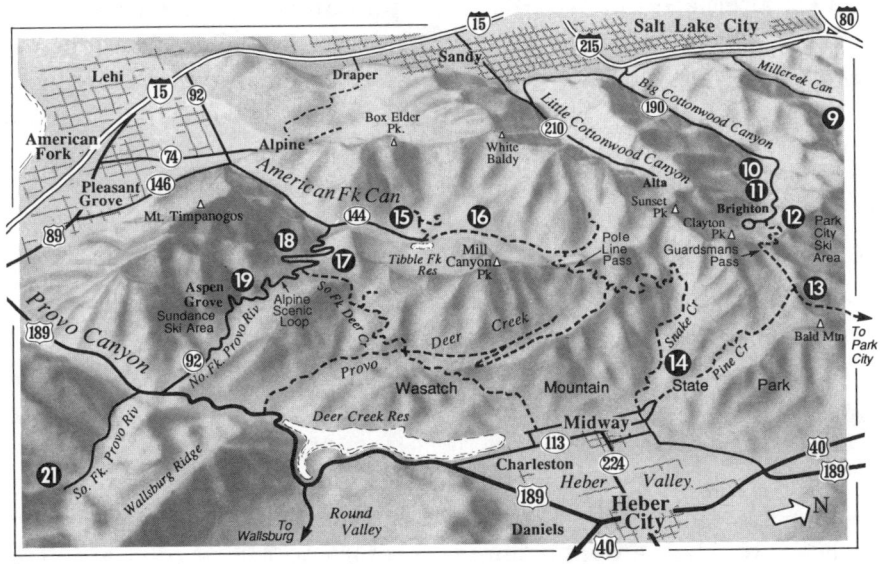

Figure 5.22 Many miles of Wasatch Mountain State Park roads are groomed for snowmobiles. Cross country skiers who like a smooth surface, as well as those who prefer deep powder, can find many enjoyable alternatives in the park.

Wasatch Mountain State Park Golf Course; the club house is located about a mile northeast of the Visitor Center.

Pine Creek Canyon goes north from the club house and climbs 3000 feet in about 9 miles to Bonanza Flat. The road is not recommended for beginning skiers due to its steepness and exposure. It starts at an elevation of only 5800 feet, and much of it faces south or southeast.

Snake Creek, a major tributary of the Provo River, is the source of most of Midway's drinking and irrigation water. It's drainage has provided considerable wood and marble for valley residents, and a few miners made their fortunes from its gold and silver. The power plant located just above the golf course was constructed near the turn of the century to provide electricity to residents of the valley, as well as to the mines of Park City and upper American Fork Canyon. Snake Creek acquired its name from the number of rattlesnakes that were found around the hot springs and mounds in the area. Early settlers are said to have killed them by the hundreds.

The Snake Creek Canyon road heads northwest from the Visitor Center. It is plowed for 3.0 miles to the Mill Flat Power Plant, where parking is available. The elevation at the trailhead is 6800 feet, so this is the best alternative in Wasatch Mountain State Park for cross country skiers. It also provides the most direct access to higher elevations. The road climbs 1000 vertical feet in 2.5 miles before crossing the stream and heading south. Skiers may prefer to turn off the road at the crossing and continue up the drainage to avoid the snowmobiles. Owners of the Brighton ski area applied for permission to expand their lifts down from Snake Creek Pass into this area, but the project was turned down by the Wasatch County Commission in 1993 due to strong opposition from residents of Midway.

After crossing the stream, the Snake Creek road traverses for 5.7 miles, gradually climbing to Pole Line Pass, at an elevation of 8900 feet. The pass provides a superb view of American Fork Canyon and the high peaks to the north. The power lines from Midway followed this route to the mines below. About four miles from the Snake Creek stream crossing, the Cascade Springs road joins the Pole Line Pass road from the left, providing an opportunity to return to Midway via a different route to be described next.

A third road in Wasatch Mountain State Park that is poplar with snowmobilers starts in the southwest corner of the town of Midway on Stringtown Road and goes to Cascade Springs, a distance of about 6 miles. The elevation gain from Midway to the ridge near the spring is only 1200 feet, so this alternative has the least climb of any tours in the park. Unfortunately, it also starts at the lowest elevation. From Cascade Springs, one can turn right (north) and ski up the canyon toward Pole Line Pass or continue southwesterly on the main roadway for another six miles to the summit of the Alpine Scenic Loop road.

American Fork Canyon

Four areas in American Fork Canyon are suitable for beginner touring: Granite Flat Campground, the upper reaches of American Fork Canyon, the Alpine Scenic Loop roadway, and the flatlands and road in the proximity of the Timpooneke Campground and trailhead.

⑮ Granite Flat Campground. Even though the Granite Flat Campground is located at the relatively low elevation of 6700 feet, its northern and eastern exposure generally guarantees better than average snow conditions. Up until the winter of 1991-92 the campground was open to snowmobiles, but since that winter the Forest Service has forbidden snowmobile use in the campground. The access road, however, must be shared with over-snow vehicles.

CENTRAL WASATCH 201

Figure 5.23 American Fork Canyon above Tibble Fork Reservoir provides excellent skiing for Utah Valley tourers.

The narrow and loopy roads within the campground are ideal for learning and practicing all touring techniques. The grades along the road are sufficiently steep to practice herringbones or telemark turns. Once cleared of snow, the picnic tables can be used for a leisurely winter luncheon.

Granite Flat Campground is easily reached from American Fork, Pleasant Grove, or Salt Lake Valley. From Salt Lake, take I-15 south over Point of the Mountain. The first exit south of the Point leads east toward Alpine, Highland, and Timpanogos Cave. Continue eastward along SR-92 into American Fork Canyon. The highway forks five miles from the mouth of the canyon; the left fork (SR-144) leads to the Tibble Fork recreation area and the right fork (SR-92), commonly known as the Alpine Scenic Loop, continues toward Aspen Grove.

Follow the left fork to the Tibble Fork Reservoir, where a large parking area has been developed for fishermen, hikers, and snowmobilers. This is probably the finest winter—or summer—trailhead in the Wasatch, and certainly one of the most heavily used. The route to Gran-

Figure 5.24 One of the most spectacular vistas in the Wasatch is the view of Mount Timpanogos from the top of the Alpine Scenic Loop highway.

ite Flat Campground follows the snowmobile road that leads northwest from near the north edge of the parking area. Granite Flat Campground is located about three quarters of a mile from the parking lot.

16 Upper American Fork Canyon. The unplowed gravel road in American Fork Canyon continues upcanyon, north and northeastwardly, from Tibble Fork Reservoir to Dutchmans Flat, then swings sharply east to ascend the previously-mentioned Pole Line Pass. The climb to Dutchmans Flat is about 6 miles along a moderately steep grade. The road is quite wide and is groomed for snowmobiles. When packed or icy the roadway may be too steep for safe descent by the rankest of beginners. The best time to tour the roadway is right after a snowstorm; the soft snow is easier to ski and provides a soft cushion during hard landings.

17 Alpine Scenic Loop Highway. Once a degree of ski control has been learned, the beginning tourer can ascend along the paved Scenic Loop road as far as abilities will permit. The road is located along south-facing slopes, so freezing of the surface can be expected late in the afternoon. The road is also popular among snowmobilers, so rutting of the trail should be anticipated.

The Alpine Scenic Loop is probably the most scenic beginner route in the Wasatch. The distance to the highway's 8000-foot summit is about five miles, with only 1500 feet of elevation gain. One does not have to tour all the way to the top to enjoy the spectacular view of Mount Timpanogos visible from this road.

The best time to undertake this ski tour is in February or March, right after a snowstorm. Start early in the morning (to get the best photographic light and to avoid the snowmobile traffic) and linger amid the spectacular scenery.

The tour commences from a small parking area at the gate that closes the highway during winter. The gate is located a couple of miles along the right fork of American Fork Canyon.

⑱ Timpooneke Area. Timpooneke is a popular summer trailhead into the upper basins of the Mount Timpanogos Wilderness. It is located along a spur road that leads to the right (west) off the Alpine Scenic Loop Highway about two miles up from the gate. A few hundred yards up the spur is a guard station (occupied only during summer) and associated picnic area, trailhead, and campground.

Just beyond the guard station, a road known as the "Timpooneke Road," branches to the right. This roadway traverses beneath the North Peak of Mount Timpanogos and ultimately winds up on Sagebrush Flat, along the west flank of Mount Timpanogos. The westward traverse is extremely avalanche-prone and not recommended for the beginner. The first two miles of road from Timpooneke, however, have minimum hazard and are ideal for learning to tour. Since these routes follow well-graded roads, deep snow is not essential to make them tourable. The roadway's northern exposure allows the powder snow to endure well between storms.

North Slopes of Provo Canyon

Most beginner tours in the vicinity of Provo Canyon are afflicted with the "low elevation syndrome." Under conditions of adequate to abundant snow depth, tours along the routes to be described can be quite delightful. Three areas will be discussed. Aspen Grove is described here; the South Fork of the Provo River and the Squaw Peak Trail are included in the next section.

CHAPTER 5. WASATCH BEGINNER TOURS

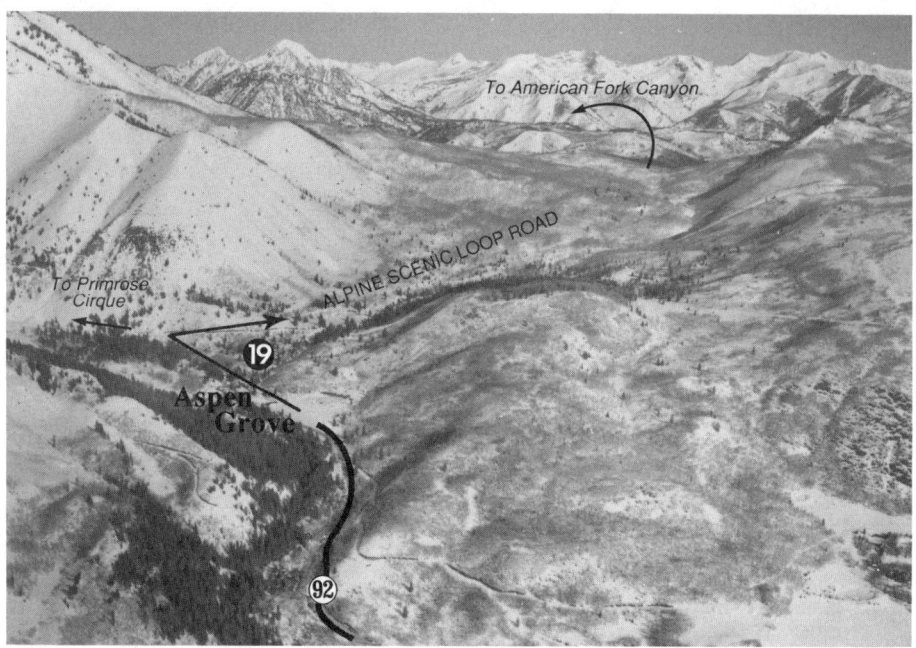

Figure 5.25 The southern part of the Alpine Scenic Loop highway is plowed as far as Aspen Grove. The upper section is a popular area for cross country skiers and snowmobilers.

⑲ Aspen Grove. Aspen Grove is a popular summer recreation area along the Alpine Scenic Loop highway (SR-92). The Grove lies on flatlands at the base of Mount Timpanogos' Elk Point. Aspen Grove's 7000 foot elevation, along with its sheltered location beneath two 11,000 foot prominences of Mount Timpanogos, assure good touring conditions at any time during the skiing season.

Beginners can test their ski legs along the flat areas of Aspen Grove, but they should avoid venturing too far into nearby Primrose Cirque where avalanches that descend from the south flank of Roberts Horn occasionally run onto the flatlands. The best beginner touring is done on—or along open slopes adjacent to—the Scenic Loop roadway.

Touring along the highway allows the option of turning back at any point along the route. As tourers become proficient, they can continue to the summit of the highway just 4.2 miles from the commencement of the tour. The Scenic Loop is a popular snowmobile play area.

Aspen Grove is easily reached from the Salt Lake and Provo areas by taking I-15 Exit 275 (Provo Canyon/800 North) and proceeding into Provo Canyon to the junction with the Alpine Scenic Loop (SR-92).

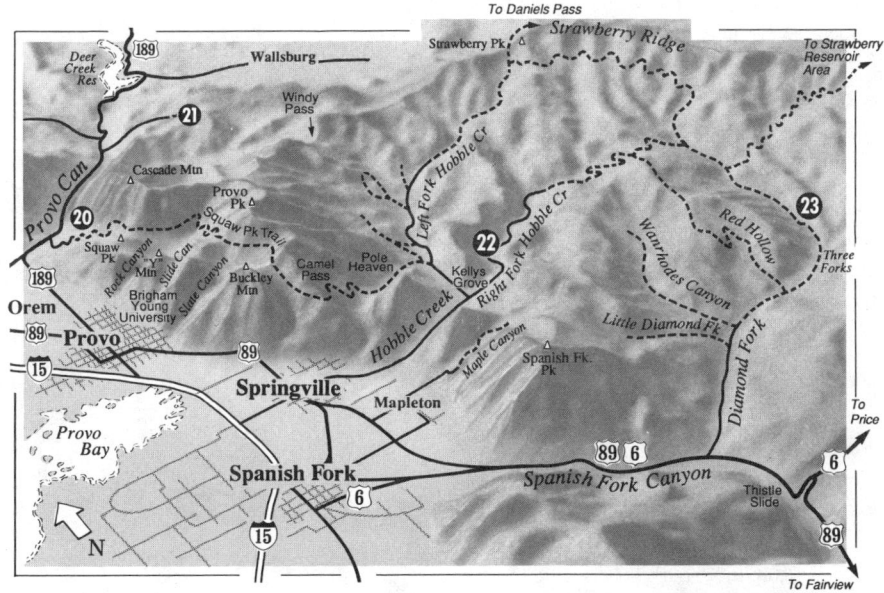

Figure 5.26 Several good opportunities can be found for beginning ski tours in the southern Wasatch Mountains.

Follow the Scenic Loop past the Sundance Ski Resort to its plowed end at Aspen Grove. Alternately, skiers from the Park City area should go south on US-40 through Heber City and take US-89 into Provo Canyon. The Scenic Loop turnoff is about three miles downcanyon from the Deer Creek Reservoir dam.

SOUTHERN WASATCH

Due to their extremely low elevations, many of the beginner touring areas in the Southern Wasatch are relatively mediocre. While the beginner touring areas in the Cottonwood canyons are located at elevations of approximately 8000 feet, most beginner areas in the southern Wasatch are more than 2000 feet lower. At such low altitudes snow accumulations are predictably—and considerably—less. Because a number of beginner areas are located on the leeward flank of the Wasatch, snowfalls there can be even less than would otherwise be expected. Since temperatures are generally warmer at the lower elevations, the touring season is considerably shorter. Most of the southern Wasatch beginner routes described are best toured between the middle of December through mid-February.

CHAPTER 5. WASATCH BEGINNER TOURS

Figure 5.27 The Squaw Peak Trail, which winds along the west slope of the Wasatch between Provo Canyon and the Left Fork of Hobble Creek, provides unsurpassed vistas of Utah Lake and the surrounding communities.

South Slopes of Provo Canyon

Ski touring areas north of the Provo River were described in the previous section, which covered the central Wasatch Mountains. The Squaw Peak/Provo Peak massif is included in the southern Wasatch.

⓴ Squaw Peak Trail. The Squaw Peak Trail is a very popular summer roadway that traverses south from near the mouth of Provo Canyon to Hobble Creek Canyon east of Springville. Much of the Squaw Peak trail is a jeep road, and during winter it is suitable only for the advanced skier. The first five or six miles of the paved roadway, partially illustrated in Figure 5.27, offers some excellent terrain for the beginner. The road is wide and ascends gradually. Nearby clearings provide numerous opportunities to test one's skill in virgin snow, and several scenic viewpoints offer places for resting. The Squaw Peak Trail is also popular among snowmobile operators, so expect to share the road with them.

SOUTHERN WASATCH

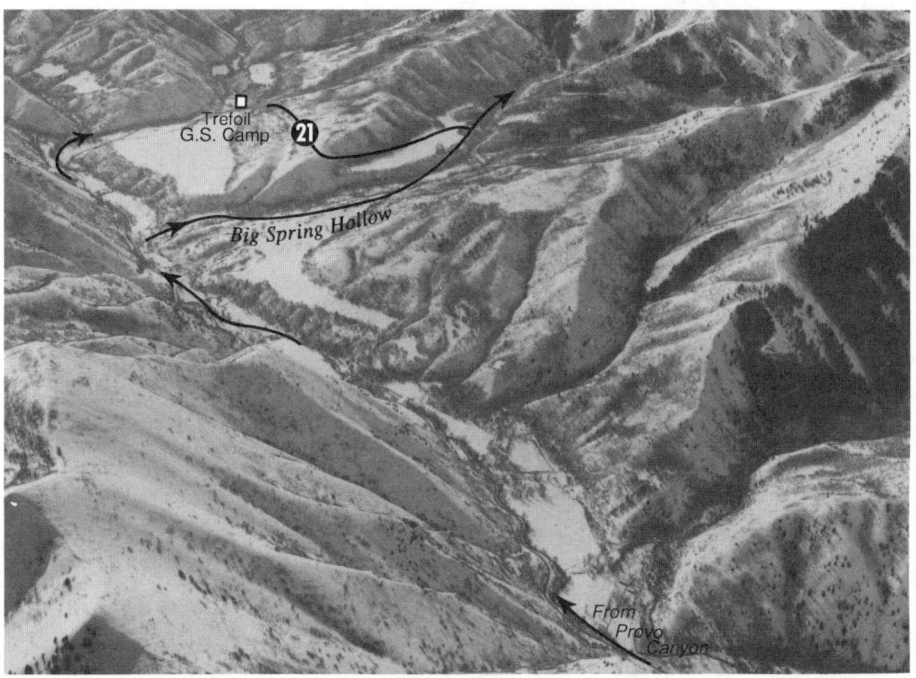

Figure 5.28   The Big Spring Hollow area provides a wonderful option for beginners when snow conditions are suitable.

The Squaw Peak Trail commences from US-189 approximately 1.5 miles into Provo Canyon. The trail's turnoff south is located 5.3 miles east of I-15 Exit 275 (Provo Canyon/800 North).

㉑ South Fork Provo River. The meadows and jeep roads in Provo River's South Fork have good potential for beginning cross country skiers. Most of the lands along the canyon's narrow access road are privately owned and rarely toured, but the City of Provo owns several hundred acres in and near Big Spring Hollow, source of a large percentage of the city's drinking water. This public property is near the end of the road at an elevation of about 6000 feet, so the skiing is often quite good between mid-December and mid-February.

Big Spring Hollow is currently under permit to the Big Spring Riding Stables, a small business that provides a horse-drawn sleigh ride service in the wintertime. According to Provo officials, the operators of the riding concession welcome cross country skiers. No snowmobiles are allowed on the property. Parking is limited in winter, but this seldom creates a problem.

From the riding stables, a jeep road and parallel bridle path follow

Big Spring Hollow westward for about two miles through wooded areas and several large open meadows to the spring. Both the road and the path can be delightful alternatives, depending on recent horse traffic. The elevation gain is about 700 feet. A spectacular waterfall can be seen below the spring, which is on the left (south) side of the canyon near the end of the road. The Provo School District has a summer camp for fifth graders at this beautiful spot each summer.

Another nice touring route to Big Spring commences at the end of the South Fork's plowed road. This alternative reduces the climb by 250 feet and increases the distance by about a half mile. Go through the Camp Trefoil gate and walk or ski for about 100 yards to a jeep road that intersects from the right (north) and traverses to a plateau that offers a superb view of the South Fork and Mount Timpanogos beyond. The road climbs for another 0.4 mile to a gate and a Great Western Trail sign. Continue beyond the gate (non-motorized traffic is welcome) for about a mile to the intersection with the Big Spring Hollow road described in the previous paragraph. The spring is about a mile farther up the hollow.

The situation in the South Fork could change drastically in the near future. A private developer is currently negotiating with the City of Provo to build a "world-class" golf resort on the Big Spring property and other adjacent land. The developer has stated that the project will also include cross country skiing. Canyon residents are naturally concerned about the effect of increased traffic on the winding road, and many Provo citizens worry that chemicals used on the golf course will negatively affect their water supply. Since the city purchased the property for the specific purpose of protecting that water, the issue has sparked considerable controversy.

The Big Springs Hollow area is reached by exiting US-189 at Vivian Park (about five miles from the mouth of Provo Canyon at the western terminus of the Heber Creeper) then taking a narrow, winding paved road southeast for 3.4 miles. The Trefoil Ranch Girl Scout camp is another mile upcanyon from Big Spring Hollow.

Hobble Creek/Diamond Fork Area

Very little good beginner touring terrain is available east of Springville or Spanish Fork. Most of the available terrain is on very low elevation lands away from major storm tracks. Snow depths are unpredictable in the two areas to be described. Those who become bored with touring in the alpine canyons of the Central Wasatch will welcome the diversion of

Figure 5.29 Since it is primarily on National Forest land, the Right Fork of Hobble Creek is the preferable alternative for cross country skiers.

touring amid the piñons and junipers along the back side of the Spanish Fork Peak massif. Only two areas are practical for beginner touring: the Right Fork of Hobble Creek, and the rolling hills terrain in the proximity of Diamond Fork.

㉒ **Right Fork of Hobble Creek.** Kelly's Grove, at the fork of Hobble Creek Canyon above Springville, is a popular summer recreation area for residents of southern Utah Valley. Initially, the canyon is quite narrow, but after it forks, both branches open and widen. Nearly all flatlands and foothills of Hobble Creek's Left Fork are privately owned; the fork has the highest incidence of threatening "No Trespassing" signs in Utah. The Right Fork of Hobble Creek is the opposite. Except for a small parcel of private land about 4 miles up the fork, all land is part of the National Forest. The two forks separate at Kelly's Grove.

The well-graded road up the Right Fork goes directly east, crosses a 7200 foot ridge, and joins the Diamond Fork drainage to be described in the following section. The initial 5 miles of roadway are relatively flat; the remainder of the road to the pass and beyond has several switchbacks on it. The initial flat portion is well suited for beginners.

The first mile of road beyond Kelly's Grove is plowed by the City of Springville. A parking area is located at the Forest Service gate. Expect some snowmobile traffic. About a mile from the gate is a Forest Service campground well-suited for a winter picnic. The flats between the gate and the campground make an excellent area for practice touring.

The City of Springville, owner of the old "Jolly's Ranch", is attempting to establish a mechanically packed track in the proximity of the ranch, but as of the 1991-92 ski season have had no success in finding funds to accomplish their goal.

To get to Hobble Creek Canyon from I-15, go east at Exit 263 (Springville/Mapleton) and follow 400 South Street into Springville. Cross Main Street and continue east on 400 South to 1300 East Street. Turn right at 1300 East onto Canyon Road and follow it into the canyon. Another mile of travel brings one to the clubhouse of the Hobble Creek Golf Course. Golf course management does not permit cross-country skiing. The pavement branches 0.5 mile past the clubhouse; the left branch leads to the Left Fork; the right branch leads to the Kelly's Grove park and campground that are operated by the City of Springville. The plowed road into the Right Fork ends 1 mile past Kelly's Grove.

㉓ Diamond Fork. Under properly abundant snow conditions, Diamond Fork offers excellent beginner touring opportunities. Uinta National Forest personnel who have skied in the area advise that touring can be "variable to excellent" during the latter part of December and through January and February.

Diamond Fork is the drainage immediately southeast of Spanish Fork Peak. Only a small part of Diamond Fork intercepts snowmelt from the east flank of the peak. Most of the water for Diamond Fork originates from the west slope of Strawberry Ridge, a major divide about 17 miles east of the Spanish Fork massif. It is included in this section only because of the scarcity of good beginner terrain in proximity of the main Wasatch ridge. As described previously, a road connects Diamond Fork with the Right Fork of Hobble Creek.

Potential tourers should be warned that Diamond Fork spans an elevation range between 5000 and 8000 feet. Touring can commence anywhere along the Diamond Fork roadway, depending on the availability of snow. The road is generally plowed until it reaches Three Forks (elevation 5600 feet), where a Forest Service gate stops any further vehicular travel. The Forest Service permits snowmobiles in Diamond Fork and one of its tributaries, Wanhrodes Canyon, but they are restricted to a 100-foot wide corridor along the road.

Diamond Fork is easily reached from I-15. Simply exit the freeway at Spanish Fork and head southeast into Spanish Fork Canyon. Diamond Fork leaves US-6/50/89 about 10 miles from the freeway exit. The Three Forks gate is about 10 miles from the turnoff.

SOUTHERN WASATCH

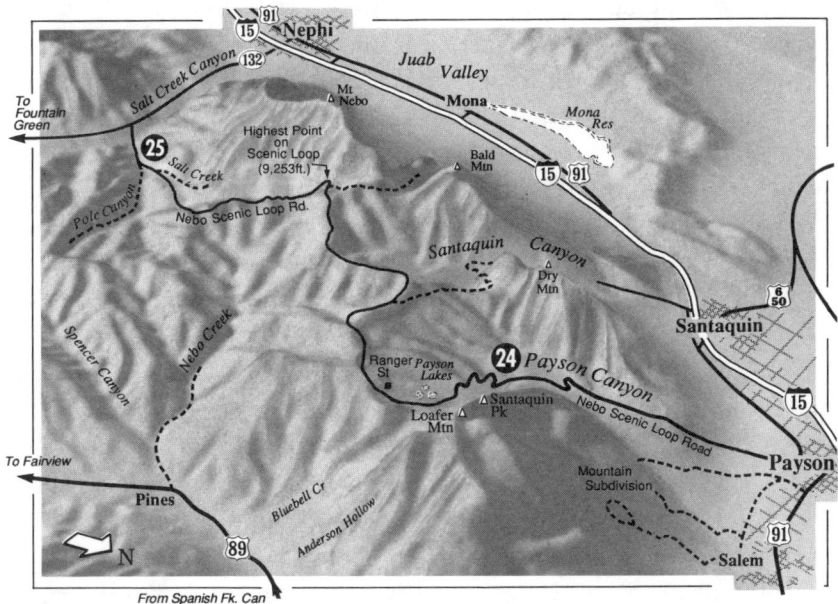

Figure 5.30 The Nebo Loop highway connecting Payson and Salt Creek canyons provides access to several touring areas for skiers at all levels.

Mount Nebo Area

The Mount Nebo massif is the southernmost massif of the Wasatch Mountains. It is one of the most spectacular regions in the range. The massif rises 7000 feet from the Juab Valley floor and terminates with Mount Nebo, at 11,877 feet, the highest summit in the range. The Mount Nebo Wilderness—the largest of the Wasatch Front wilderness areas—protects the most scenic region from any future commercial exploitation.

Most of the canyons that access the massif are impractical for beginners. Payson Canyon, however, provides an indirect access from the north, and Salt Creek Canyon provides direct access from the south. The Nebo Loop, a 24-mile paved Scenic Byway, connects Payson and Salt Creek Canyons.

Three areas have terrain suitable for beginners: Payson Canyon, Salt Creek, and Pole Canyon.

㉔ Payson Canyon. Of all the beginner touring areas of the southern Wasatch, Payson Canyon stands out as best. The beginner route commences at the Forest Service gate near the mouth of Payson Canyon and follows the Nebo Scenic Loop. Because the road is paved, wide, and of gentle grade and smooth curves, the ability to turn on one's skis may not even be necessary. The entire 24-mile length of the Scenic loop is groomed weekly for snowmobiles, so if a tourer becomes incapacitated, help is usually close at hand. The road is sufficiently wide that collisions between man and machine can be easily avoided. Perhaps the nicest feature of the route is its capacity to function as a gauge of one's abilities: the more skillful one becomes on skis, the farther he may wish to proceed along the highway. Payson Canyon's northern aspect almost guarantees good quality snow, especially during the colder months of winter.

The first three miles of roadway follow the bottom of the canyon, but during the next two miles the road switchbacks onto a gently-ascending, wide plateau with many open areas for practice turning. As the terrain opens, so do the mountain panoramas of nearby Santaquin Peak, Loafer Mountain, Utah Valley, and distant Mount Timpanogos.

Payson Canyon is most easily reached by leaving I-15 at the Payson Exit and following Main Street into town. At the traffic light turn east onto 100 North Street (also known as SR-6) and continue east to Sixth East Street. Turn right (south) and follow Sixth East Street past the beautifully restored Peteetneet School through the city and into Payson Canyon. The road is gated at the Maple Dell area, about five miles from Payson.

㉕ Salt Creek Canyon. Salt Creek flows south along the eastern flank of Mount Nebo before swinging westward to dump into Juab Valley at Nephi. Its canyon is very narrow and confining with little room for offroad exploration. An unplowed Forest Service road that follows the creek provides several miles of good touring when snow conditions allow. A couple of campgrounds along the way are convenient rest stops.

To get to Salt Creek Canyon, take the SR-132 exit off I-15 at Nephi and drive east about 4.5 miles to a fork. Bear left toward the Nebo Scenic Loop. The road is closed to motor vehicles about a half mile from its junction with SR-132. The elevation at the end of the plowed highway is 5800 feet.

Skiers can follow the road up Salt Creek Canyon for about five miles where it ends at a picnic area. The road is open to snowmobiles, but they are restricted to a 100 foot corridor along the roadway.

Pole Canyon. Pole Canyon is a tributary to Salt Creek. It joins Salt Creek about 2 miles from the turnoff at SR-132. Pole Canyon has a road in it that is also open to snowmobiles. One can continue along this road as far as snow and physical conditions permit.

SOUTHERN WASATCH

Figure 5.31 Mount Nebo is the southernmost and the highest peak in the Wasatch Mountains.

Nebo Scenic Loop. The south terminus of the Nebo Scenic Loop joins Salt Creek about two miles upstream from Pole Canyon. The Scenic highway's pavement is black and south exposed (hence not particularly attractive for those seeking fluffy powder), but it can be toured under proper conditions and by those "desperate to go somewhere."

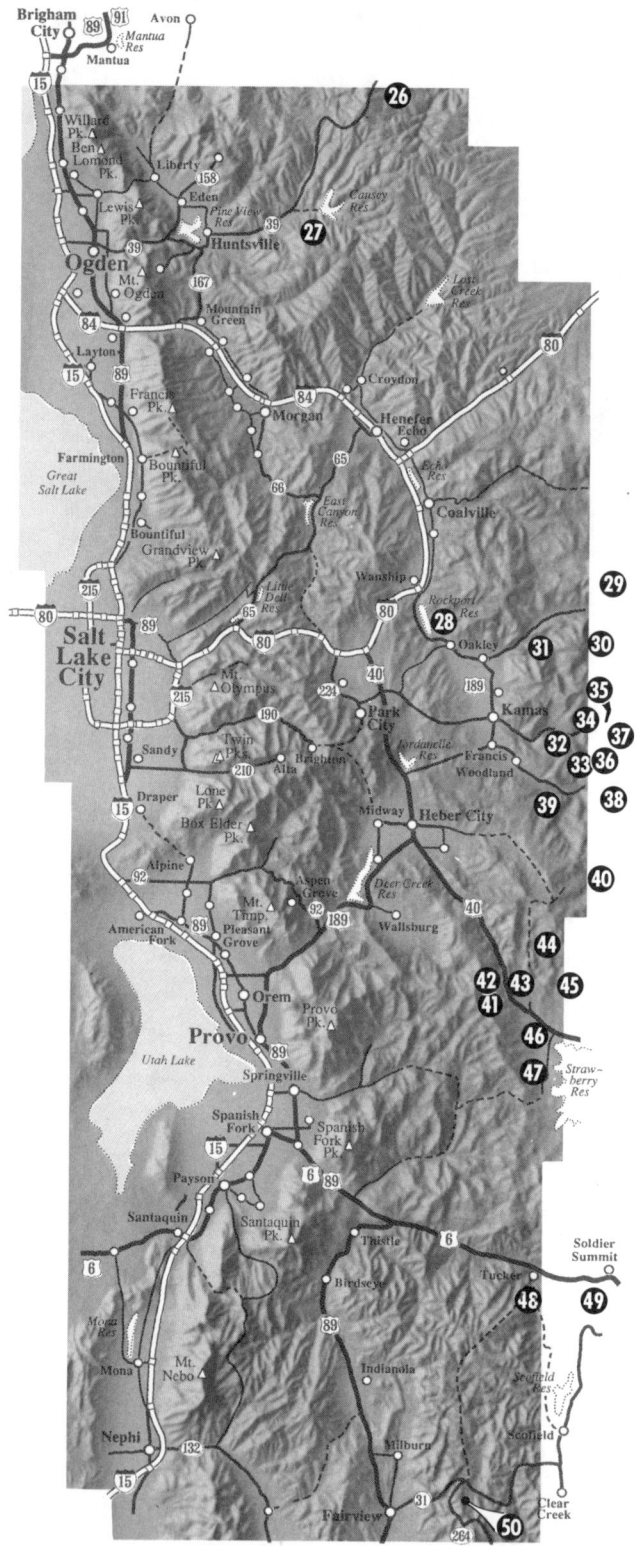

BEGINNER TOURS NEAR THE WASATCH

NORTHERN AREA

26. Monte Cristo 215
27. Causey Reservoir 216

WESTERN UINTAS

28. Rockport State Park .. 216
29. Upper Weber River ... 219
30. Smith-Morehouse 220
31. South Fork Weber R. . 220
32. Beaver Creek 222
33. Pine Valley 222
34. North Fork Provo R. .. 223
35. Mirror Lake Highway . 224
36. Soapstone Basin 226
37. Iron Mine Mountain .. 227
38. South Fork Provo R. .. 228
39. Bench Creek 230
40. Lake Creek 230

DANIELS SUMMIT/ STRAWBERRY

41. Daniels Summit 232
42. Lodgepole Cmpgnd.... 234
43. Telephone Hollow 235
44. Upper Strawberry R. .. 235
45. Co-op Creek 236
46. Doe Knoll 237
47. Strawberry Ridge 237

SOUTHERN AREA

48. Tucker 241
49. Soldier Summit 241
50. Wasatch Plateau 242

Chapter 6

BEGINNER TOURS NEAR THE WASATCH

Because ski area expansions and real estate developments have eliminated so much ski touring terrain in the proximity of Salt Lake City, we felt it necessary to include descriptions of beginner tours that are located outside of the Wasatch Mountains. This chapter covers a number of routes for novices in the Monte Cristo area, the western end of the Uinta Mountains, the Daniels Summit/Strawberry Reservoir area, Soldier Summit, and at the northern end of the Wasatch Plateau.

NORTHERN AREA

A number of ski touring alternatives can be found within a 45-minute drive of the Ogden area along SR-39, which goes east through the town of Huntsville, over 8800 foot Monte Cristo summit, and down to Woodruff on the Wyoming border.

㉖ Monte Cristo

Early in the season, SR-39 is drivable all the way to Monte Cristo summit and provides access to a number of roads and trails into the nearby National Forest. One superb ski tour is a Forest Service road that follows the ridge crest north for several miles with spectacular views of the Uinta Mountains to the east and the Wasatch to the west. Best of all, its elevation is sufficiently high to guarantee good snow when the golfers are still happily playing around in the valley.

In mid-winter, SR-39 is plowed only to the Ant Flats road, about

17 miles beyond Huntsville. Most of the snowmobilers seem to prefer to stay on SR-39, so Ant Flats is usually a quieter touring alternative. One can ski north all the way to the Hardware Ranch on a very gentle route that drops from 7050 to 5600 feet elevation in about 15 miles. Both the Ant Flats road and SR-39 over Monte Cristo are groomed for snowmobile use, so on busy weekend days ski tourers may find the many side roads and trails to be more inviting.

㉗ Causey Reservoir

The South Fork of the Ogden River is one of the main tributaries of Pineview Reservoir. The river parallels SR-39 for about 8.5 miles east of Huntsville and then forks. The right fork flows near a county road, also plowed in winter, that goes in a southeastward direction to the Causey Reservoir dam. Several jeep roads and trails around and near the reservoir are suitable for skiing, but much of the surrounding terrain is too steep for beginners. The easiest touring alternative, Skull Crack Canyon, drains into the south arm of the reservoir and is fairly gentle for two or three miles. Elevation at the reservoir is 6700 feet, so skiing is best in mid-winter.

WESTERN UINTAS

The west end of the Uinta Mountains is located about 50 miles from Salt Lake Valley and provides many touring opportunities for those willing and able to drive that far. Figure 6.1 provides an overview of options to be discussed in this section. The touring route and terrain information presented here is not detailed. Anyone wishing to explore this area may want to purchase appropriate topographical maps and/or Alpentech's *Uinta Backcountry Map #1*. Information is also available from the Forest Service's Kamas Ranger District Office (783-4338) and the Heber Ranger District Office (654-0470).

㉘ Rockport State Park

The town of Rockport was an early settlement on the Weber River at the mouth of Three Mile Canyon. It received its name in 1867 when a stone fort was built there to protect residents from marauding Indians. The site of the old town has long been covered by the waters of Rockport Reservoir, part of Rockport State Park.

WESTERN UINTAS

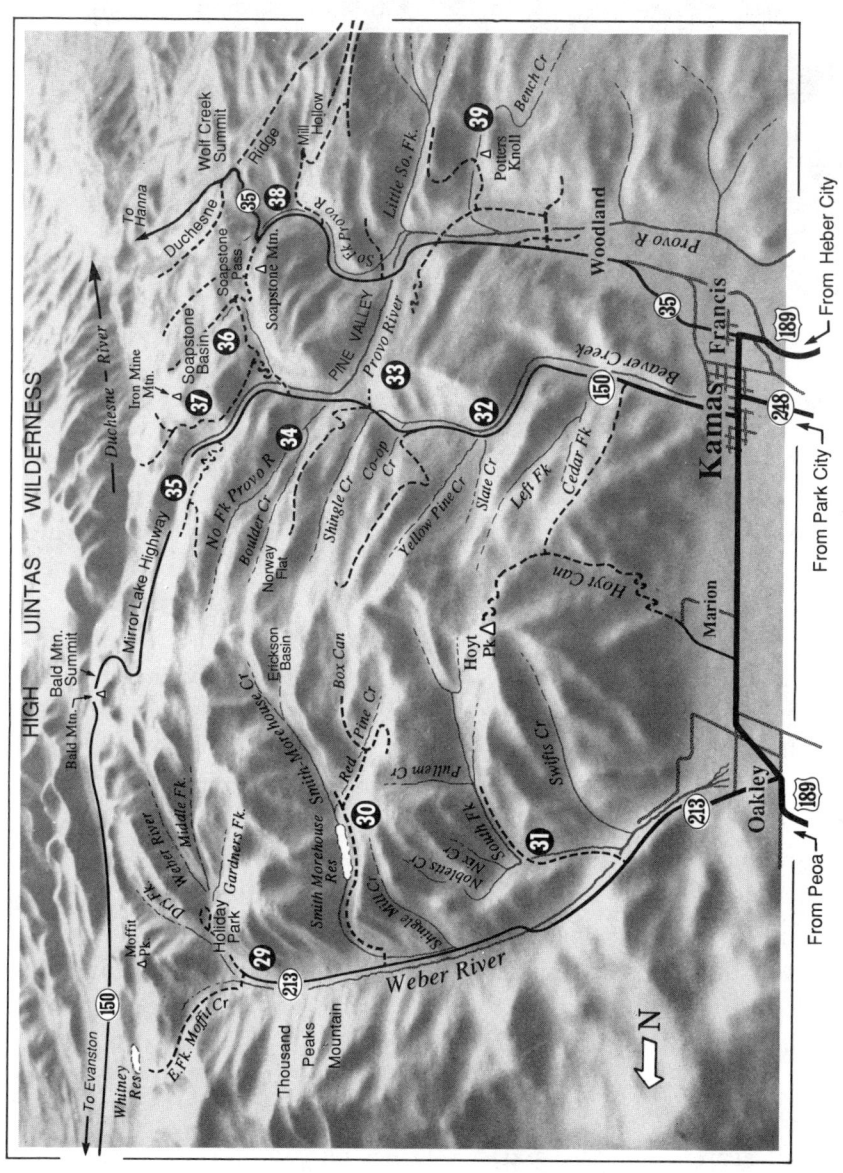

Figure 6.1 Increasing numbers of Wasatch Front ski tourers are making the 50-mile drive to canyons near Oakley, Kamas, and Woodland for their winter recreation.

Figure 6.2 Mary Hanscom enjoys a day of skiing and wildlife observation in Cotton Canyon, near Rockport State Park.

Traditionally, the park has been busy for only about three months of each year when it is invaded by boaters and sailboarders. During spring and fall, a few fishermen visit the park, but the place has been almost deserted during winter. A few years ago, directors of the Utah Division of Parks and Recreation decided to increase winter visitation by grooming a few miles of trail in and near the reservoir for cross country skiing. The area provides winter range for deer, eagles, and many smaller mammals and birds, so it's a delightful place to tour during the cold months of the year. Snowfalls were so marginal during the early 1990's that the track was never set. 1993 was a different story; record snow depth and low temperatures enabled Park personnel to maintain excellent tracks for much of the winter.

Rockport Reservoir is just south of Wanship, a small town located approximately 27 miles east of Salt Lake City on I-80. From Wanship, drive south on US-189 for 5 miles to the park entrance. The trail system starts at the end of the plowed road (about 3 more miles) on the east side of the reservoir. A small daily fee may be charged for use of the park.

The trail system has two parts, one in the campgrounds near the reservoir and the other in a nearby canyon. Both are suitable for beginners. The easiest loop is about two miles long and follows roads through the Cedar Point and Juniper campgrounds. The other trail is on private land in Cotton Canyon, but the landowner has granted permission for people to ski two or three miles up to a locked gate and corral. The

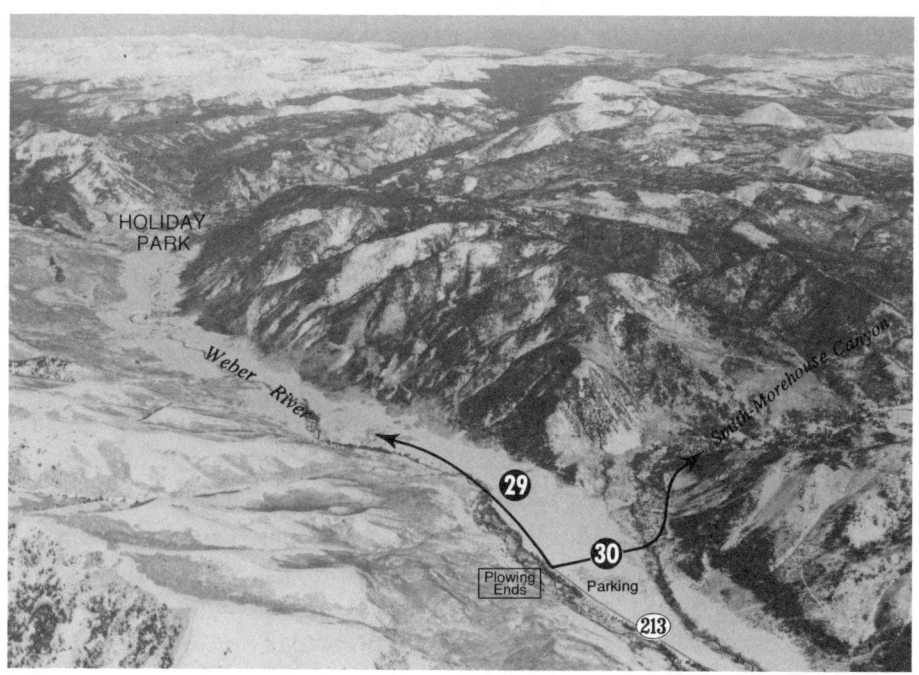

Figure 6.3 The road in the Weber River valley above the Smith-Morehouse turnoff is not plowed in winter and is ideal for cross country skiers.

upper part of this canyon is the most likely area to view deer and eagles, so it is highly recommended that tourers ski all the way to the gate.

㉙ Upper Weber River

SR-213 leading east from Oakley parallels the Weber River for about 20 miles to a summer home area known as Holiday Park, first settled near the turn of the century by Feramorz Little, a former Mayor of Salt Lake City. Four main tributaries of the Weber River converge at this beautiful spot. Only the lower 12 miles of SR-213 are paved and plowed. Tourers can park at the end of the pavement and follow the unplowed roadway to Holiday Park.

This section of the Weber flows through an almost flat, wide-open canyon with views of the mountains all around. The property on both sides of the road is privately owned and posted, *but the road is maintained by the county and open to the public.* The tour begins at an elevation of 7400 feet, which guarantees a long snow season, and rises only 600 feet in more than seven miles. The Weber River drainage bends to the southeast at Holiday Park, and the Middle Fork of the

Weber branches off to the south. Both lead to National Forest land with excellent intermediate and advanced touring areas.

③⓪ Smith-Morehouse Canyon

For almost 100 years, Smith-Morehouse Canyon has provided wood and water to settlers in the Kamas Valley. The canyon was named for an early logging company that operated in the area. In about 1920 the farmers of Oakley and Marion began work on a dam and a ditch to deliver irrigation water to their fields. The impounded lake has been a popular summer recreation destination ever since. The dam and reservoir were recently expanded by the Weber River Water Conservancy District and the canyon is being considered as a source of water for the rapidly expanding Park City metropolitan area.

The road into Smith-Morehouse Canyon branches from SR-213 about 12 miles east of Oakley, then ascends gradually through wooded terrain for 2.4 miles and 300 vertical feet to the reservoir. The road into the canyon is usually not plowed, so the tour normally commences at the end of the maintained section of SR-213. Problems with the dam in recent years have required that the roadway in Smith-Morehouse Canyon be plowed. If this situation continues, tourers may be able to drive to the dam and park there.

The Smith-Morehouse Canyon road continues 1.8 miles beyond the dam to Ledgefork Campground. Skiers who wish to follow the canyon beyond that point should bear left on a campground road that goes across a bridge to a summer parking area and trailhead. The trail crosses a foot bridge just beyond the parking area and follows the drainage on the right (west) side of the stream. From there, the canyon narrows and the the trail becomes more challenging. The next 2.6 miles is appropriate for a novice skier, although a couple of steeper spots may require a few traverses and kick turns. Most tourers will want to turn around at the base of the large cliff that separates the main Smith-Morehouse trail from the fork that goes right (southwest) up to Erickson Basin.

③① South Fork of the Weber River

Another cross country skiing alternative in the upper Weber River area is the South Fork of the Weber. Access to this drainage is gained by a road that goes eastward from SR-213 about five miles from the town of Oakley. The turnoff will be recognized by a large "Camp Oakley" sign. The lower 2.2 miles of the South Fork road is sometimes plowed by the

Figure 6.4 Smith-Morehouse Canyon is more popular in summer when fishermen are sometimes seen standing shoulder-to-shoulder along the shores of the reservoir. The canyon is more pleasant in winter when cross country skiers may encounter only an occasional snowmobile.

owners of the houses and cabins in the canyon, but it isn't sanded. The skiing can be excellent in a year when there is plenty of snow and when the temperature remains cold. The bottom of the canyon has two gates and many "No Trespassing" signs, *but the road is open to the public.* The gates are kept unlocked, and the signs state that the road may be used, but not the adjacent property. Please respect the wishes of the land owners. Since there is no place to park up the canyon, cars must be left beside the highway.

The road into South Fork Canyon climbs gently, gaining only about 100 feet of elevation over a distance of 2.0 miles, to a large open area with several summer homes. At that point, the road makes a sharp right turn and bridges the river. (Another road goes up more steeply to the left where the main road turns to cross the bridge, but this is not recommended for beginning skiers.) Immediately beyond the bridge the main road turns sharply to the left and continues along the south side of a meadow. (Again, there is another road that goes straight at that point, but that one is a private access road for cabin owners.) The elevation at this point is about 7000 feet.

At the far end of the meadow, the South Fork road bears right and continues climbing gradually in a southwesterly direction. The canyon narrows and becomes steeper, but beginners will enjoy about two more miles (another 400 feet of climbing) before turning around. More advanced skiers can continue as far as they like.

㉜ Beaver Creek Trail

For several years, the Forest Service has maintained a machine-packed track along the south side of Beaver Creek, parallel to the Mirror Lake highway (SR-150). The track starts 5.7 miles east of Kamas and basically follows the road, which gently climbs from 7100 to 7600 feet over 4.6 miles to the Pine Valley campground, where the highway drops down to cross the North Fork of the Provo River. Along the way, several access points are well marked and have areas plowed for parking. These provide a number of opportunities for up-and-back tours or point-to-point outings.

According to Forest Service signs, *the Beaver Creek trail is closed to foot traffic, dogs, and snowmobiles.* It is on the opposite side of the valley from the road, making traffic hardly noticeable. Several campgrounds along the way have picnic tables and outhouses to provide all the comforts of home. A number of nearby side canyons may be explored if the snow is good, but these are a bit steeper and more difficult than beginning skiers may want to attempt.

㉝ Pine Valley

The Pine Valley Campground is about 10.5 miles from Kamas on SR-150. The Utah Department of Transportation (UDOT) plows a parking area for skiers and winter campers at the end of the campground access road, and the Forest Service is considering establishing a groomed track in the area. At present, tourers can ski around the campground and adjacent valley, connect with the the Beaver Creek Trail that ends nearby, follow a trail that traverses along the west side of Pine Valley to Woodland, or cross the Provo River and ski along an old jeep trail to the Soapstone road.

One popular touring option involves parking a car at the lower end of the Beaver Creek Trail and driving another car to the Pine Valley Campground to start the tour. After a short initial climb to intercept the Beaver Creek trail, the remainder of the five-mile tour is mostly

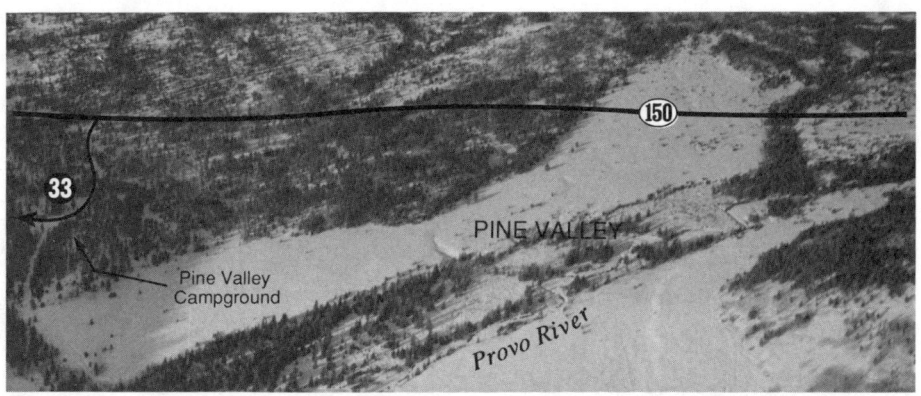

Figure 6.5 Pine Valley descends gradually for 4.5 miles from SR-150 (east of Kamas) to SR-35 (east of Woodland). The lower half of Pine Valley is privately owned, but beginners can enjoy the open, publicly-owned forest lands near the Mirror Lake highway.

a gradual downhill slide. Finding the trail is the only tricky part of this tour. The Pine Valley Campground is quite large, extending down from the highway almost a mile to the Provo River. Follow the road toward the Lower Provo River Campground. Just after the turnoff to the Group Campground, bear right off the road and cross the stream. A trail climbs up the hill in a westerly direction and intersects the Beaver Creek Trail.

The trail to Woodland starts at this same intersection. Instead of turning right (west) to go down Beaver Creek, simply bear left and head south along the west side of Pine Valley. This trail is much less traveled and may not be packed, but it is generally quite easy to follow. If in doubt, continue traversing at approximately the same elevation through open areas along the natural bench above the valley. The south end of the trail joins the Cedar Hollow jeep road, which descends to SR-35.

When the snowpack is sufficiently deep, skiers may want to cross the Provo River at the lower campground and follow a trail along the south side of the river that parallels the Mirror Lake highway for 4.2 miles to the Soapstone Basin road described in a later section. This route is not used very much, so it may be necessary to climb around a few fallen trees, but the sights and sounds of the river are worth the trouble.

34 North Fork of the Provo River

The North Fork of the Provo River crosses SR-150 about 11.4 miles above Kamas and flows into the main Provo River just south of the

Figure 6.6 The North Fork of the Provo River provides access to the upper lakes region of the western Uintas. It is also the location of The Utah Nordic Alliance's yurt.

highway. Good ski touring routes on both sides of the North Fork's streambed follow Forest Service roads and trails into the upper drainage. The canyon climbs very gradually for several miles and becomes quite narrow in spots. The first three miles are not a problem, but the stream must be crossed one or more times in order to go much farther. The area is closed to snowmobiles.

35 Mirror Lake Highway

The Mirror Lake Highway (SR-150) is currently plowed for 14.3 miles east of Kamas. A parking area is maintained at that point for snowmobilers and other National Forest users who wish to explore the west end of the Uinta Mountains in winter. A gate, closed from late autumn to late spring by UDOT, keeps the off-road vehicle drivers from messing up the snow.[1] The elevation at this point is 7760 feet.

The highway continues climbing gradually eastward and northward for another fifteen miles to Bald Mountain Pass before dropping into

---

[1] The Forest Service is planning to move the snowmobile trailhead down the road about three miles to the North Fork crossing, where a 100-car parking lot would be constructed. The current plan is to continue plowing SR-150 to the existing gate to facilitate skier access to nearby touring areas. A groomed trail would be constructed parallel to the highway for snowmobiles.

Figure 6.7 The upper part of the Mirror Lake highway, passing through the "lumps and lakes" region of the western Uintas, affords many delightful options for spring skiing after the road has been plowed.

the Mirror Lake area. The entire length of the highway is groomed for snowmobilers and receives very heavy use. The elevation of Bald Mountain Pass is 10,700 feet, so this area has snow when beginners have nowhere else to ski. Unfortunately, the gate is sometimes closed before the snow covers the lower part of the road, so it might be wise to call UDOT (965-4104) or the Forest Service Ranger Station in Kamas (783-4338) before driving all the way from the Wasatch Front early in the season.

Most beginners will not be able to ski far enough in a day to get very close to Bald Mountain Pass, so late spring is the best time to plan a tour in this area. UDOT usually opens the highway over the pass sometime in June, long before the snow has melted off the high rolling terrain dotted by lakes and steep rocky peaks poking up like mushrooms from the alpine plateau (see Figure 6.7). Again, one should check with UDOT or the Forest Service to find out when the road is plowed. Good access points for skiers are Trial Lake, Lilly Lake, and Bald Mountain Summit. The best skiing is on the northwest side of

226 CHAPTER 6. BEGINNER TOURS NEAR THE WASATCH

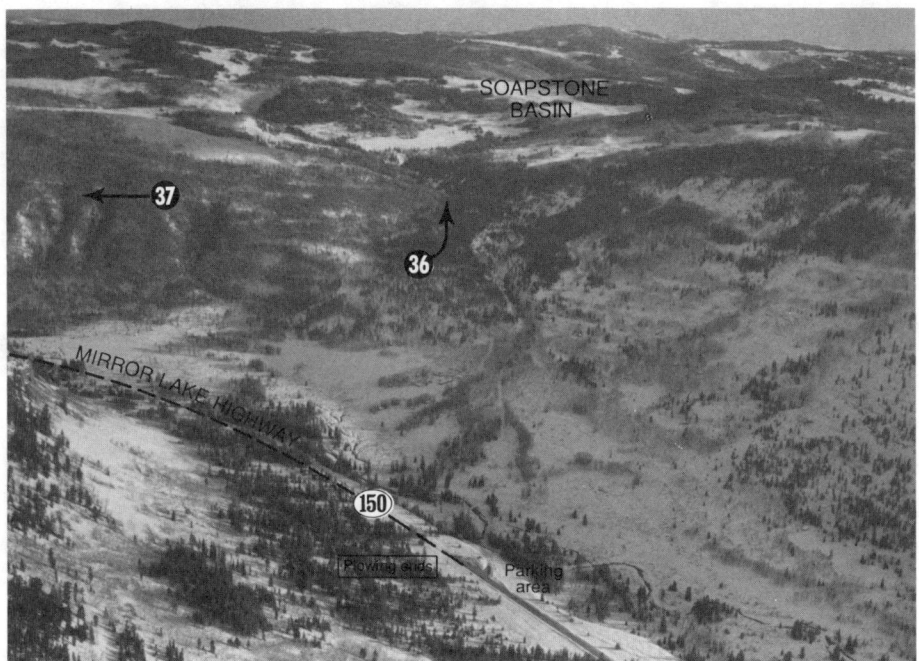

Figure 6.8 Soapstone Basin is a popular destination for skiers and snowmobilers. Its high elevation guarantees good snow for at least six months of each year.

the highway, and the best time of day is early morning, when the snow surface is sufficiently hard to support the weight of a skier.

㊱ Soapstone Basin

Another touring alternative from the end of the plowed section of SR-150 is to follow the groomed snowmobile road that branches to the right (south) and leads to Soapstone Basin. (See Figures 6.8 and 6.9.) The route passes Camp Roger, a summer camp operated by the Salt Lake YMCA, and climbs about 1300 feet over 5.8 miles on a winding road to Soapstone Pass, a high ridge overlooking the South Fork of the Provo River to the west and south. Along the way, numerous open meadows and powder slopes provide terrain for practicing one's skiing skills.

The road enters Soapstone Basin 4.1 miles from the Mirror Lake Highway and crosses the basin on the way to the pass. There are two excellent ski touring opportunities in this area with significantly less traffic than the groomed road. First, at the sharp right switchback just before the last climb up to Soapstone Pass, an ungroomed road goes

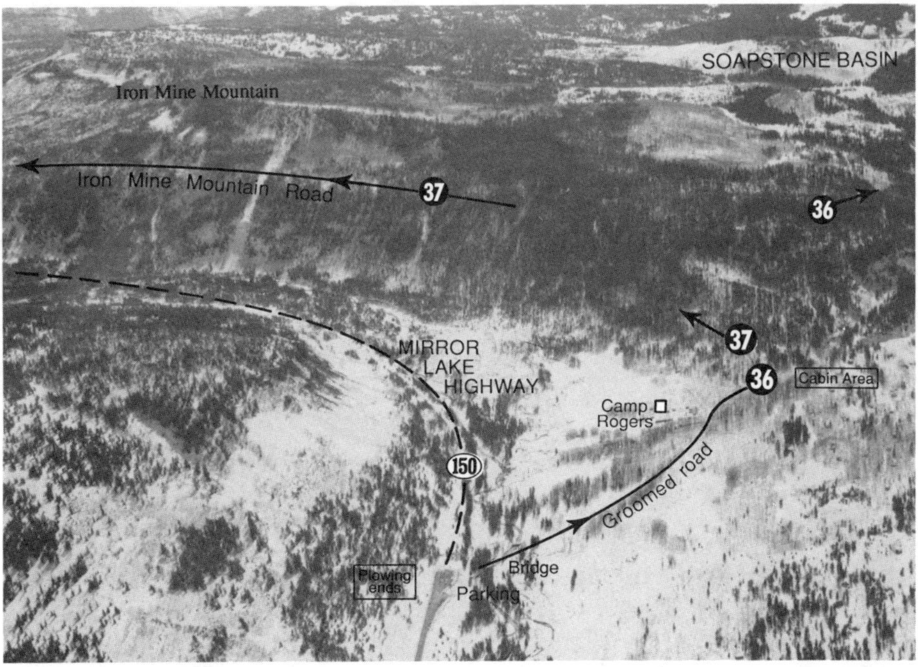

Figure 6.9 The road along the north flank of Iron Mine Mountain often has good snow early in the season when the Mirror Lake highway is not ready for skiing.

straight and continues east up through the valley for 5.3 miles, rising only 950 feet to an unnamed pass before dropping into the Duchesne River drainage. The second possibility in Soapstone Basin is a road that traverses east from Soapstone Pass. The road stays at about constant elevation along the north-facing slope and is sheltered by trees most of the way.

A final alternative that should be mentioned is to follow the groomed Soapstone road as it continues south over Soapstone Pass to join SR-35, which descends to the Woodland trailhead described in the next section. The disadvantage of this point-to-point tour is the 25-mile car shuttle.

㊲ Iron Mine Mountain Road

The Iron Mine Mountain road, partially pictured in Figure 6.9, is one of the most delightful areas for beginning skiers in the Uinta Mountains. The tour commences from the parking area described in the previous section and for the first two miles follows the groomed Soapstone road. The Iron Mine Mountain road is a less-traveled jeep road that continues straight at a sharp right switchback about half way to Soapstone Basin. Few snowmobilers choose this option since they usually follow the path of least resistance along the groomed roadway. The Iron Mine Mountain road gains about 1200 feet over 5.6 miles as it traverses along the north side of the mountain, high above the Mirror Lake highway. Views of the valley below are superb, and the snow is protected from sun and wind by aspens and firs all the way.

More ambitious tourers can continue by bearing right (south) at a fork in the road and climbing another 1.4 miles to a ridge with an incredible panorama of the "High Uintas." From the ridge, the road descends gradually for 1.4 miles to Iron Mine Lake, a fine spot for lunch and a well-deserved rest. For tourers who feel *really* ambitious, the return trip to the car can be accomplished by continuing over the ridge south of the lake and dropping down through Soapstone Basin.

38 South Fork of the Provo River

SR-35 going east through Francis and Woodland leads to a number of ski touring areas suitable for beginners. The main Provo River turns north 5.5 miles east of Woodland and passes through private land in Pine Valley to join the Mirror Lake highway. The South Fork continues straight east, adjacent to SR-35, to its headwaters at Wolf Creek Summit. This road is currently plowed about two miles into the South Fork drainage, and a snowmobile parking area is maintained at that point. The future, however, is uncertain. Despite vehement opposition of many National Forest users, local residents, and nearby land owners, intense lobbying by oil interests resulted in an "improvement" project that will widen and pave this road for tanker trucks shuttling between the Uinta Basin oil fields and refineries in Salt Lake.

Cross country skiers can follow one of three groomed roads, or a number of quieter but steeper side canyons may be explored. The main road (SR-35) climbs for 8.3 miles to almost 9500 feet elevation at Wolf Creek Pass on the Duschesne Ridge before descending eastward to Hanna and Duchesne. If this pass is the destination, be sure to turn right (south) where the road forks about 5.1 miles from the trailhead. If the snow isn't too deep, one can view a monument in the center of the fork commemorating the death of Macashi Coto, a Japanese aviator who crashed nearby on July 4, 1929, while flying over America. Unfortunately, a few modern-day "pioneers" have seen fit to disfigure the monument with their rifles, so each year the commemorative text becomes more difficult to read.

WESTERN UINTAS

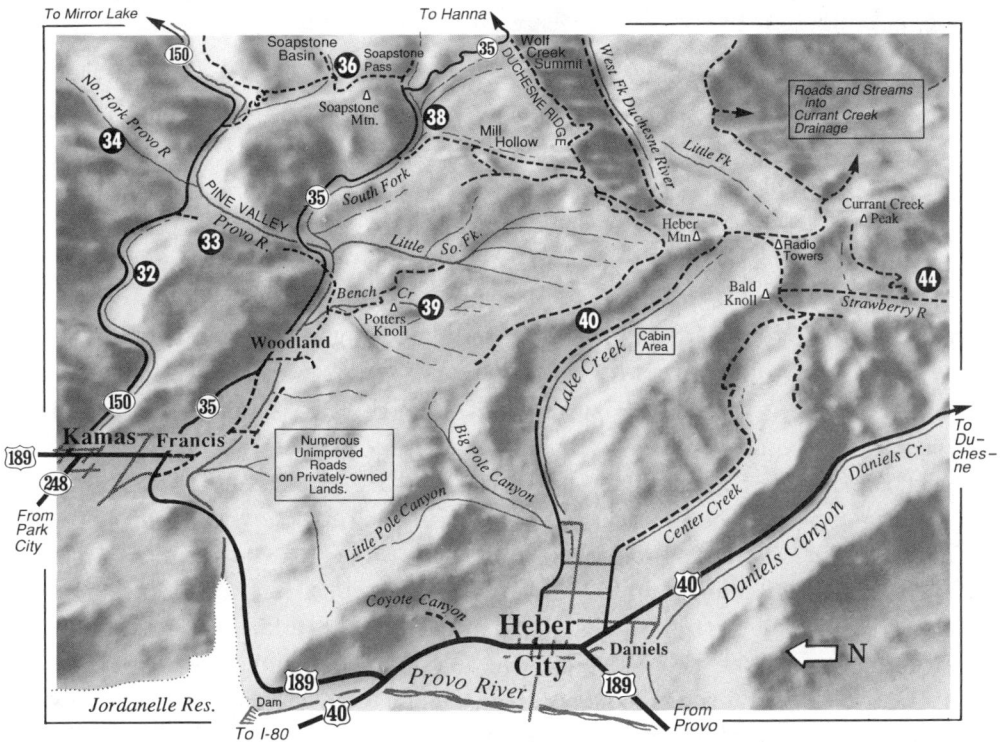

Figure 6.10 Novice ski tourers will find many enjoyable touring options in the hills and forests above Woodland and Heber.

Bearing left (east) from SR-35 at the above-mentioned monument leads to 9080 foot Soapstone Pass, described in a previous section. This route follows a groomed roadway through Dry Hollow for 1.9 miles to the pass. Several other routes may be taken to Soapstone Pass that avoid most of the snowmobile traffic, but all are likely to involve trail-breaking, and all traverse somewhat steeper terrain. Two examples are the Nobletts Creek and Iron Mine Creek trails, which climb northward to the ridge and intersect jeep roads that go east along the shoulder of Soapstone Mountain to the pass. Watch for National Forest trail signs along SR-35.

The third groomed road in the South Fork drainage passes through Mill Hollow. The road bears off to the right (south) from SR-35 about 2.7 miles from the parking area. It climbs in a southwesterly direction for 3.5 miles to Mill Hollow Reservoir and then continues for another 3.0 miles to a 9750 foot pass on the Duchesne Ridge. The road is packed for snowmobiles all the way to Lake Creek, east of Heber, as described in a later section.

㊴ Bench Creek

Bench Creek is another delightful alternative for beginning cross country skiers in the Western Uintas. Bench Creek drains into the Provo River from the south just above Woodland. To reach the trailhead, turn right on Bench Creek Road (between the Woodland Cash Store and the LDS church) and follow it across and up the Provo River for 3.4 miles. The trailhead is on the right between two brown houses. The touring route looks like a private road, but it is a public right of way that provides access to the National Forest. The only parking is along the highway, so be sure to pull over as far as possible.

After about a mile of basically flat skiing, the road bends to the left (east) and crosses Bench Creek. Skiers can follow the road as it climbs over a ridge and drops into the Little South Fork drainage, but some sections may be too steep for a novice. *Be sure to turn around before climbing a slope that is too steep to descend safely.* A better alternative is to turn right (south) immediately after crossing Bench Creek and to ascend the trail that parallels the stream. A trail follows the drainage all the way to the ridge overlooking Lake Creek above Heber, about 4.7 miles and 1600 vertical feet from Bench Creek Road. Only a few spots are sufficiently steep to cause concern, and these can be bypassed with a couple of switchbacks through the trees. Most of the trail passes through wooded areas with an occasional open meadow, and the ridge provides a spectacular panorama for those ambitious enough to go all the way to the top.

㊵ Lake Creek

SR-169, a road that leads to the headwaters of Lake Creek in the mountains east of Heber City, is groomed for snowmobiles in the winter. To get to the Lake Creek trailhead, take Center Street east out of Heber City (one block north of the traffic light) and drive about seven miles to where the plowing stops. The elevation at that point is 6600 feet. From there, Lake Creek climbs steadily for 9.0 miles to a 9700 foot pass south of Heber Mountain that overlooks the Duchesne River to the east. The snowmobile route drops into this drainage before turning north and climbing to the pass, described in a preceding section, at the head of Mill Hollow.

A nice loop tour (that involves quite a long car shuttle) is to ascend Lake Creek and to descend, via Mill Hollow and the South Fork of the Provo, into Woodland.

Figure 6.11 Many beautiful ascent routes can be found in the Lake Creek drainage east of Heber City. With its spectacular view of Mount Timpanogos, return trips are even more delightful. *Inset:* Bill Stenquist enjoys a skating workout on the Lake Creek road.

DANIELS SUMMIT/STRAWBERRY

Strawberry Reservoir, completed in 1912, stores water that is collected from the Colorado River Basin and delivers that water to the Wasatch Front via a 3.8 mile tunnel into Diamond Fork, a tributary of Spanish Fork River. Main sources of water for the reservoir are Strawberry River and Co-op Creek, whose headwaters are in the southwest part of the Uinta Mountains. Strawberry Reservoir is located near the head of Daniels Canyon, about 20 miles southeast of Heber City on US-40.

Due to the distance from the metropolitan areas of the Wasatch Front, few skiers travel to this area, but this is expected to change as touring near the Front becomes more congested and as more skiers discover Daniels Summit and the Strawberry Basin. The owners of the Daniels Summit Inn are also planning to expand their operation to include maintaining a packed track and opening a restaurant and shop with cross country ski rentals.

The Forest Service has recently designated a few areas in the vicinity

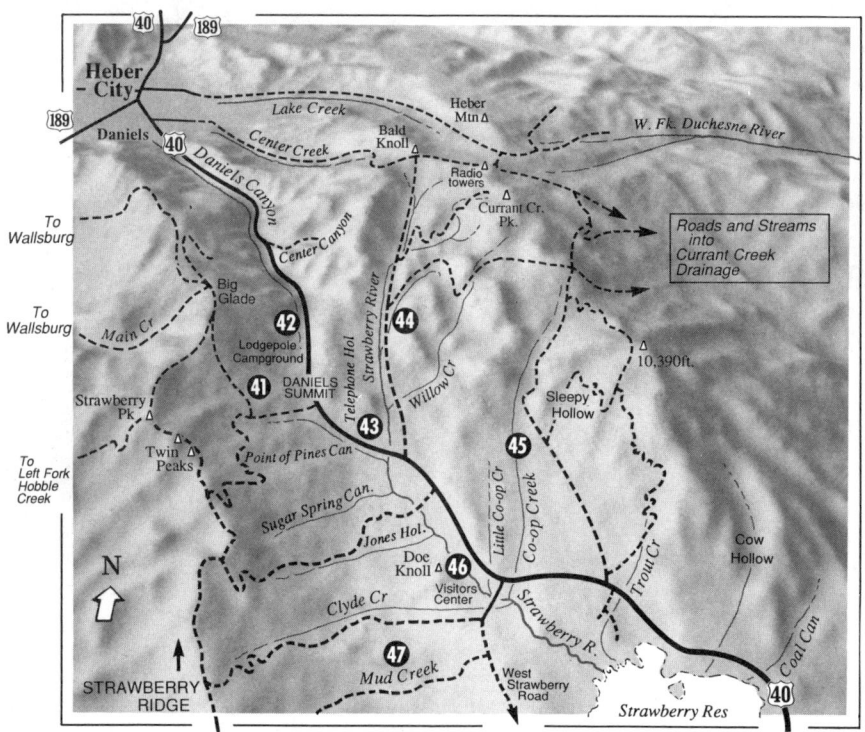

Figure 6.12 The area in the proximity of Daniels Summit and Strawberry Reservoir provides excellent opportunities for beginning ski tourers. Its high elevation assures good snow when other trails may not be suitable for skiing.

of Daniels Summit and Strawberry Reservoir for cross country skiers. Snowmobiles and other over-snow vehicles have not been restricted, but signs have been (or will be) erected to let everyone know that skiers are likely to be on the trail. Figure 6.12 depicts several touring possibilities.

㊶ Daniels Summit

At an elevation of 8000 feet, Daniels Summit is the high point along US-40. The summit is located about 17.5 miles from Heber City. Old timers reminisce nostalgically of a summit tavern, where one could purchase bootlegged liquor during Prohibition. Today, Daniels Summit is a favorite jumping-off place for winter recreational activities, with ski touring opportunities in all directions. This is a popular spot for snow machines, so it's best to avoid weekends if possible. No designated parking area exists at the summit, so care must be exercised to leave vehicles far enough to the side of the highway to avoid interference with traffic.

DANIELS SUMMIT/STRAWBERRY

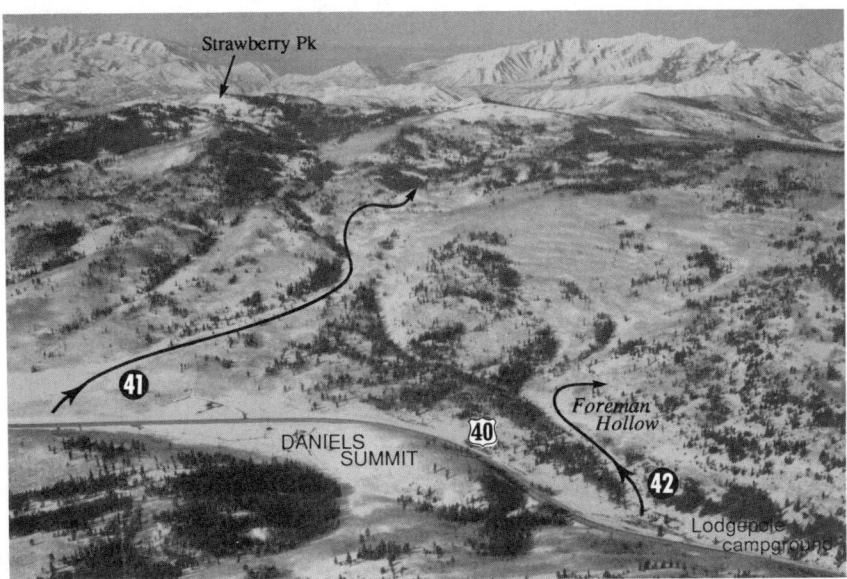

Figure 6.13 US-40 provides access to many touring routes in the vicinity of Daniels Summit. Skiers can enjoy incredible views of the Wasatch Mountains to the west from the Strawberry Ridge.

The best skiing near Daniels Summit is on the southwest side of US-40, on the slopes of Strawberry Peak. This peak is the beginning of Strawberry Ridge, which rolls gently to the south for almost 40 miles, so the touring possibilities in the area are limitless. The ridge achieves elevations as high as 9700 feet, assuring superb views and a long season of quality snow. Tourers may follow a number of Forest Service roads, but the terrain is sufficiently gentle and open to permit a tourer to ski almost anywhere. Avalanche hazards, while present, are less severe than in the steeper canyons of the Wasatch.

A particularly interesting possibility is to follow the Forest Service road system down along the north end of the Strawberry Ridge. The access road starts just southeast of Daniels Summit (at the Main Canyon sign) and climbs in a westerly direction for 1.6 miles to an intersection. One road bears left and traverses south along the Strawberry Ridge to Buck Springs. The other road—a better alternative for beginners— bears right (north) and traverses in a northwesterly direction along a ridge that provides great views of Heber Mountain to the east and many Wasatch peaks to the west.

Several roads intercept this route from the left (southwest). The first (4.8 miles from Daniels Summit) climbs back toward Strawberry Peak.

About one half mile beyond that, a second road drops down very steeply from a large open plateau called Big Glade and ends up in the town of Wallsburg near Deer Creek Reservoir. A combination of the terrain, the exposure to sun, and the 5700 foot bottom elevation make a tour to Wallsburg unsuitable for beginning skiers. Other roads branch off to the right (northeast) and descend to US-40. These are less exposed to sun, but they are also quite steep and not recommended. Most tourers prefer to return to their cars via their ascent route.

42 Lodgepole Campground

Lodgepole Campground is located about a mile northwest of Daniels Summit, near mile post 34. The Forest Service has designated and marked a four-mile loop west and south of the campground for hiking and cross country skiing. Signs along the trail inform visitors of local flora and geology. The lower end of the loop in and near the campground is suitable for beginning skiers, but the upper part is quite steep and heavily wooded.

The best touring option for a novice is to stay on the roads and in the open areas. In particular, one can ski from the lower end of the campground on a road leading down along Daniels Creek. In about a mile, a fenced area is encountered, but this can be bypassed on the uphill side by anyone wishing to continue farther downcanyon. The terrain becomes too steep for beginners about a half mile beyond the fence.

More adventurous tourers can follow the marked ski trail that ascends Forman Hollow, traverses north to Shingle Hollow, and then returns to the start. To get to this trail, turn right immediately after entering the campground and follow the signs with blue diamonds. You will soon go left on a trail that climbs up Forman Hollow. The trail ascends gradually for a few hundred yards and then steepens. The marked trail soon turns right and leaves the hollow. It switches back and forth up to a ridge and then traverses to the northwest for a mile or so. This section of the trail is high enough to allow a skier to overlook Daniels Canyon—a beautiful view indeed. The tough part is the descent. The trail enters a gully (Shingle Hollow) that it follows back down to the road mentioned in the previous paragraph. It's not too steep, and there's room for traversing and making kick turns, but this route is not for the faint of heart or the first-time tourer.

DANIELS SUMMIT/STRAWBERRY

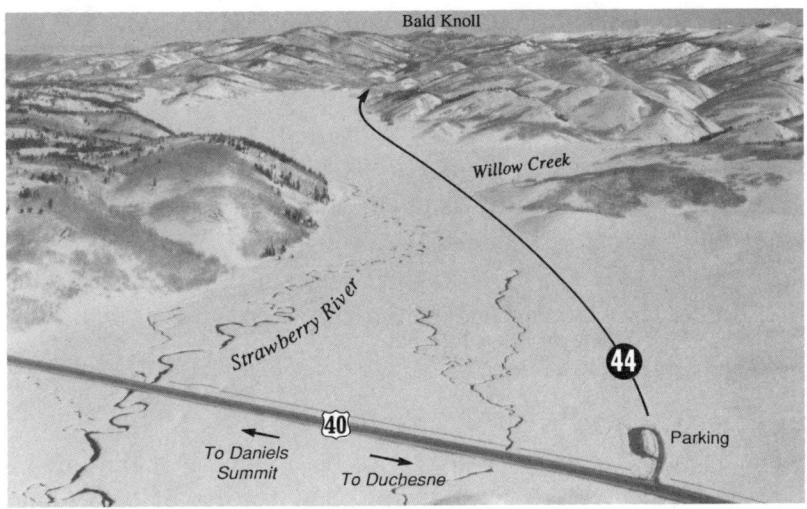

Figure 6.14 The upper Strawberry River meanders through a wide flat valley after descending from the slopes of the southwest Uinta peaks.

㊸ Telephone Hollow

The only area designated by the Forest Service for ski touring on the northeast side of US-40 is Telephone Hollow, which starts about 1.1 miles southeast of Daniels Summit, near mile post 37. The road up the hollow climbs gently in a northerly direction for about a mile to an intersection. Turn right (east) at that point and climb about 100 yards to the top of the ridge. The road continues over the ridge and drops down into the Strawberry River valley, which is described in the next section. An equally good alternative (without snowmobiles) is to go left (north) and follow the ridge. You can ski as far as you like through comfortably-spaced aspens and firs.

㊹ Upper Strawberry River

During the summer of 1888, some 700 soldiers from Fort Douglas (Salt Lake City), Fort Duchesne (the Uinta Basin), and Fort Bridger (southwestern Wyoming) assembled in the valley of the Strawberry River for major Army maneuvers, only the second of its kind to be carried out in the West. Each summer in recent years, the Uinta National Forest has sponsored an archeological dig at the site to unearth artifacts from that historical event.

As illustrated in Figure 6.14, winter visitors to the upper Strawberry River will not find evidence of the early soldiers or their modern-day investigators. The valley, a wide snow-covered meadow with several streams meandering through it, extends north from US-40 about 3 miles east of Daniels Summit. The only signs of civilization are the snowmobiles that use the road along the east side of the valley to access the high peaks and canyons to the north.

One of the best times to visit the upper Strawberry is late winter, when the snow in lower areas is no longer suitable for ski touring. Migrating birds visit the area on their way south in March and April. Sandhill cranes, hawks, and eagles may be observed in abundance early in the morning as they feed along the river. If you're lucky, you may see an occasional coyote or fox venture out of the nearby hills to join a groggy ground squirrel for breakfast.

A parking area, complete with portable toilets, is maintained adjacent to the highway. Ski tourers can follow the road north along the right (east) side of the valley. Peace and quiet are more likely on the west side of the valley near the river, but it may be necessary to cross a few side streams along the way during early or late winter. The first 5.8 miles of the valley are almost flat, rising only about 500 feet. The road crosses to the west side of the river at that point, just beyond a large corral, and begins to climb a bit more steeply. Energetic skiers can continue for another 4.2 miles (and 1850 feet of elevation) to Bald Knoll, which overlooks Lake Creek and provides a vantage point for the high Uinta peaks.

Several drainages along the east side of the Strawberry valley are equally pleasant. The first is Willow Creek, which joins the Strawberry valley about 1.4 miles from US-40. Novices can enjoy following this canyon north and east to its crest—the ridge above Co-op Creek—about 4.6 miles and 1150 vertical feet from the Strawberry River. A second recommended alternative is Bjorkman Hollow, about 4.5 miles from the parking area. The route into the hollow is a bit steeper, but nice for a couple of miles. A third side drainage suitable for skiers begins at the large corral mentioned in the previous paragraph. Instead of crossing the river, one can bear right on a road that traverses along the east side of the river and then climbs more steeply to the summit of Currant Creek Peak on the ridge between the Strawberry River and Co-op Creek.

④⑤ Co-op Creek

The next major drainage east of the Strawberry River is Co-op Creek, so named because of a community livestock grazing arrangement in the area. Like the Strawberry River, it provides access to the peaks of the southwestern Uintas and is popular with snowmobilers. Also like the Strawberry, it is a delightful place to ski, particularly in early and late winter. A parking lot is plowed just east of the Strawberry Visitor Center on the north side of US-40.

The road along the main drainage of Co-op Creek climbs 1500 vertical feet in the first 8.2 miles to the ridge overlooking Currant Creek. Several Forest Service roads join at this point, all of which are good options if you want to proceed farther. The Currant Creek Feeder Canal, which crosses the road at that point, is part of the Central Utah Project that diverts water to the Wasatch Front via Strawberry Reservoir.

The only side canyon along the way that might be of interest is Sleepy Hollow, which comes in from the right (east) about 3.4 miles from the car. This route is a bit steep, but less traveled.

46 Doe Knoll

The Strawberry Visitor Center, visible in Figure 6.15, is located just off US-40 on the West Strawberry access road, about seven miles southeast of Daniels Summit. The building is not open in winter, but a nearby parking area is maintained for skiers and snowmobilers. The West Strawberry road is not plowed.

Doe Knoll is a small hill located across a large meadow behind the Visitor Center. It has been designated for cross country skiers. No established trail exists, but the vegetation around the knoll is sparse enough to allow one to follow any route that looks inviting. A nice four-mile loop circles the knoll, crossing a saddle on the north side and returning to the start. For those who wish a longer tour, much terrain is available to explore in the Jones Hollow drainage north and west of the knoll.

47 Strawberry Ridge

The West Strawberry road is not plowed beyond the Visitor Center parking area, so skiers can follow it all the way to the south end of the reservoir and beyond. Several ridges and drainages west of the road provide access to Strawberry Ridge, and most are ideal for cross country skiing. *Touring on the reservoir's ice is not recommended.*

Less than a mile south of the parking lot, a Forest Service road branches right (east) across a meadow and up the Clyde Creek drainage. The terrain is gentle at the lower end, but the road steepens as it approaches Strawberry Ridge. One can climb as far as endurance and

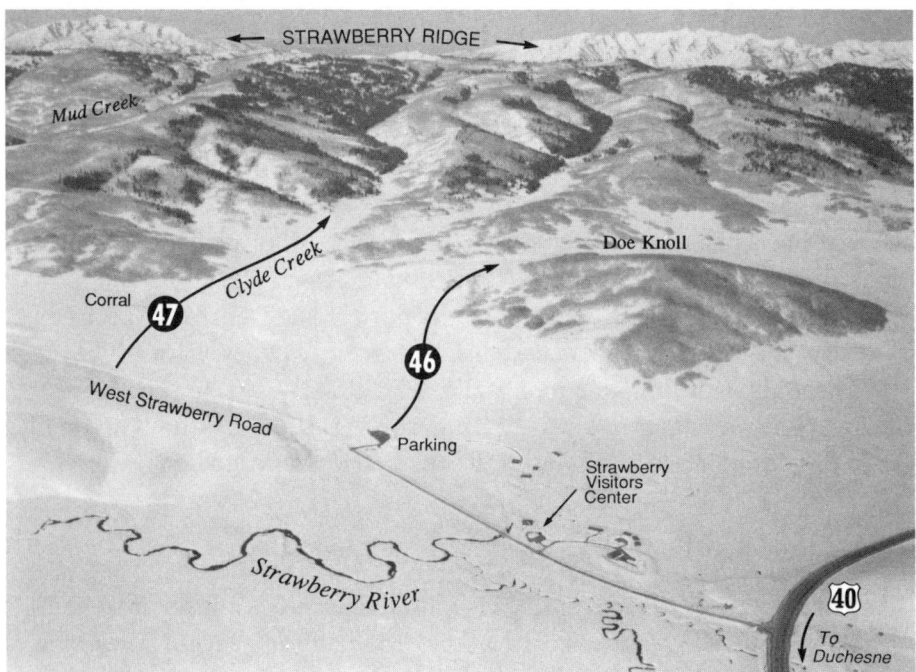

Figure 6.15 Strawberry Ridge, which extends about 40 miles south to Spanish Fork Canyon, is accessed from US-40 via several short canyons that intercept the West Strawberry Road.

skiing ability permit. Snowmobilers use this area, but not heavily. The total climb to the ridge is 1700 feet over a distance of about six miles. From the top, the view to the west and south is spectacular; the Wasatch peaks are just as impressive from the back side as they are from the front. From the top of the Clyde Creek drainage, one can ski southward along the ridge for about a mile to connect with the Mud Creek road, or return to the car via the ascent route.

Mud Creek intersects the West Strawberry road about 2.7 miles south of the Visitor Center. Like Clyde Creek that it parallels, the Mud Creek drainage climbs gradually for a couple of miles but steepens as it approaches Strawberry Ridge. Beginning skiers may not want to venture all the way to its crest.

A number of other roads ascend to the ridge from the southwest corner of Strawberry Reservoir, but all involve a considerably longer tour. Skiers who enjoy skating across the snow's crusty surface in springtime might even consider following one of these roads all the way to the Diamond Fork drainage described in the previous chapter.

SOUTHERN AREA

The average annual snowfall at the 8800 foot elevation of the Brighton-Alta area of the Central Wasatch is approximately 480 inches. Compacted, the snowfall results in a maximum seasonal snowpack of about ten feet, a more-than-adequate depth to cover the largest boulders and deadfalls. With the exception of some isolated alpine areas (such as the Mount Timpanogos massif) snowfall totals generally decrease as one radiates outward from the Central Wasatch. Snowfalls also diminish due to drops in elevation and to an area's location along storm tracks. Park City, at an elevation of 6900 feet and located only a few miles from Alta, receives only half the total snowfall as does Alta.

While tourers usually prefer deep snowpacks, they don't often require them. It is not unusual to view skiers (usually nordic!) scooting along snowpacks not even deep enough to cover dried June grass. Some tourers, for whom the sport has become a religion, kick and glide on faith alone.

This section has been assembled for the beginning tourer who would "break new ground" in search of the solitude often no longer available in the nearby canyons or along the west end of the Uinta Mountains. The tourer who doesn't mind sharing his trail with an occasional sagebrush or pinon pine—and associated wildlife—may find two areas of special interest: Soldier Summit and the Wasatch Plateau.

Soldier Summit

Soldier Summit (elevation 7450 feet) is a gently rolling pass at the head of Spanish Fork Canyon, a major drainage that transects the Wasatch near the southern end of Utah Valley. Spanish Fork Canyon contains two U.S. highways and a transcontinental railroad track. Numerous jeep roads radiate from the highway to public forest lands that commence generally a mile or two from the paved roadways. The forested areas located to the north of the canyon are part of the Uinta National Forest; those that lie to the south are managed by the Manti-LaSal National Forest.

Soldier Summit and Soldier Creek are named, at least according to one believable account, in honor of some Union soldiers who died there in a blizzard while enroute to die in the Civil War. The desolation of the area did not prevent its development as a community. The first scattered residences were established in the 1860's, and major growth commenced after railroads began laying tracks across the high pass.

240   CHAPTER 6. BEGINNER TOURS NEAR THE WASATCH

Figure 6.16   During the railroad's occupation of Soldier Summit, the desolation of the windswept community was eased considerably by the presence of a saloon. Today, the small community is on the verge of becoming a ghost town. Saloon Photo courtesy of Utah State Historical Society.

In 1919, after officials of the Denver & Rio Grande Western Railroad declared the summit a "division point," construction started on a hotel and 40 employee cottages.

Soldier Summit continued growing, eventually to include many new company-owned homes, a YMCA building, a swimming pool, a billiard parlor, and a schoolhouse. The presence of a saloon is rarely mentioned in writings describing the town's amenities; the presence of a brothel is never mentioned. Railroad maintenance operations at the summit included a classification yard, a passenger and freight station, a roundhouse and locomotive shops. Between 1925 and 1930, when the railroad abandoned it as a division point, the community housed some 300 residents.

Today, Soldier Summit is nearing the status of ghost town—that's what makes it an attractive locale for backcountry touring. Beginning tourers who venture to Soldier Summit should not expect to be greeted by magnificent panoramas of forest and alp. The broad and treeless expanse of the summit plateau will seem more like the desolate arctic than the familiar Wasatch. Potential tourers should be aware that the summit area is frequently swept by winds so fierce that one can capture the arctic ambiance without leaving the car. In touring at the Summit, novices are urged not to depart from established roadways when "whiteouts" caused by low clouds or drifting snow make route retracing along the flatlands almost impossible.

Outings to Soldier Summit should be planned as all-day affairs. The drive from Salt Lake Valley to the mouth of Spanish Fork Canyon takes about an hour, and it's nearly another hour's drive up the canyon to the summit. A brief, contemplative pause at the Thistle Slide overlook (about eight miles up Spanish Fork Canyon) is highly recommended.

48 Tucker. Tucker is a rest stop along US-6 about 10 miles up-canyon from the Thistle slide overlook (about 7 miles west of Soldier Summit). Tucker is located at the confluence of Soldier, Clear, and Starvation creeks. During the coal mining booms of the past, it served as an important railroad junction. Some 500 residents are reported to have occupied the area at one time or another. Ski touring is very limited from Tucker. Only during winters of particularly deep snowfalls can one ski along the graded forest road leading west from the rest stop. For the first two miles the roadway traverses private lands; it then continues into the Manti-LaSal National Forest, eventually ascending the Wasatch Plateau to be described in a subsequent section.

49 Soldier Summit. Soldier Summit is surrounded by non-public lands, so any touring in its proximity should be done only with permission of land owners. A forest access roadway departs eastward from the highway about 0.5-0.7 mile from the official Soldier Summit elevation sign. A wide area at the turnoff is used to park snowmobile trailers. The forest road forks about 0.5 mile from the turnoff; the left fork goes north, then northwest, following the Left Fork of White River into the Uinta National Forest. The right fork of the road branches eastward, then follows (northeastwardly) the Right Fork of the White River. Either fork of the roadway can be toured for as long as stamina—and interest and enthusiasm—warrant.

Figure 6.17 At timberline elevations of 10,000 feet, the terrain along the crest of the Wasatch Plateau resembles that found in the north-European countries where nordic skiing originated.

50 Wasatch Plateau

The northern region of the Wasatch Plateau is destined to become one of the finest ski touring areas in Utah. The Plateau is high, cold, sparsely timbered, gentle, and scenic. Most of the forested terrain is public, under the management of the Manti-LaSal National Forest. The plateau is easily accessed by paved highways.

The Wasatch Plateau, a north-to-south landform located east and south of the Nebo massif of the Wasatch Range, has been described as the largest flat-topped plateau in Utah. It rises from the 6000 foot elevation at its base to crests as high as 10,000 and 11,000 feet. Not much has been written about weather patterns that affect the plateau; 200 inches of snowfall is thought to be the approximate average annual snowfall. The temperatures along the higher regions are sufficiently low to permit accumulation of powder snow and to prevent its rapid transformation to less desirable forms. While present, avalanche hazards are not as severe in the Plateau region as they are in the Wasatch Mountains.

The Wasatch Plateau is most frequently accessed from the Sanpete County community of Fairview (about 90 miles south of Salt Lake City, reached via I-15 and US-89). It can also be accessed from Scofield or from the Price/Huntington area. From Fairview, SR-31 ascends

Figure 6.18 The upper regions of Huntington Canyon contain endless miles of gentle, beginner terrain. The arrow points at a small roadside avalanche.

eastward through Fairview Canyon approximately eight miles to the plateau's crest, where it branches. SR-31 continues southward along the ridge for six or seven miles, then commences a gradual descent down Huntington Canyon toward Price. SR-264 departs SR-31 at the branch, drops gently (for the next eight miles) into the upper reaches of Huntington Canyon before crossing a pass east into Pleasant Valley and the community of Scofield.

The best beginner touring is to be found along the upper reaches of both highways. Figure 6.17 depicts typical ridge-crest terrain found along SR-31; Figure 6.18 shows the canyon-bottom area along SR-264. Would-be Wasatch Plateau tourers should take time to drive along the upper reaches of both roads to familiarize themselves with the lay of the land and parking/touring possibilities. The U.S. Forest Service's or Bureau of Land Management's *Nephi* 1:100,000 scale Metric Series topographical map shows most of the graded roads in the vicinity. SR-264, however, is a recent addition to the state's highway system and may not appear on some editions.

Sunrises and sunsets can be especially beautiful along the crest of the plateau. It is not very difficult to plan an outing to take advantage of either event. The wide-open terrain and its easy accessibility also lends itself to unsurpassed moonlight touring.

Bob Athay (l) and Steve Lewis take a break from public hearings to do "field work." Thirty years of community activism has led to Congressionally-designated protection for several unique Wasatch areas. Continued--and growing--public participation is vital to prevent commercial exploitation of remaining unprotected areas.

Chapter 7

PRESERVING THE WASATCH

From the first visit of Carrington, Brown, et. al. to the summit of Twin Peaks in August 1847, the nearby Wasatch Mountains have served as an "urban park" for residents of Wasatch Front communities. During the 1920's, as the smog from coal fired home and industrial heating systems choked the valleys, discovering the canyons and summits became the avocation of many a lover of clean air and exercise. Skiing, at that time exclusively cross country, began its rise to popularity during that decade. Late in the 1930's at Alta, a home-built ski lift creaked into operation to serve growing ranks of local skiers. Growth of "mechanized" skiing continued through the 1940's and 1950's; the only new development, Solitude, occurred in 1958, and it too was geared to serve the local clientele.

Within fifteen years of Solitude's opening, three additional ski areas commenced operation and others expanded. The Park City resort opened late in 1963. With ski runs and ridges scraped to bedrock, the Park West ski area came to life a few years later. The Snowbird complex opened in 1971. At Alta, lift operations expanded into the hallowed ski touring terrain of Albion Basin.

While the 1960's witnessed unprecedented development in the local canyons, it also witnessed the germination of a philosophical movement kinder and gentler toward the Wasatch Mountains. Nationally, the '60's focused to a great extent on preservation of the public domain. Congress passed several resource protection and management laws that would direct federal agencies to manage public resources in a more regulated manner. The National Wilderness Preservation Act, to authorize preservation of areas for their wilderness values, was enacted in 1964. Authorized four years later, the National Environmental Policy Act (NEPA) mandated use of a structured environmental evaluation process to precede any federal actions.

Utah's First Wilderness. As the Wilderness Act neared passage, University of Utah chemistry Professor Cal Giddings (at that time an active ski tourer and mountaineer) proposed the Lone Peak area as a prime candidate for inclusion into the wilderness preservation system. Officials of the Uinta and Wasatch national forests received the proposal warmly—then shelved it indefinitely. Seven years passed before members of the Wasatch Mountain Club renewed the effort to protect the Lone Peak area from what many believed to be imminent commercialization.[1]

Based on presentations by members of the Wasatch Mountain Club and a strong endorsement from the Salt Lake County Commission, U.S. Senator Frank E. Moss initiated a Senate bill to designate the Lone Peak area as Wilderness. Officials of the Forest Service balked, effectively killing the legislation. They insisted that "an intensive study and review process" precede any Congressional action.

The Lone Peak wilderness debate became a debate over high density versus low density recreation. Many understood the issues involved; few explained them better than the 1972 Congressional candidate Wayne Owens. "The great majority of the acreage in the Wasatch Front is already being used for high density recreational purposes," he wrote to a Congressional subcommittee. "Unless we act now," he warned, "we face a future in which our children, and most certainly our children's children, will never have a chance to experience what unspoiled nature was like." Once elected, Congressman Owens joined Senator Moss in introducing a second wilderness proposal to Congress. Again the Forest Service balked. They were undergoing the Roadless Area Review and Evaluation (RARE) process mandated by Congress and could not endorse the legislation.[2]

---

[1] Sometime during the 1960's a tramway was proposed to the summit of the Pfeifferhorn; a summit restaurant was discussed also. Snowbird officials had also proposed a tramway, with rotating summit restaurant, for American Fork Twin Peaks. A large map, prominently displayed on a Snowbird realtor's wall, depicted a tramway to continue to Red Baldy, at the head of White Pine gulch, and another one to continue farther west to the top of White Baldy. At the east edge of the Salt Lake valley, Mount Olympus was also discussed for a tramway and restaurant.

[2] The Forest Service's RARE process itself was highly flawed. In 1972 a federal court found RARE to be biased against wilderness. A new review and evaluation process (RARE-II) was initiated to comply with the court's interpretation of con-

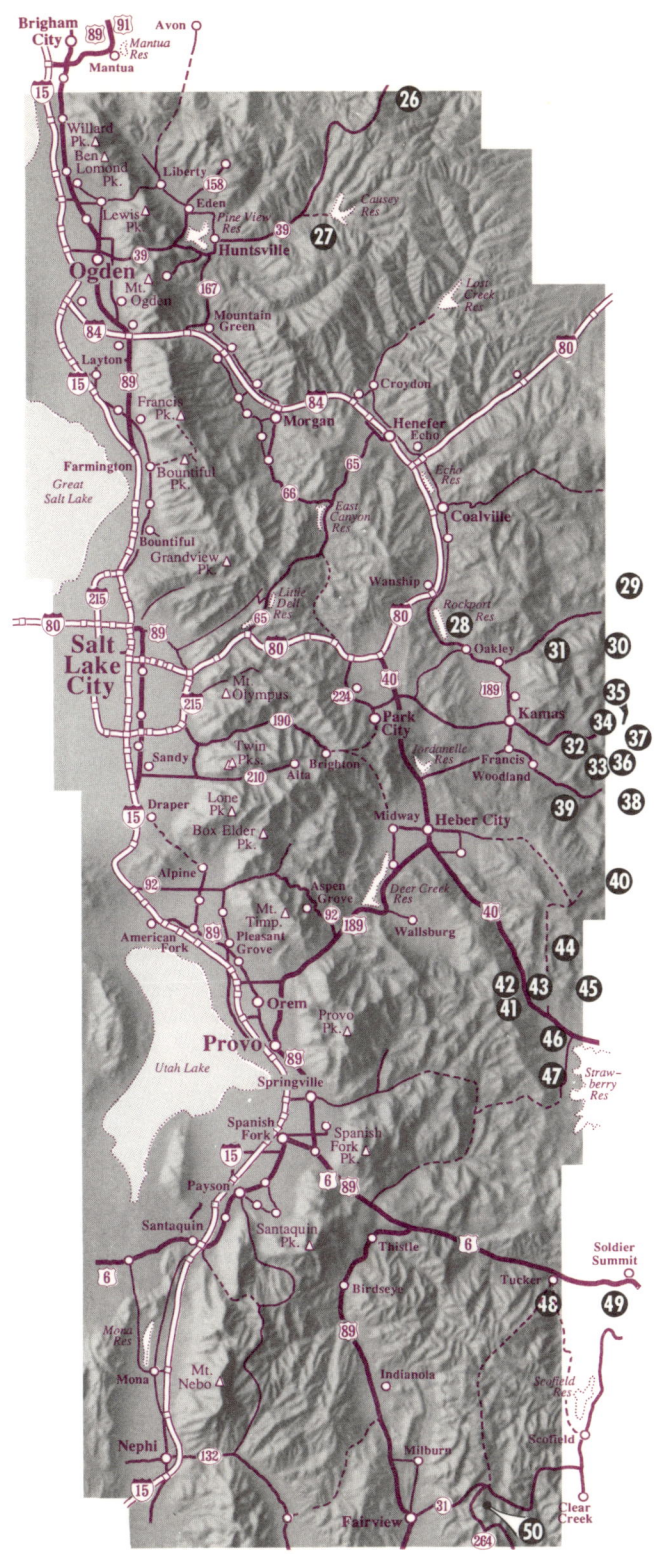

BEGINNER TOURS NEAR THE WASATCH

NORTHERN AREA

26. Monte Cristo 215
27. Causey Reservoir 216

WESTERN UINTAS

28. Rockport State Park .. 216
29. Upper Weber River ... 219
30. Smith-Morehouse 220
31. South Fork Weber R. . 220
32. Beaver Creek 222
33. Pine Valley 222
34. North Fork Provo R. .. 223
35. Mirror Lake Highway . 224
36. Soapstone Basin 226
37. Iron Mine Mountain .. 227
38. South Fork Provo R. .. 228
39. Bench Creek 230
40. Lake Creek 230

DANIELS SUMMIT/ STRAWBERRY

41. Daniels Summit 232
42. Lodgepole Cmpgnd.... 234
43. Telephone Hollow 235
44. Upper Strawberry R. .. 235
45. Co-op Creek 236
46. Doe Knoll 237
47. Strawberry Ridge 237

SOUTHERN AREA

48. Tucker 241
49. Soldier Summit 241
50. Wasatch Plateau 242

Dave Hanscom

A native of Maine, Dave Hanscom started skiing at the age of two. He skied competetively in high school and at Middlebury College, specializing in cross country and jumping. After graduate school, he and his wife Mary moved to Utah, where they have raised their two sons, Brett and Greg.

While Ski Touring Director of the Wasatch Mountain Club in the early 70's, Dave observed that Utah tourers needed less-crowded alternatives for their winter outings, and that many had little understanding of the hazards associated with the sport. The first edition of *Wasatch Tours* was published in 1976.

Dave has taught many classes in avalanche safety and has written numerous articles on ski touring for local publications. A founder of the Utah Nordic Ski Association, he has worked to preserve opportunities for ski touring in the state. Dave is Director of the Wasatch Citizens Series and continues to be an active participant in, and organizer of, cross country ski races.

Alexis Kelner

Alexis Kelner was born in northern Europe, where ski touring is a way of life from birth. World War II displaced him, and he has resided in Utah ever since. After spending several years lift skiing, he took up touring in 1956 to escape the overcommercialization of the resorts.

Alexis is the author of *Skiing In Utah,* a comprehensive illustrated history of the sport in the state. He is also the author of *Utah's Olympics Circus*, a light-hearted examination of promoters' numerous efforts to impose a winter Olympics on Salt Lake City. Kelner's extensive knowledge of avalanche science led to a contract to illustrate the U.S. Forest Service's *Avalanche Handbook*.

Since the mid-1960's Alexis has been an outspoken advocate for the preservation of the Wasatch Front's canyons and actively participated in efforts to secure Wilderness status for Lone Peak and other nearby areas. Today, through writings and speaking engagements, Alexis continues his conservation activism.

ISBN 1-884744-02-8

Wasatch Front residents' hopes for a Lone Peak Wilderness were further dashed when conservative (and anti-wilderness) politicians Jake Garn, Orrin Hatch, and Dan Mariott were elected to Congress. Idaho Senator Frank Church and Arizona Representative Morris Udall recognized the uniqueness of the Lone Peak area and highlighted it in their Endangered American Wilderness Act. Almost predictably, officials of the Wasatch National Forest jumped onto the opposition's bandwagon.[3] The Forest Service's opposition quickly vanished when Pres. Jimmy Carter replaced the Department of Agriculture official opposed to wilderness with one who favored it.

During the legislative process, opposition by Utah's Congressional delegation gradually softened. After Salt Lake Mayor Ted Wilson obtained the City Commission's endorsement of a Lone Peak Wilderness, Senator Garn signed on as co-sponsor of the legislation. The remainder of the Utah delegation followed suit. With President Carter's signature on the Endangered American Wilderness Act of 1978, Lone Peak became Utah's first official Wilderness.

Throughout the 1970's, public opinion polls indicated a growing constituency concerned with preservation of the nearby canyons. Utah's Congressional delegation paid heed to the changing demographics. It took nearly 14 years to include Lone Peak under the Wilderness Act's protective umbrella, but considerably less time was needed to affect wilderness designation for the Twin Peaks, Mount Olympus, Mount Timpanogos, and Mount Nebo areas. Much of the ground work for the new wilderness legislation was laid by the Utah Wilderness Association, a citizens' group that had been organized by former Wilderness Society coordinator Dick Carter.

Planning for the Future. If the 1960's were the "decade of environmental awakening" for the Wasatch Mountains, the 1970's and 1980's should be considered as the "decades of public planning." Uinta National Forest officials deserve accolades for initiating the first *major* forest planning effort in Utah. Their "Proposed Land Use Plan" was released for public comment in 1973.

Almost concurrently, Salt Lake County government commissioned

---

gressional intent. RARE-II was challenged by a group of concerned citizens in Idaho. Their successful appeal (called the Gospel Hump decision) prompted the Forest Service to commence yet a third round of evaluations that became known as "Son of Rare II."

[3] Since the area was "within the sights and sounds of a major metropolitan area," they argued, it was "impure" and therefore did not qualify as wilderness. The "sights and sounds" argument was challenged by the Utah chapter of the Sierra Club and was strongly condemned by the Endangered Wilderness Act's sponsors.

two San Francisco consulting firms to undertake a planning process to regulate development *on private lands* in the vicinity of Alta and Snowbird. The ensuing plan, known as the *EDAW* study, offered much to minimize canyon urbanization and was unanimously endorsed by the staff of the County's planning office. Noting that "we now have solid guidelines for the control of development," County Commissioner Pete Kutulas expressed "little doubt that the County Commission will unanimously adopt this study." Snowbird's executives had other ideas. They initiated a massive—and ultimately successful—lobbying effort to derail the study's recommendations.

The 1970's saw several new federal laws enacted that would further influence forest planning. By 1976, forest-wide plans and public involvement started to become commonplace.

By the time the Wasatch/Cache National Forest officials initiated their public involvement process early in the 1980's, the local population was well-prepared to defend their canyons from further exploitation. Grandiose plans for a trans-canyon tunnel between Alta and Brighton (to make the areas more accessible as a winter Olympics site) further outraged the citizenry. When the Forest Service's proposed plan was made public late in 1984, it attracted over 500 written responses.

Many of the responses were from ski tourers and hikers. Numerous comments strongly opposed expansion of Snowbird, Solitude, and Park West onto adjacent National Forest areas. Continued loss of cross-country terrain, due to ski area expansions and the Forest Service's failure to effectively control commercial helicopter skiing, was frequently lamented.

As the final *draft* was being prepared, groups of individuals were summoned for a "sneak preview." Those working for backcountry preservation were in a state of near-euphoria when told that Snowbird's expansion into White Pine and Solitude's expansion into Silver Fork would not be authorized during the first 10-15 year planning cycle.

But Snowbird's Dick Bass was not to be impeded. He helicoptered Utah's Senator Orrin Hatch and other power brokers into White Pine and exposed them to *His* master plan. When asked how the White Pine and Silver Fork restrictions came to be deleted from the *published* forest plan, a frustrated Forest Service official replied that "it was scuttled."

Late in the 1980's, after constant prodding by Forest Supervisor Arthur J. Carroll, Salt Lake County officials commenced developing a planning document for private lands located within or adjacent to lands under Forest Service control. A "citizen's advisory committee," well-balanced between environmental and development interests, was orga-

It's Time to Stop Taking Our Canyons for Granted

Tom Wharton
Outdoors Editor

Most of us grew up taking the canyons east of Salt Lake City for granted. They served as our playground. They were the places where we enjoyed our first hike, went fishing and hunting with our fathers and learned to ski. They were spots for July 4th picnics and camping trips.

The fact that they provided much of our drinking water was easy to overlook. So was the reality that a great deal of the land in the area was private. And the economic benefits of the ski resorts located in the canyons were largely ignored.

The canyons were simply there, with their beautiful alpine scenery, high mountain lakes, bubbling brooks and fascinating geology. We would always be able to enjoy them.

Or so we thought.

Developers intent on making money off the canyons have started to threaten them in a slow process that could destroy the reason so many of us have visited them for so many years.

Family-owned ski areas like Brighton and Alta somehow seemed to fit in with the general feel of the canyons. They had been there since the early 1940s and had turned a nice profit without having to build huge condominiums. Their growth was slow and well planned. They were like old friends.

Solitude, with its many changes of ownership and small-time atmosphere, also seemed like a part of the skiing scene. Until recently, when its present owners began to suffer illusions of turning this resort into something much larger, Solitude captured the same type of rustic resort flavor as its two older neighbors.

Things really began to change in the canyons when Snowbird came on the scene in the early 70s. The issue of whether this resort, with its brightly colored tram and monolithic concrete condos, should have been built in the first place turned many young college students into environmentalists.

Though well-planned and executed, this was a huge resort many didn't feel belonged in the canyons. The concept of a ski resort was fine. Lifts and a lodge or two were acceptable. It was the damned condos, high-priced lift tickets and big-time resort atmosphere folks hated. Many still do.

It was at about this time that Utah suddenly discovered the ski industry as a major tourist attraction. The Park City area, with its hodge-podge of ugly condominiums, fake-funky boutiques and psuedo-mining town atmosphere, should have given the U.S. Forest Service, Salt Lake City and County and state planners an example of how not to develop a resort. When the last few remnants of the old Main Street were prostituted, it became obvious that Park City could serve as a perfect showplace of unplanned development gone haywire.

That obvious display of ugliness should give wiser folks in Salt Lake County pause for reflection on what is becoming decision-making time for the future of the canyons east of the city.

Frankly, now is the turning point for the precious canyons of the Wasatch Front. The developers are starting to come forward with their plans. To someone who loves the natural beauty of these canyons, these plans are frightening.

Solitude wants to turn itself into Big Cottonwood Canyon's version of Snowbird, complete with its own monolithic condos. In the process, it is looking at even more ski lift expansion into Silver Fork Canyon, a once-pristine area it has already partially ruined.

Snowbird, not satisfied with its present profit structure, wants to continue to expand, looking to put new lifts into the public lands of White Pine and American Fork Canyons.

Foothill development continues to creep up the mountains. Rich folks building huge homes on mountain slopes destroy the wildness of the Salt Lake Valley, eating up huge chunks of wildlife range, blocking hikers' access to public land and slowly destroying the majesty of the Wasatch in the process.

And, as the canyon developments continue to increase in size, how are the small roads going handle the increased traffic, something the obsolete roads often have difficulty doing now? What of the future if the proposed developments take place?

The fragile nature of these canyons and the developers' awful plans for them are causing local citizens to take a look at the future. The Utah Museum of Natural History's Wasatch Front lecture series, which began Monday at Highland High School and will run through the next eight weeks, is taking an objective look at things.

Before new sewers are built, new developments and lifts are allowed and more concrete creeps into the mountains of the Wasatch, isn't it time for government agencies to start working on a master plan to protect these precious resources for future generations?

Range scientists use a term called "carrying capacity" to describe the maximum allowable grazing that can be tolerated by the land. It appears as though the Wasatch Front canyons will soon reach their carrying capacity for people, if they haven't already.

A friend of mine, mourning the loss of a trout stream, once said that you can give a developer millions of dollars and he can build you a modern highway, a mall or a golf course.

But, no matter how many millions a man may have, he can't create another trout stream. Or, for that matter, a mountain.

The mountains and canyons of the Wasatch are too precious to be turned over to the care of people who worry more about the bottom line than they do about future generations of Salt Lakers.

These wild areas have reached their carrying capacity.

Now is the time to tell the developers to take their condos and ski lifts elsewhere.

Reprinted by permission of the Salt Lake Tribune.

Figure 7.1 Throughout the 1980's, numerous articles by the *Salt Lake Tribune's* Outdoors Editor, Tom Wharton, and the Deseret News' Environmental Specialist, Joseph M. Bauman, publicized canyon preservation and conservation issues.

nized. A local consulting firm was contracted to oversee the project. Well-advertised meetings were scheduled to define issues and to provide the general public opportunities for input. One meeting attracted more than 1,000 concerned individuals. Planners also widely distributed a comprehensive canyon user's questionnaire. Even though a half-hour's effort was required to thoughtfully respond to the multitude of questions, nearly 1,000 surveys were completed.[4]

As approved by the County Commission in September 1989, the plan allows ski resorts to expand skiing nearly 50% during the next two decades, but the expansions may occur *only within existing permit boundaries*. White Pine and Silver Fork drainages are preserved for backcountry recreation. Expansion of resort areas onto adjacent private lands is allowed, but only after meeting stringent requirements. Olympic events are to be excluded from Big and Little Cottonwood canyons, and "interconnection" of the Cottonwood ski resorts with Park City will require further consideration.

The thousands of area residents who influenced the outcomes of the County and Forest Service plans have much to be proud of. While some feel the plans are "ten years and a thousand condominiums late," they are the only game in town for the 1990's.

Current Issues and Ongoing Concerns

It has taken nearly 40 years to awaken Utahns' environmental conscience. As we enter the mid-1990's, concern for preservation of local canyons exists in every community located near the Wasatch. Support for wilderness designation is at an all-time high. The phrase "Quality of Life" has become an integral part of every politician's vocabulary.

Related to backcountry touring, four major issues will face the next generation of residents, activists, and community leaders: (1) curtailment of ski resort expansion to prevent further loss of backcountry terrain, (2) rigid control (or elimination) of helicopter skiing, (3) preservation of public access to public lands, and (4) continuation—or increase—of public involvement in land management decisionmaking.[5]

---

[4] The great majority of respondents preferred no more commercial developments or additional lodging in the canyons. Preservation of existing backcountry ski terrain, and confinement of commercial skiing to existing permit boundaries, attracted an equally high majority. One facet of the study was especially heartening: 700 of the respondents considered themselves as downhill alpine skiers.

[5] Wasatch preservation issues beyond the scope of this book include: (1) control, through zoning and other regulatory means, of private lands along the foothills and in canyons, (2) public acquisition of critical private lands within and adjacent to

Control of Commercial Ski Area Expansions. Confronted by all the self-congratulatory boosterism disseminated by ski industry, tourism, and economic development agencies—and repeated by the local media—Wasatch Front residents could conclude that Utah's ski industry forms a major bulwark of the State's economy and that it is undergoing massive growth in utilization.

The facts indicate otherwise.

In analyzing 1987-88 Utah ski tourism statistics, State Representative David Jones found that the $200 million spent in Utah that season by non-resident ski vacationers amounted to only 10% of the $2 billion spent annually by all tourists in Utah and that non-resident skier expenditures amounted to only 0.83% of the State's $24 billion gross product.

Ski resort visitation data, reported by the Utah Ski Association and tabulated in Figure 7.2, dispels the notion that Utah's commercial ski recreation is experiencing major growth. So meager has been that growth that lobbyists recently convinced Utah's legislature to grant the ski industry a direct public subsidy for lift construction.

Utah's stagnant ski market reflects the state of the industry nationally. In the January, 1990 *McKinsey Report,* commissioned by the National Ski Areas Association, analysts reported that "the first evidence of industry-wide decline are showing." Demographics and macrosocietal trends "will at best be neutral for the ski industry."[6]

When ski touring was being "rediscovered" during the 1960's, large tracts of the Wasatch were available for those seeking the backcountry alternative to commercial skiing. But during the past 30 years—due to expansion of commercial ski operations—much of the publicly-owned terrain has become unavailable for the rapidly-growing sport. Approxi-

---

public lands, (3) abandonment of economically, socially, and environmentally undesirable canyon transportation proposals such as "Interconnect," and (4) reevaluation of public land use policies that favor "destination" use over use by local residents.

[6]Utah ski industry proponents' optimism for continued growth is based on three premises: (1) that marketing of the state as "America's Choice" to host the Winter Olympics will stimulate an influx of tourist skiers, (2) that Utah's resorts can siphon market shares from adjacent states, primarily Colorado, and (3) that Utah's ski-age demographics will remain positive.

National demographics show the number of ski-aged adults declining in the 1990's. Due to its inordinately high birth rate, Utah's ski-aged adult population is still increasing in the '90's (although at a somewhat reduced rate than in the '80's). But a large segment of Utah's ski-aged population tends to have large families. Combined with the astronomically—and increasingly—high costs of commercial skiing, it is questionable that that segment of the population will contribute significantly to the growth of Utah's ski industry.

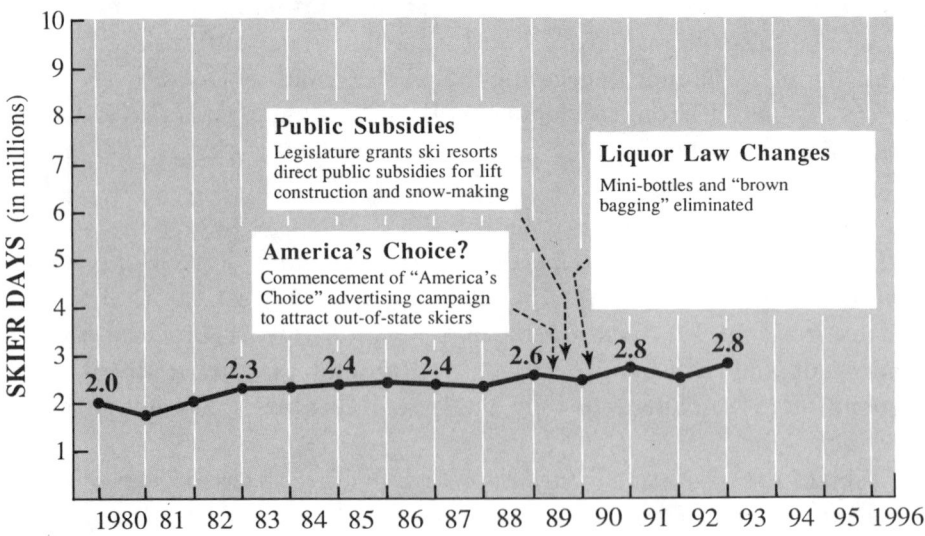

Figure 7.2 Utah ski visits have increased very little in the past decade despite industry marketing efforts and direct public subidies.

mately 50% of the beginner and intermediate touring routes in Big and Little Cottonwood canyons described in the first edition of *Wasatch Tours* in 1976 are now part of commercial ski areas.

In Little Cottonwood Canyon, Albion Basin had provided the finest backcountry winter recreation opportunities in the canyon until Alta's lift company expanded its operation. White Pine Gulch is the only drainage in Little Cottonwood that remains free of commercial development that is suitable for all levels of touring. The Salt Lake County Canyons Master Plan has set White Pine apart for back-country recreation, but the plan comes up for revision in a few years. Snowbird officials are likely to launch a strong lobbying effort to absorb White Pine into their operation. The prospects for Big Cottonwood Canyon are as grim as those recently experienced in Little Cottonwood.

In their Forest Plan, officials of the Forest Service recognized the "dramatic growth" of backcountry touring and the shrinking areas available for its use. Throughout recent planning and resort expansion debates, they assured backcountry advocates that loss of touring terrain would be "mitigated." As yet, no concrete proposals for such mitigation have been advanced.

Backcountry recreationists must be especially watchful that they are not forced into the absurd situation where the "destination skiers" (who burn up immense quantities of aviation fuel getting to Utah) get to utilize the choicest ski terrain adjacent to Salt Lake City, but backcountry users who live adjacent to the mountains get "mitigated" to the Uintas, Stansburys, or the Wellsvilles for their recreation.

Helicopter Skiing. When the helicopter skiing concession first commenced operations near Alta, some town residents expressed outrage at the disruption it caused to the serene mountain environment. "F__ Helicopters," painted in three-foot block letters on the roof of one Alta official's residence, denoted the intensity of feelings.

By the end of 1990, the helicopter skiing concession had sewn up (under its Special Use Permit) most of the skiable non-wilderness terrain in the Wasatch Mountains. At the same time the ranks of backcountry tourers had increased beyond the wildest expectations of the handful who rediscovered the sport in the 1960's. A recent Forest Service analysis indicates that the Central Wasatch alone receives 80,000-90,000 backcountry skiing day visits annually. Heli-skiing, on the other hand, accounts for only 1,000-2,000 skier days. Concerned tourers began asking Forest Service officials how they could justify allowing so few heli-skiers to spoil and endanger the backcountry recreational experiences of so many. Many canyon residents also complained of noisy helicopter overflights that disturbed their serene environments.

When the heli-ski Special Use Permit came up for renewal in January 1991, forest officials initiated a "professionally directed" mediation process to resolve mounting friction between the two user groups. The backcountry skiers' representatives' goal was resolution of conflicts. In a lavish brochure distributed to their clientele, the heli-ski concession declared that their permit could not be revised "to the satisfaction of both parties," essentially a No Compromise position. Alternate weekends use patterns or alternating terrain usage proposals, that would have assured both user groups *equal* access to undisturbed terrain, were rejected by heli-ski negotiators. After several sessions of failure to compromise, mediation was discontinued.

Forest Service officials then continued the process required for permit renewal. That the officials favored the heli-ski concession became obvious on reading the range of alternative actions they published.[7] All alternatives appeared to have taken at face value the heli-ski permittee's claims that any modification of their permit would lead to the concession's demise. Forest officials discounted all substantive proposals to resolve conflicts proffered by backcountry advocates.

---

[7] Those who desire additional information on the heli-skiing controversy should ask for the "Heli-skiing File" at university libraries.

The heli-skiing issue's undesirable outcome will be debated again in 1995 or '96, when the permit comes up for renewal. It would be prudent for concerned backcountry recreationists, canyon residents and visitors to become informed of the issues and to pledge vigorous participation in the renewal process.[8]

Public Access. Access to public lands in the Wasatch Mountains is less of a problem for tourers than it is for hikers. Few skiers wish to attempt an outing along the populated areas of the Wasatch Front due to the low elevation and steep, rugged terrain. Most of the serious access problems are found in Morgan, Summit, and Utah counties where ranches are situated between highways and National Forest lands. Most of these private properties are used for crops and grazing in warmer months, but lie idle in winter, and most include terrain that would be very suitable for skiers.

The "No Trespassing" restrictions placed by some land owners are only partly caused by selfishness. Most ranchers or farmers can tell stories of hunters who trashed their properties, tore down fences, or killed domestic animals. One act of vandalism can fester in the mind of an isolated rancher for years, souring his outlook towards responsible land users for the rest of his life.

Whenever we've discussed the necessity of entering or crossing private land to commence a ski tour, we've encouraged participants to obtain the land owner's permission. Respecting the property rights of land owners will reap benefits in respect gained by tourers.

Continued Public Participation in Land Use Planning. Due to its proximity to metropolitan areas, the Wasatch-Cache National Forest has become one of the most heavily used recreational forests in the U.S. As southern Wasatch communities expand, the nearby Uinta National Forest may follow suit. Future management philosophies and directions, developed with considerable public participation, are spelled out (though not always clearly) in thick and detailed Land and Resource Management Plans commonly called Forest Plans. These are revised on ten or fifteen year cycles.

Supervisors of the Wasatch-Cache National Forest have commenced their Forest Plan revision process; they are asking concerned individuals to submit their names so that they may be kept informed of opportunities for public input. The Uinta National Forest's managers will commence a 5-year revision process for their plan in 1994.

---

[8] In skiing regions all over the world—except in the crowded Wasatch—helicopter skiing operations are allowed only in remote non-public areas, far from highways and public transportation, residential, and business environments.

We urge every reader of this book to get on the mailing lists and to participate vigorously in the revision process. Ski industry and other commercial interest lobbyists are already at work attempting to undermine some Plan provisions. To get on the mailing lists, write or call:

Wasatch-Cache National Forest
125 S. State Street, Room 8236
Salt Lake City, UT 84138
(801)524-5030

Uinta National Forest
88 West 100 North
Provo, UT 84603
(801)377-5780

Through experience and insights gained over a combined 60 years of conservation activism, we offer readers the following suggestions:

- *Write letters.* When elected (or Forest Service) officials perform in your interest they should be praised lavishly; condemnations of improper actions should be polite, with well-reasoned suggestions of how—and why—stands should be altered.
- *Individual letters have greatest impact.* Officials give less weight to form letters, surveys, and signed petitions.
- *Numbers are important.* It's vital that officials receive many letters. Public hearings should overflow with concerned individuals.
- *Join and contribute to activist organizations.* Their newsletters will keep you informed of issues and *conservationists' proposals* for resolving land-use conflicts.
- *Elect politically correct representatives.* As is evident from the Snow Basin land exchange decision and several other examples, Forest Service officials too often favor politicians who are influenced by narrow special interests over common individuals who represent a broad spectrum of the population.
- *Never Give Up!* Political situations aren't always as bad as they seem, and eventually they change. The 14-year effort for Lone Peak Wilderness serves as a good example.

Throughout this volume, we've tried to point out important issues that can adversely affect the quality of Wasatch backcountry recreation. Recreational users must unite and participate more vigorously in the political and bureaucratic management of public lands. Major environmental victories have been won in the Wasatch against immense opposition by the "traditional" power brokers of the state; similar land-use victories can be won again, but it will take commitment.

The future of the canyons is up to you! Get involved today!

Coming:

WASATCH TOURS
Volume 2 – the Northern Wasatch

Intermediate and advanced tours in the Northern Wasatch

- covers the Wasatch north of the Utah County---Salt Lake County boundary
- more ski tour descriptions
- more, and larger, high resolution aerial photographs
- more and better touring route maps
- canyon urbanization *versus* canyon preservation philosophies

(To be available April 1994)

In the meantime, you'll enjoy:

SKIING IN UTAH--A History

SKIING IN UTAH--A History explores in great detail the personalities, adventures, and achievements of many individuals who helped shape Utah's early skiing. *SKIING IN UTAH* is illustrated with over two hundred historical photographs and is fully annotated with references. An excellent reference work.

Price: . . . . . $ 15.50 *(includes Utah sales tax)*

UTAH'S OLYMPICS CIRCUS

UTAH'S OLYMPICS CIRCUS is both a light-hearted and serious examination of Utah Olympics promoters' numerous efforts (stretching over a period of thirty years!) to impose a Winter Olympics on Salt Lake City. Numerous cartoons and songs for Utah's traumatized taxpayers.

Price: . . . . . . $ 8.50 *(includes Utah sales tax)*

ORDER FORM

NAME _____

STREET ADDRESS _____

CITY, STATE _____ ZIP _____

MAIL TO:
WASATCH TOURS PUBLISHING
1451 MORAY COURT
PARK CITY, UTAH 84060

Prices include Utah sales tax.

☐ WASATCH TOURS, Vol. 1 . . . . $13.50

☐ SKIING IN UTAH $15.50

☐ UTAH'S OLYMPIC CIRCUS . . . . $ 8.50

Postage/Handling . . . . $ 3.00

TOTAL ENCLOSED:

☐ Put us on your mailing list for announcements of future publications.

☐ We would appreciate receiving alert notices on canyon preservation issues.